IMAGES
of America

MADISON HEIGHTS

On the Cover: In this late 1940s image, Antonina Bucciarelli (also known as "Mrs. B") waits on patrons in her popular restaurant, the Madison Drive-In, later nicknamed "the Loop." Viola Bricker sits on the near stool with her son Kenny, while her friend Birdie Northcutt (right) looks on. Located close to Madison High School, it was a welcome venue for students and their families, complemented with warm hometown service. (Courtesy of Teresa Bucciarelli Hoskins and the late Angelina Bucciarelli Joyce.)

IMAGES
of America

MADISON HEIGHTS

Margene Ann Scott and Roslyn Fay Yerman

ARCADIA
PUBLISHING

ISBN 978-1-4671-1092-1

Published by Arcadia Publishing
Charleston, South Carolina

Printed in the United States of America

Library of Congress Control Number: 2013938250

For all general information, please contact Arcadia Publishing:
Telephone 843-853-2070
Fax 843-853-0044
E-mail sales@arcadiapublishing.com
For customer service and orders:
Toll-Free 1-888-313-2665

Visit us on the Internet at www.arcadiapublishing.com

Dedicated to the memory of my parents, Arnold and Eleanor Yerman.
—Roslyn

Dedicated to the love and blessings of my late parents, Eugene and Marian Seyler.
—Margene

CONTENTS

FOREWORD

This is a tale of two cities. The dickens is, this book is about one city, and that is Madison Heights. It is a must-read for everyone who has ever stepped foot in my hometown.

I was born and raised in what is now called Madison Heights. I spent the first 50 years of my life there, minus my time at Michigan State University.

My wife, Pat, is a Madison Heights native. My mom, Lois, was on the school board for years. My brother, Jack, was superintendent of the Madison School District. So I definitely have the pedigree.

Still, I have always thought of Madison Heights as a divided city. Not quite the two cities that Charles Dickens wrote about back in the 1800s, but there definitely was a division. That perspective probably stems from my background first as a high school athlete at Madison High and later as a teacher and a coach at my alma mater. Two completely separate school districts equaled one very heated rivalry.

The Madison High Eagles versus the Lamphere High Rams—go to your respective corners, and when the bell rings, come out swinging.

This book is a real knockout. It takes us far beyond that divide and illustrates the threads that tie our city and its residents together.

I am proud to be from Madison Heights.

—Jim Myers
former teacher and coach
also known as George "The Animal" Steele
World Wrestling Entertainment

ACKNOWLEDGMENTS

Thanks to my parents for their love and support in providing the foundation for the person I have become. My father was a Center Line High School counselor for years, and it was a chance encounter that afforded me the opportunity to interview in Madison Heights. My appreciation goes to former Madison Heights Public Library director William Miles for his friendship and for the opportunity to serve as library director and work with the Madison Heights Historical Commission, thereby paving the way for me to work on this book.

Thank you to my sister, Sue Yerman, and my brother, Howard Yerman, for their love and support. My appreciation goes to the staff of the Madison Heights Public Library for their patience and support during the writing of this book. Thank you to city staff, colleagues, and friends in my "second home" of Madison Heights for your support, input, and enthusiasm for this project. Finally, thank you to the Madison Heights Historical Commission, in particular Joy Davids for her recollections and efforts on behalf of this project, and to city residents for making the trip down memory lane with us.

—Roslyn

I acknowledge my family that gives me a reason for being. My extraordinary husband, Jack Scott, is the joyful love of my life, whose constant support gives me strength and purpose. Thanks to my cherished daughter, Kristen Johnston Gregory, and her talented husband Jim, and to my admired son, Kraig Johnston, and loving memories of his beautiful wife, Jill. My life's true blessings are my adored grandchildren: Christopher Adams, Chelsea Adams, Dylan Johnston, Cory Johnston, our "angel" Ian Johnston, and my own beloved grandma, the late Anna Ploof.

Jack's love thankfully brought my step-family dividend: children Linda Scott Hanneman and her husband, Steve; Michael Scott and his wife, Eveline; Mark Scott and his wife, Kathleen; and our sweet sister Joanne Basford. Bonuses are grandchildren: Kurtis and Lucas Scott, Clayton Scott, and Matthew and Katie Hanneman. I give grateful thanks for "flowers" of my life: true friends, including "cupids" Lila and Jim Richards. Lastly, thank you for many who share my passion for history and work to preserve it.

—Margene

Introduction

Major growth took place in the area that would become Madison Heights following World War II, with many residents employed in the auto industry. The city of Madison Heights was incorporated on January 17, 1955, when residents of the east side of Royal Oak Township voted for incorporation by a 372-vote margin. The name "Madison" came from the Madison School District, which serves part of the community, and while the land is generally low and flat, "Heights" was added for aesthetic reasons when charter commissioner John B. Michrina filed the petitions in Lansing.

As the population grew close to 40,000, the area offered a wide range of prices in housing, two public school districts, one parochial school district, and something for everyone, including variety in recreation, sports, churches, opportunities for community involvement, and membership in national organizations.

Emphasis has shifted from auto manufacturing to light industrial, medical, and technology. Claims to fame include a wide variety in housing market costs, educational opportunities, and an identifiable multicultural diversity in both its residential and business populations. Two major interstates cross in Madison Heights, allowing easy access to surrounding areas and states. The community is known for its spirit of volunteerism and hometown warmth.

The divisions that do exist are the threads that tie the city and its residents together, such as the heated rivalry between the sports teams from the city's two school districts. The strong concentration on team sports for youngsters contributes to the foundation of teamwork and more, which benefits them throughout their lifetimes.

The city is also known for award-winning schools, a senior center, and five high-occupancy senior apartment towers featuring food programs. Numerous churches provide many denominations for various beliefs. The city attracts visitors every day to participate in numerous recreational activities at sites such as a golf course, wave pool, "lazy river" water trail, water slide and park, soccer complex, baseball complex, nature center, wooded walking trails, sled hill, bowling lanes, dog park, and indoor pools in the schools, the public library, and the Heritage Rooms museum. The massive Red Run drain meanders diagonally through the city but it was covered in the early 1960s, allowing the county to provide recreational land use along its length.

Important individuals include Wyland, local high school graduate and native son, world-renowned marine artist, and environmentalist. He is famous for his more than 100 "Whaling Walls"—murals of ocean life painted on major buildings throughout the world. Jim Myers, local graduate, teacher, and longtime coach, went on to world fame as George "The Animal" Steele, movie actor and WWF wrestler. Other sports heroes include Ken Dallafior, former professional football player for the Detroit Lions and San Diego Chargers; Berney Gonzales, Junior World Olympic wrestling gold medalist and a member of the Michigan Wrestling Hall of Fame; professional football player Grady Alderman; and pro hockey players Shawn Penn and Pat Peake. Madison Heights is the home of the late Jessie Byam, at 98 the oldest person to graduate from high school in the United States, and Miss Senior Michigan 1991 Edna Brown, as well as one of the first Rotary Clubs to admit women (in 1987).

Historically, Madison Heights originated from pioneering families and their many contributions, such as the Lamphere family, who first gave the community land in 1888 for the schoolhouse at 13 Mile and John R Roads, and brothers Albert, August, and Joseph Kendall of the Kendall family, who gave their land in 1926 when the schoolhouse was moved from John R Road and Greig Avenue to their farm. Additional farmers owned farms along many of the city's major roads and can be documented through the census. These farm families came here in the early 1900s from other countries for the opportunity to start fresh and be self-sufficient, farming their land and often working to buy it. They recognized they had a golden opportunity to start their own business and be successful with their independent life. The goals of these families were to be productive and to provide a happy life for their families rather than to be rich. These farm families gave rise to the life and hope of the community that became Madison Heights.

Visitors to Madison Heights enjoy the varied recreational opportunities. In the winter, visitors and residents enjoy sledding on the large hill at the civic center; a main attraction in the warmer months is the wave pool, water slide, and water park. The annual run/walk is held in the spring, and thousands of families attend our annual festival and fireworks. Motor enthusiasts attend the local car/cycle show in conjunction with the renowned Woodward Dream Cruise. There are five well-known hotels and inns for the many corporate employees who travel and need to stay in the Detroit metropolitan area.

After surveying many places to stay in or reasons to visit the city, Madison Heights sees annual counts of close to 25,000 stays from each of its major hotels and inns. The Oakland County Wave Pool water complex in our city reports 100,000 to 130,000 annual visits depending on the heat of the summer. The county golf course reports 19,622 golfers annually. The county dog park is enjoyed by 22,249 visitors and their dogs.

The Madison Heights Historical Commission and the former Greater Federation of Women's Clubs Madison Heights Junior Women's Club have written and compiled a series of three books about the history of Madison Heights. Mainly consisting of text, there are also limited photographs and drawings in the books. The original *Madison Heights Heritage Book* covers the period prior to 1900 through 1965, when the city was 10 years old. The *Heritage Book Update* covers the period from 1966 to 1992. The *Heritage Book Update II* covers the period from 1993 to 2005 in commemoration of the city's 50th anniversary.

The history of Madison Heights illustrated here will reach a broader audience and supplements the previous work with more high-quality photographs along with a more personal touch to the citizens, the city's progress, and what makes the city unique.

It covers the areas of the city of Madison Heights and Royal Oak Township, north of 8 Mile Road, south of 14 Mile Road, west of Dequindre Road, and east of Campbell Road and Stephenson Highway (south of 12 Mile Road). The history will cover from about 1834 at the advent of the Lamphere Schools to the current day. Considering that the title could be *Madison Heights: City of Progress*, the emphasis is on how the city has progressed in terms of type of employment, population growth, advancement of technology, and opportunities and activities offered to its citizens. At its core, it will highlight the fact that Madison Heights has always exhibited a hometown atmosphere and that the spirit of involvement and volunteerism is predominant.

One

Prelude to a City

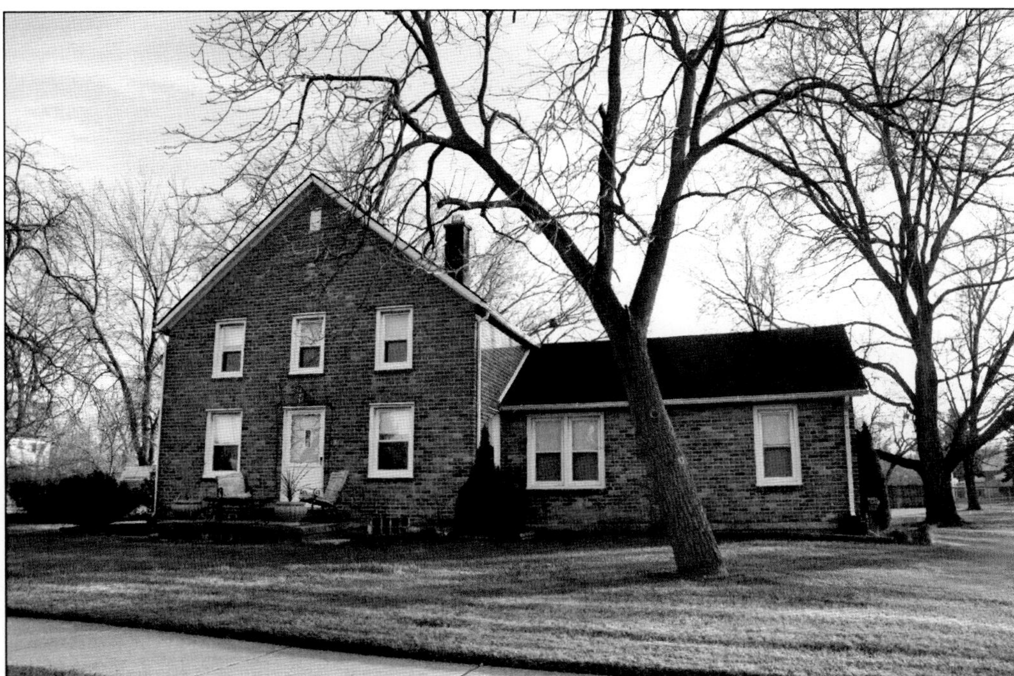

The oldest home to remain standing today in Madison Heights is at 1560 East 13 Mile Road. Councilman Robert Corbett helped run a Seaver Title Company search, tracing the property to the last name Millard, who received the government land in 1834. In 1839, the property was deeded to another family by the last name of Noyes, whose children attended the first schoolhouse in the Lamphere district. The house is one of many structures among newer developments, including homes from the 19th century once surrounded by fields. (Photograph by Margene Scott.)

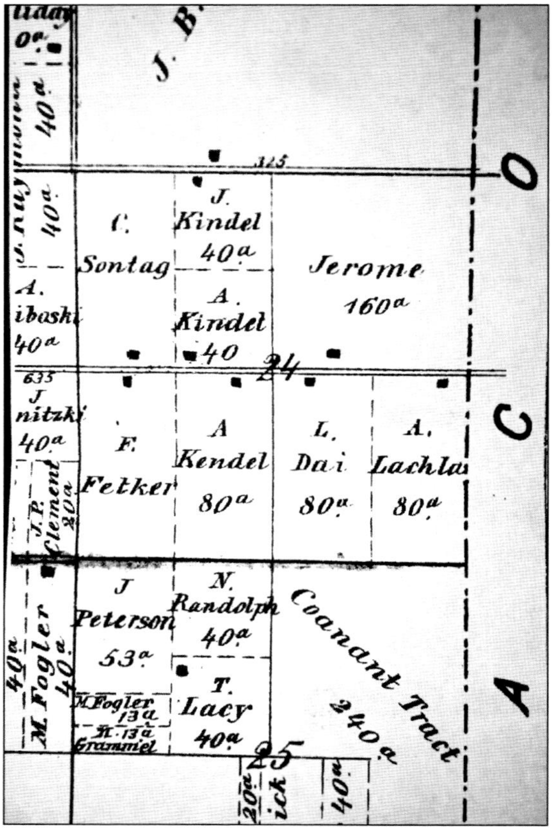

Some of the earliest pioneer families were the German/Prussian descendants of William Kindel. His three sons came to the United States in 1867 and worked as laborers for the Ladensack family in Detroit. By 1880, the brothers had each bought adjoining property totaling 160 acres. The lots are shown on a portion of this late 1800s southeast Oakland County map. The section number 24 in the center of the map is on East Lincoln Avenue, with the bold dotted line on the right representing Dequindre Road and the western border of Macomb County. The Kindel farms were on the north and south side of East Lincoln Avenue, reaching from 10 Mile Road north to 11 Mile Road. (Courtesy of Julie Halpin McMillan.)

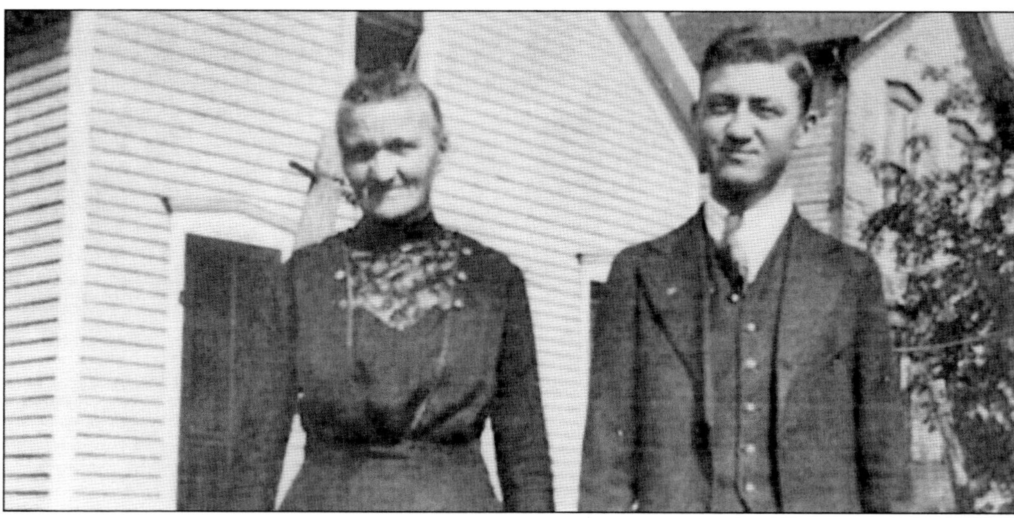

Farm owner Joseph Kendall married Julia Gendernalik in 1873, and the family continued to live in what was then Royal Oak Township. Their son William Paul Kendall served on the Madison Board of Education, and married Julia Neusius from another area pioneer family. Another son, Frank (pictured with his mother), and his wife, Ada, deeded a section of their farm in 1926 at the northeast corner of East Lincoln Avenue and Wolverine Street for the District 10 school, after which it was renamed Kendall. One of the Kendall farm homes still stands at 735 East Lincoln Avenue. (Courtesy of Julie Halpin McMillan.)

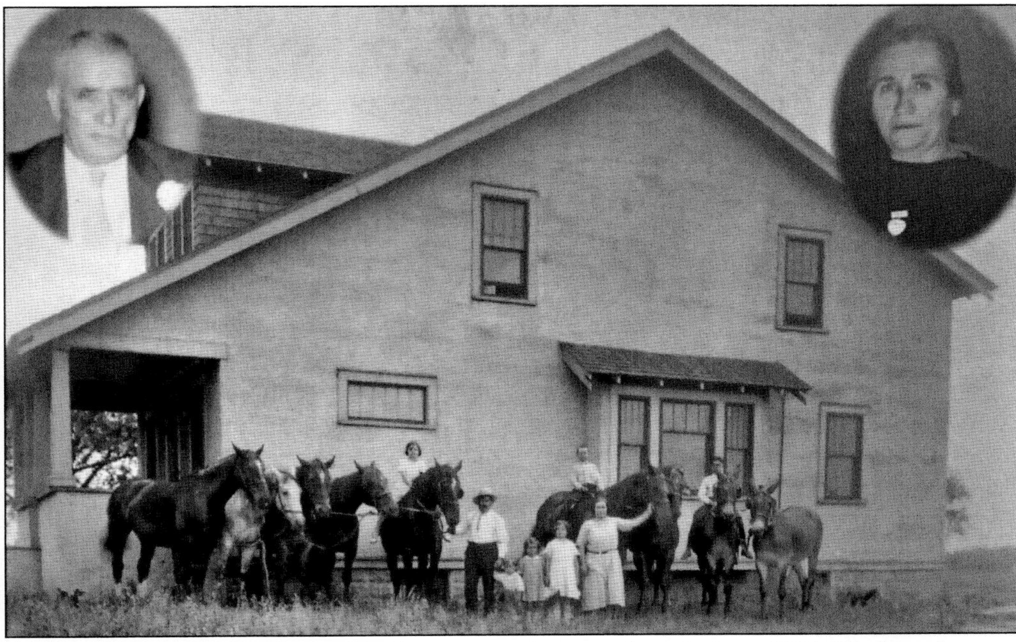

Stefano Acciacca was only 18 when he came to America from Italy in 1904. Working first as a teamster, he cut subdivisions and dug basements with a team of nine horses. At 16, the enterprising Stefano met Eufemia; they were married and later moved to 10 1/2 Mile (Lincoln) Road on the southwest corner of Wolverine Street. Youngest child Norma remembers walking across the street to the Kendall School and family gatherings every Sunday with bocce ball competitions. On the homestead, her father sold grapes, raised vegetables, and slaughtered pigs. The house still stands today at 950 East Lincoln Avenue, beautifully restored by owner Wayne Reif. (Courtesy of Norma Acciacca Turkette.)

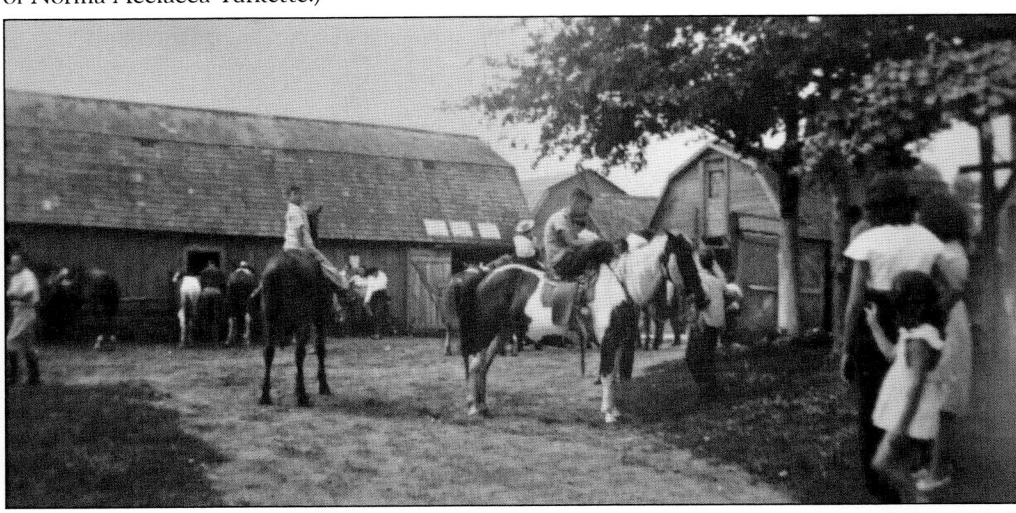

The second youngest of seven children, Dante "Don" Acciacca graduated from Madison High School and built a home just west of his parents on East Lincoln Avenue near Wolverine Street. He began a popular riding stable and held frequent races throughout the neighborhood. Don's father, Stefano, was hesitant about riding, but when World War II ended in August 1945, he grabbed a bottle of wine and rode up Wolverine Street to the neighbor's house and celebrated. (Courtesy of Norma Acciacca Turkette.)

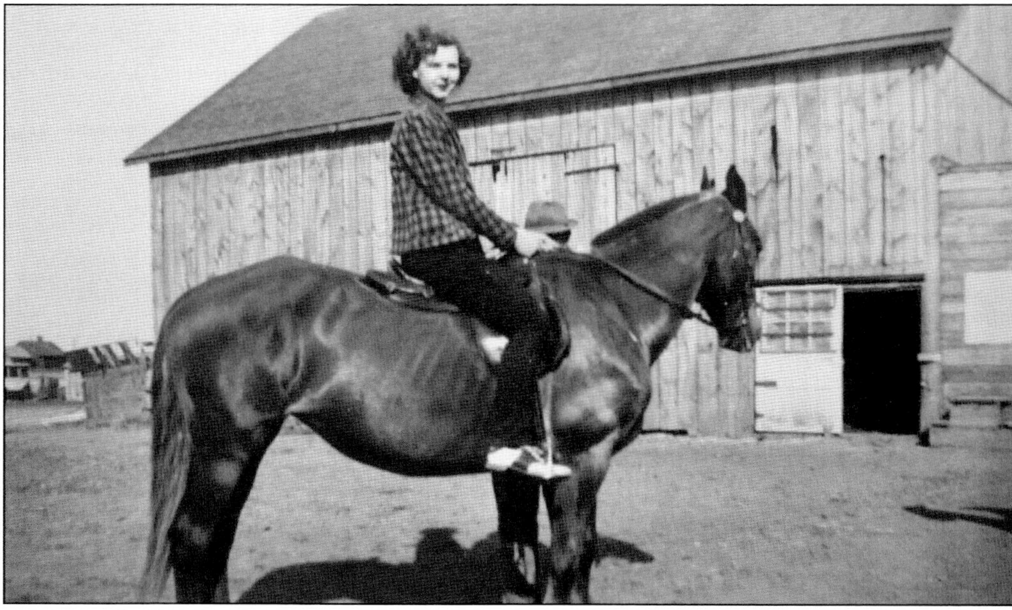

Anna Mudloff and Leo Koss were married in 1915 and purchased their farm at 1141 East 11 Mile Road, where they sold their crops of strawberries and tomatoes at a roadside stand. Daughter Frances grew up on the farm shown in this photograph from 1942. Later, voters elected to purchase the site for $13,000 where the small, wooden Koss School was built. The site at 27107 Hales Street was followed by the larger, brick Vandenberg elementary school, later renamed Schoenhals. (Courtesy of John and Terry (Cottrell) Wilkinson.)

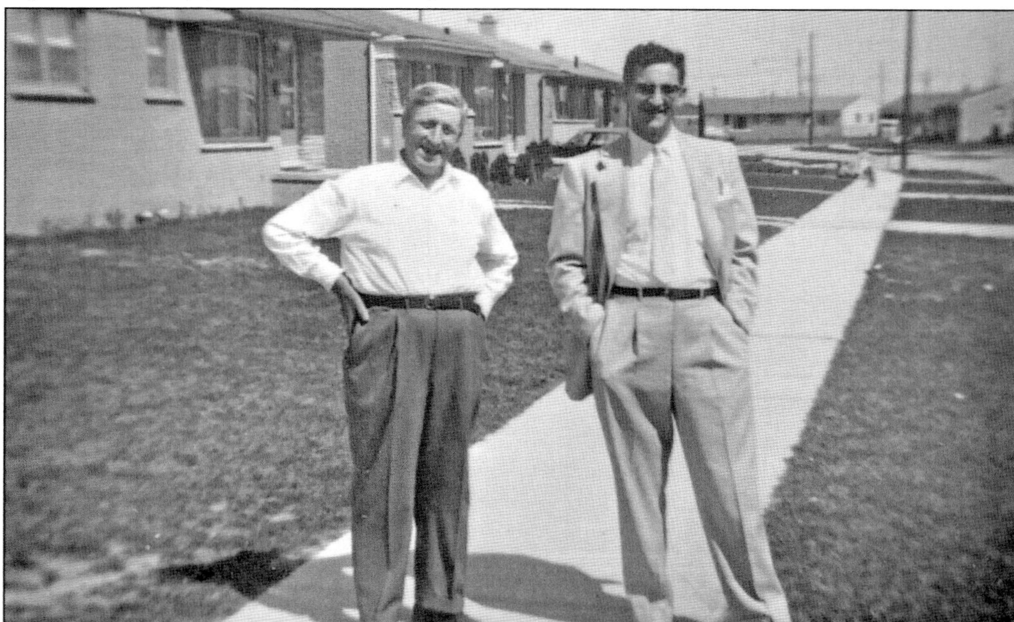

The Koss farm stretched from 11 Mile Road north on Hales Street to the Rosie's Park area. Following his sale, Leo moved to 305 East Parker Avenue, which was a new subdivision at the time. He stands here on the left chatting with neighbor Stephen Sweik. (Courtesy of John and Terry (Cottrell) Wilkinson.)

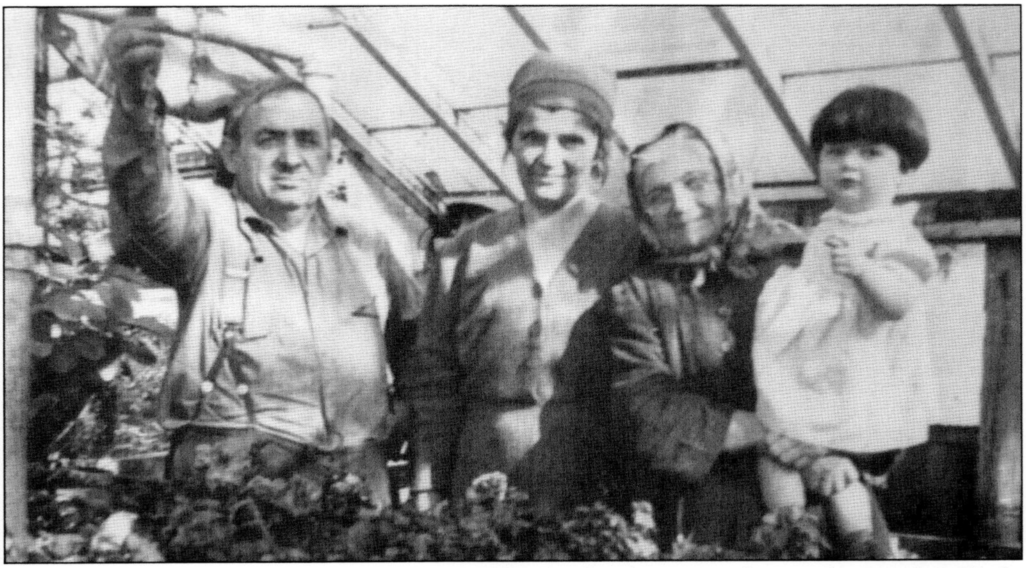

From left to right, Millan and his wife, Julia Illich; the family matriarch Grandma Pauline Illich; and Judy Illich pose inside the family greenhouse in 1942. Emigrants from the Austro-Hungarian Empire, they married in December 1918, eventually moving to Michigan. In 1925, needing a bigger home for their 10 children, they moved to Royal Oak Township, where they could have space for their children to play. An inexpensive home on a site near Lincoln Avenue west of Stephenson Highway was purchased and moved by a farmer to 466 West Harwood Avenue. (Courtesy of the Illich family and Daisy Illich.)

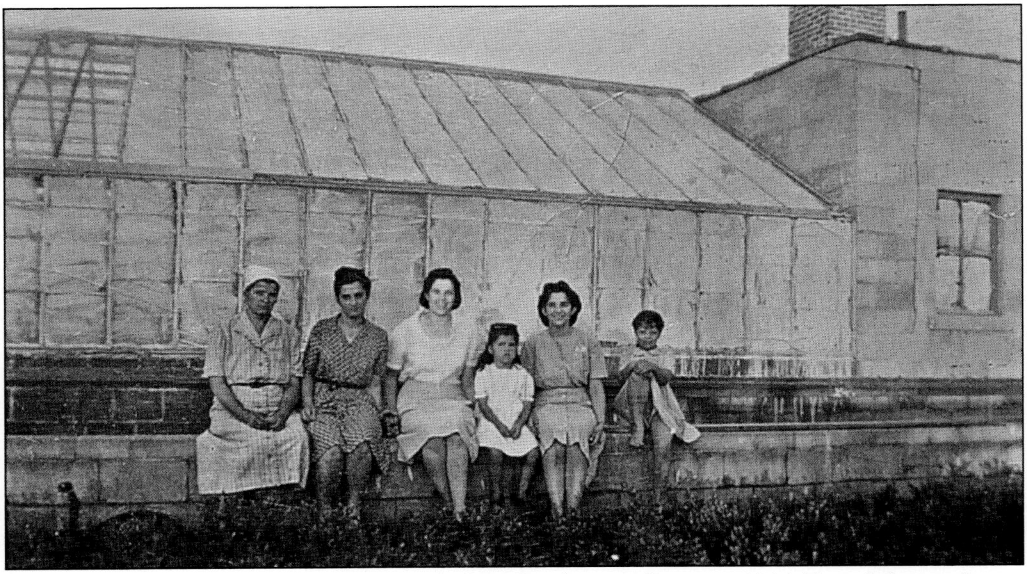

The Illich women pose outside of the Oak View family greenhouse in 1946. From left to right are Julia, Mildred, Pauline, Judy, Helen, and Ruth Ann. Millan Illich worked as a brick mason before transitioning to the greenhouse business. In 1930, the couple started greenhouses on Lincoln Avenue behind the family home. As soon as a child could carry a flowerpot, he or she was put to work when not in school. The greenhouse took its name from the practice of picking up free pots from the Oakview Cemetery. Julia died in 1951, and Millan carried on the business until 1956. (Courtesy of the Illich family and Daisy Illich.)

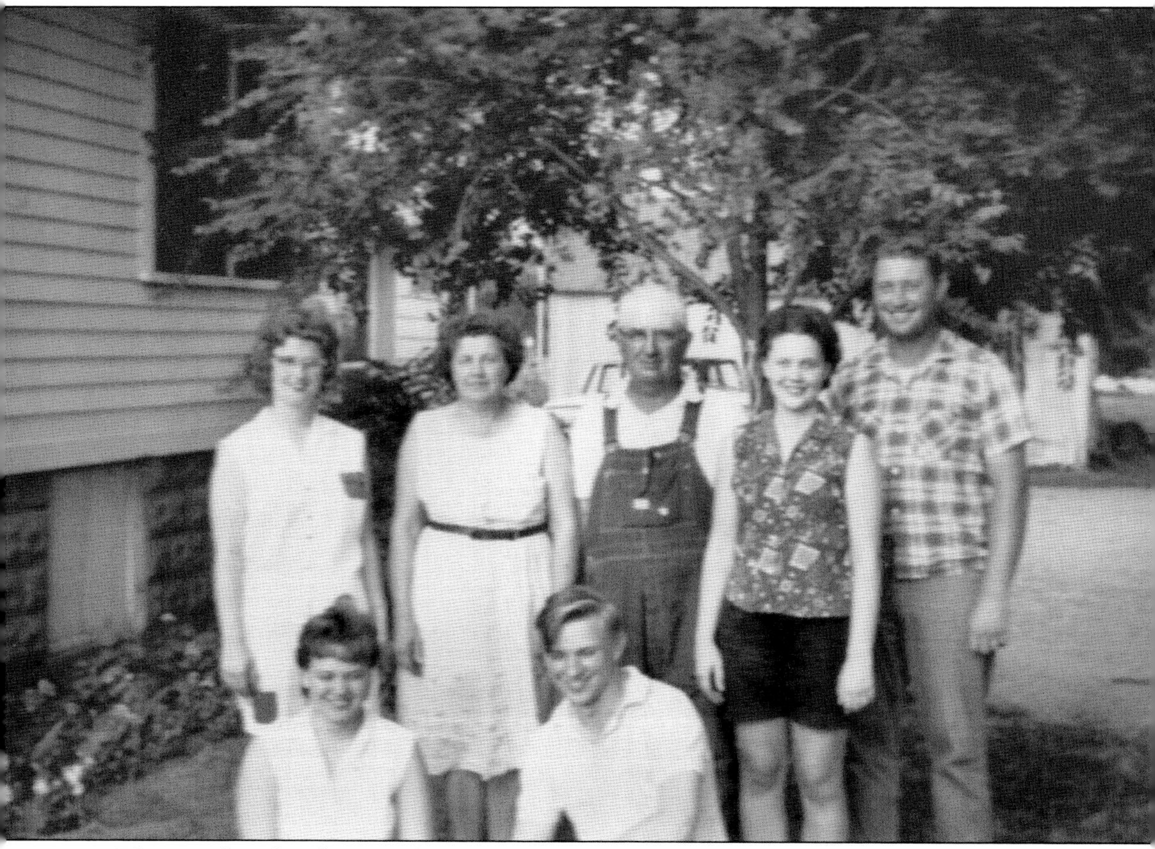

The Kutchey family poses behind their home in the mid-1960s. From left to right are (first row) Catherine Ellen Kutchey and Lawrence David Kutchey, who would pass away in Vietnam in 1968; (second row) Mary Jane Kutchey, family matriarch Mathilda (Minda) Kutchey, father Raymond Charles Kutchey, daughter Rose Ann, and son Raymond Joseph Kutchey. Not pictured is Leslie George Kutchey, who died in 1964. (Courtesy of Mary Jane Kutchey Guc and Raymond Joseph Kutchey.)

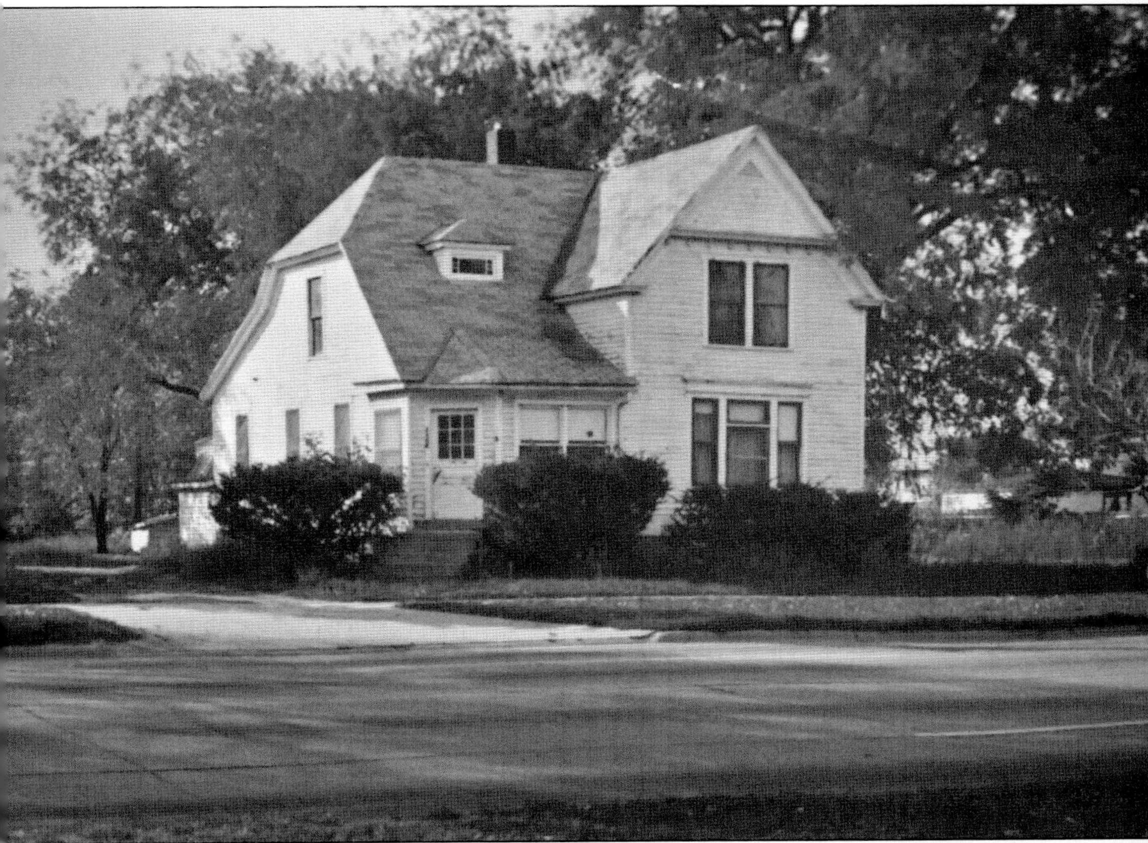

While the Kutchey family lived in their ancestral home, flowers and produce were grown and sold in small stands on two-lane 12 Mile Road. The freshness of their stock was appreciated, and it became a popular stop. Their 80-acre property at 1186 East 12 Mile Road expanded a half-mile south to Gardenia Avenue, with other Kutchey family farms around the area. (Courtesy of Larry Campbell.)

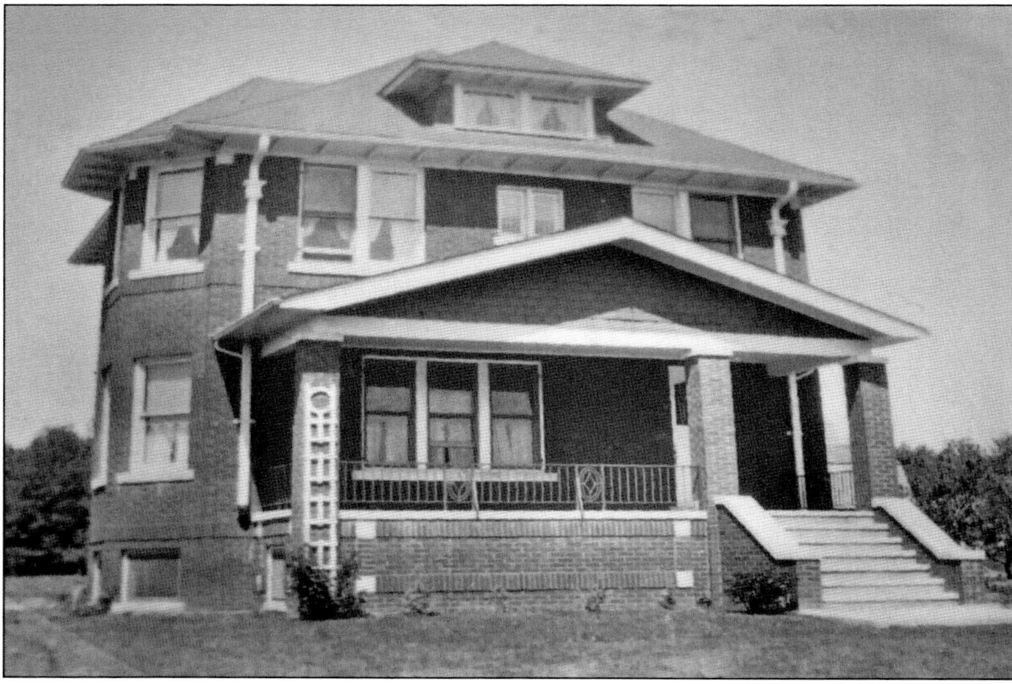

The Horkey farmhouse was located at 29825 John R Road, north of 12 Mile Road, on the west side of John R. The Horkey and Diesing farms were adjacent on the north and south side of 12 Mile, west of John R. The Diesing farm had 12 Mile as its northern border. (Courtesy of George Horkey Jr. and Marietta Horkey Walden.)

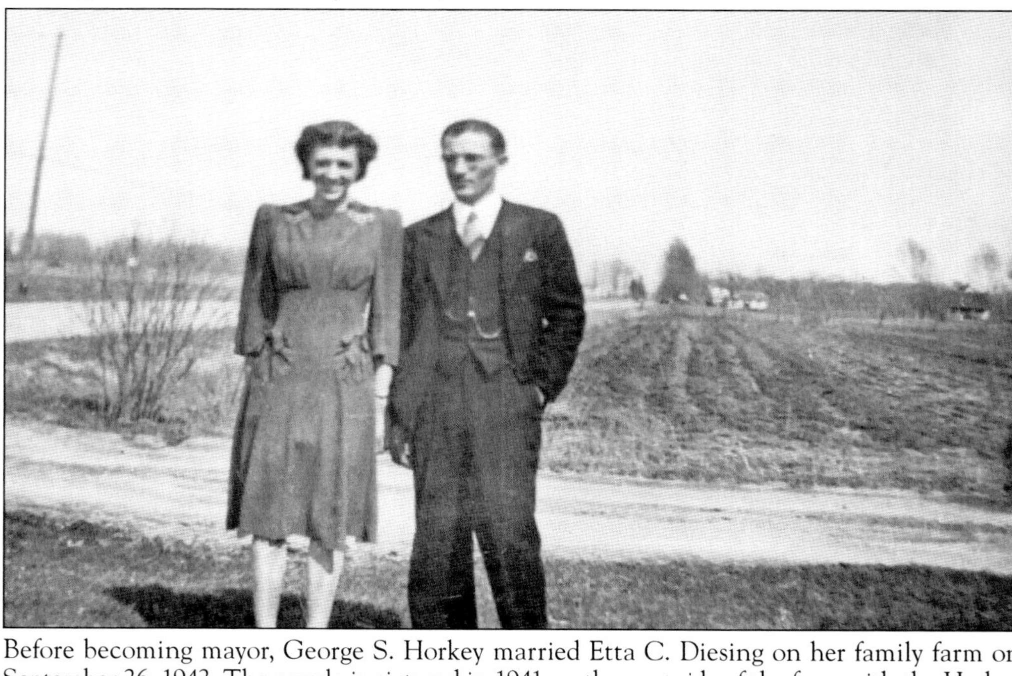

Before becoming mayor, George S. Horkey married Etta C. Diesing on her family farm on September 26, 1942. The couple is pictured in 1941 on the west side of the farm with the Horkey property on the left. In the engagement notice, Horkey is described as an active farmer in Royal Oak Township. (Courtesy of George Horkey Jr. and Marietta Horkey Walden.)

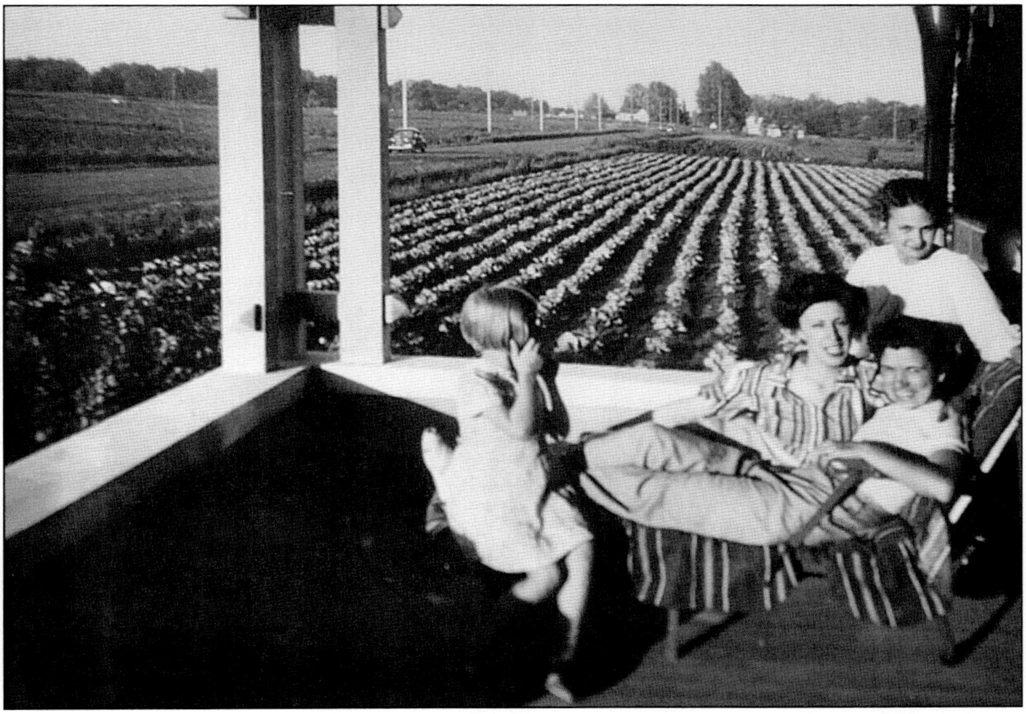

Members of the William and Nellie Diesing family relax on their porch watching traffic go by on 12 Mile Road. The property consisted of 30 acres at 433 West 12 Mile. Their house was a Sears and Roebuck cinder-block construction. Their farmland was eventually turned into subdivisions, but Diesing Street still remains. (Courtesy of George Horkey Jr. and Marietta Horkey Walden.)

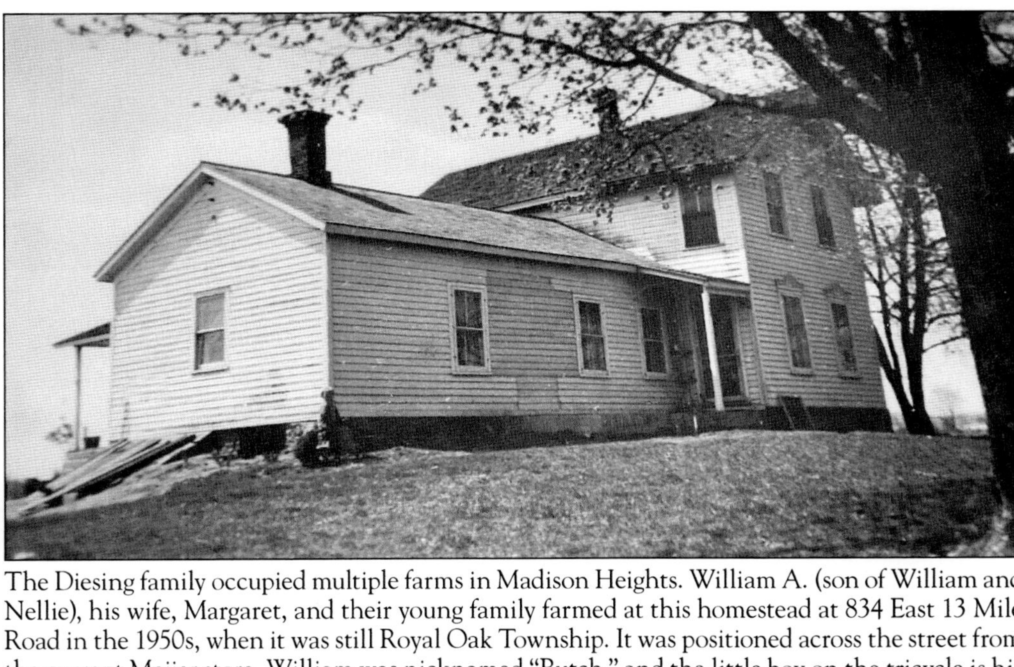

The Diesing family occupied multiple farms in Madison Heights. William A. (son of William and Nellie), his wife, Margaret, and their young family farmed at this homestead at 834 East 13 Mile Road in the 1950s, when it was still Royal Oak Township. It was positioned across the street from the current Meijer store. William was nicknamed "Butch," and the little boy on the tricycle is his son Glen. (Courtesy of Marietta Horkey Walden and George Horkey Jr.)

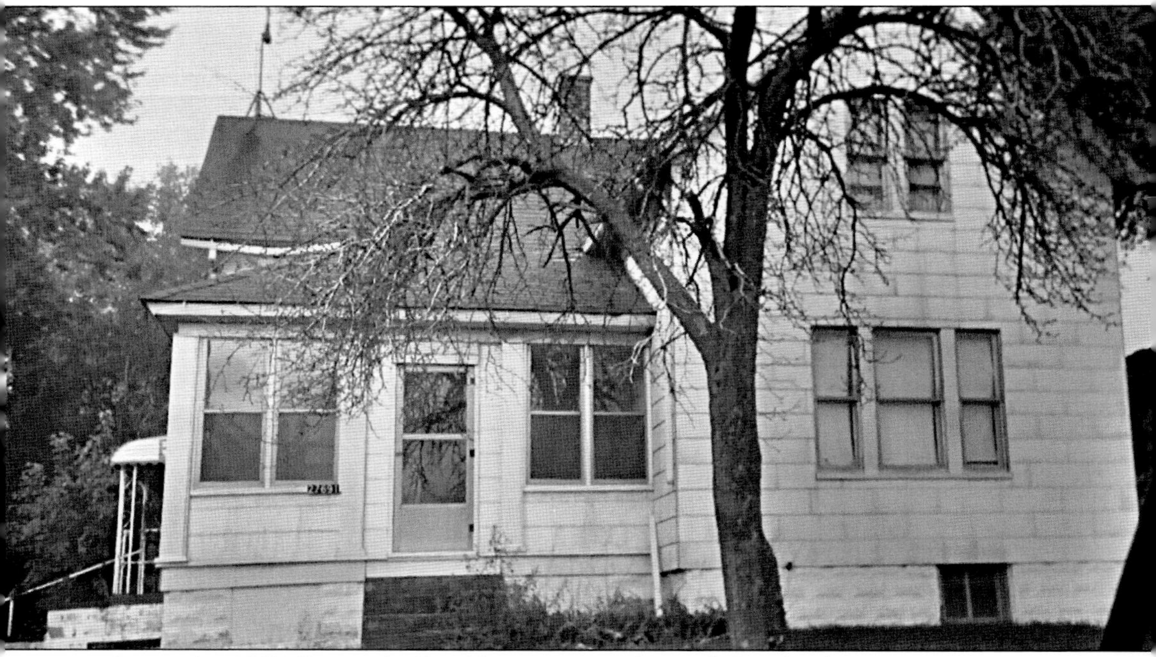

Located at 27691 Dequindre Road between 11 and 12 Mile Roads, Slovenian immigrants Bernard Travnikar and wife, Marie, raised their four children Bernice, Bernard Jr., Vladimir, and Richard in this home. Their oldest son, Bernie Jr., was born in Highland Park on May 28, 1915. Three years later, the family moved here to then–Royal Oak Township. Throughout his lifetime, Bernie Jr. was instrumental in the growth and development of the city. A 1934 Madison High School graduate, he took many criminal justice courses before becoming a police officer in 1943 with Royal Oak Township. In 1953, he purchased a bar in the city, which he owned for several years. Bernie Jr. was married to Margaret over 50 years, and the couple lived in seven different Madison Heights locations during their married lives. Younger brother Richard Travnikar also served on the police force as one of the city's first detectives. (Courtesy of Mary Merkel.)

Two

Growth of a City

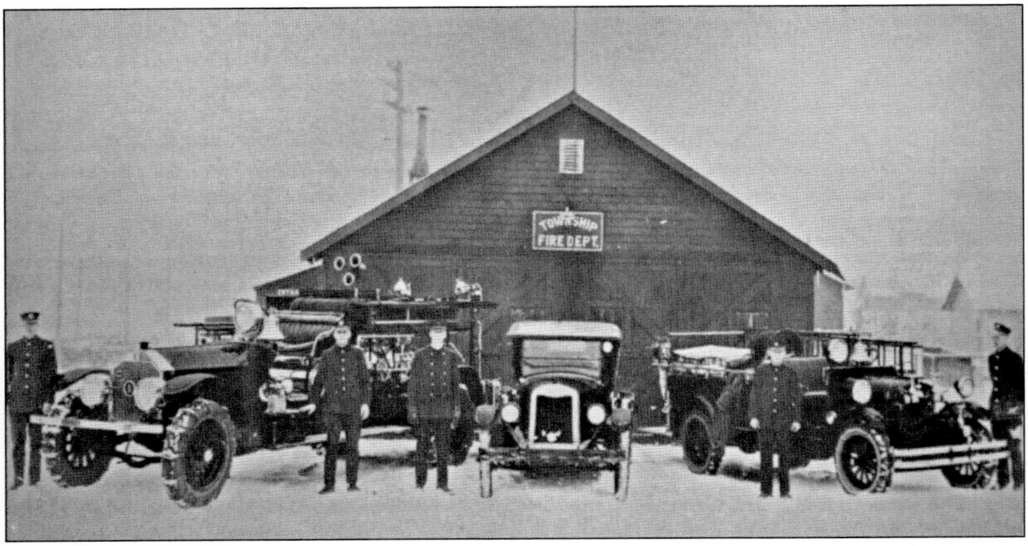

The area of Royal Oak Township now known as Madison Heights experienced significant growth during the 1920s. Prior to 1942, the township fire department was located in Hazel Park. When that area was incorporated in 1942, the department moved its headquarters to John R Road and Sixth Street. Township offices were also moved from Hazel Park to a small building at 27452 John R. (Courtesy of Madison Heights Historical Commission.)

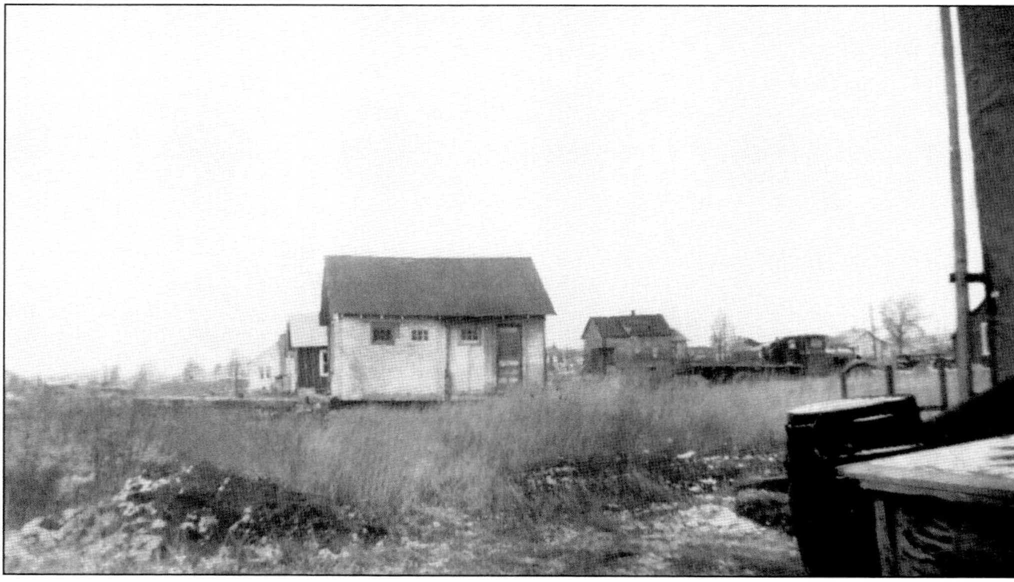

When the original pioneer families found their homestead lots, they were often without a place to live while they built their future homes. This former goat barn was delivered in November 1937 to Ted and Fran Carlson at what is now 26555 Alger Street. They managed to live in the structure while they built their home on the property at 26547 Alger. The couple's daughter occupies the enlarged and renovated house today. (Courtesy of Delores Carlson McCalvey.)

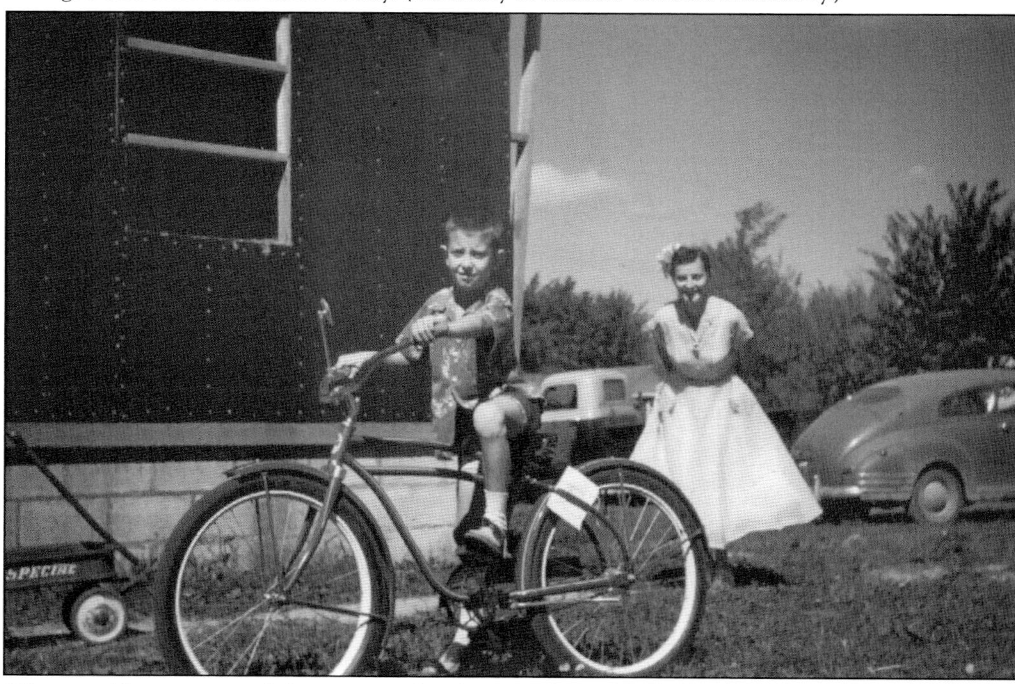

Often, residents occupied their incomplete homes adorned with just tarpaper. In this 1954 image, young Ron Huxtable is teased by his mother Anne Perkins Huxtable at their tarpapered homestead at 26531 Brush Street. Ron and his younger sister, Diane Huxtable Stouffer (not shown), both went on to graduate from Madison High School. Tragically, Ron was killed in Vietnam. He lost his life nine days after his 22nd birthday in 1970. (Courtesy of Diane Huxtable Stouffer.)

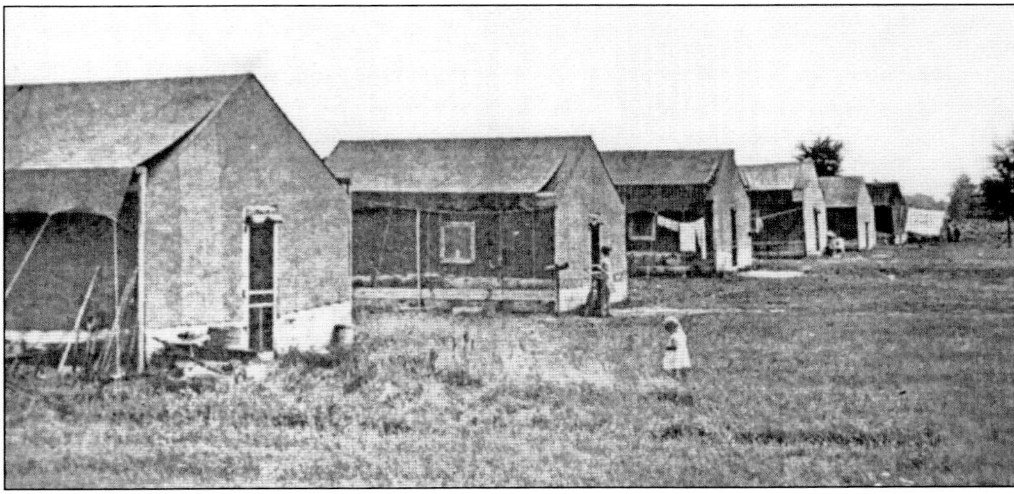

The "Tent City" was the name given to an area inhabited by welfare recipients south of 13 Mile Road and east of John R Road. It was across from the original Lamphere High School when it was a two-story building constructed in 1928. In 1937, the Lamphere School District refused to accept students from this area. Administrators advised state officials that most came from other communities with no source of funding for their education. (Courtesy of the *Daily Tribune*.)

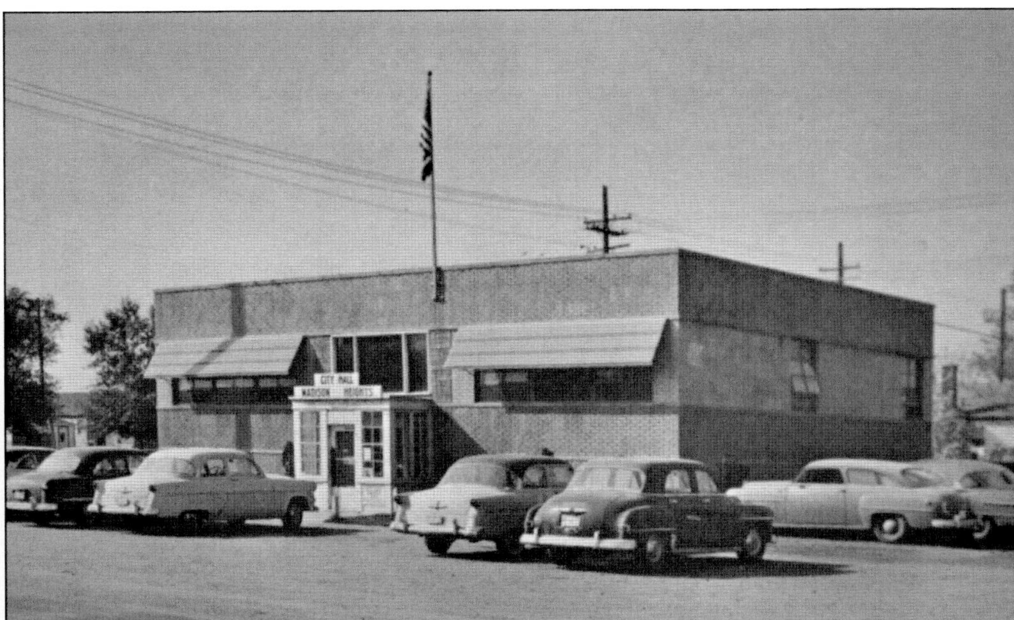

Instrumental in the passage of the city charter was a young charter consultant named Donald Smith who was appointed as city manager in February 1956. There was limited available office space, as Royal Oak Township was using most of it. Additionally, Smith faced the prospect of running a city on borrowed money and the problems of equally dividing the assets of the old Royal Oak Township. Township officials requested a formal census for this purpose. City officials set up offices in the city-township hall at 26305 John R Road. The building still exists today. (Courtesy of Madison Heights Historical Commission.)

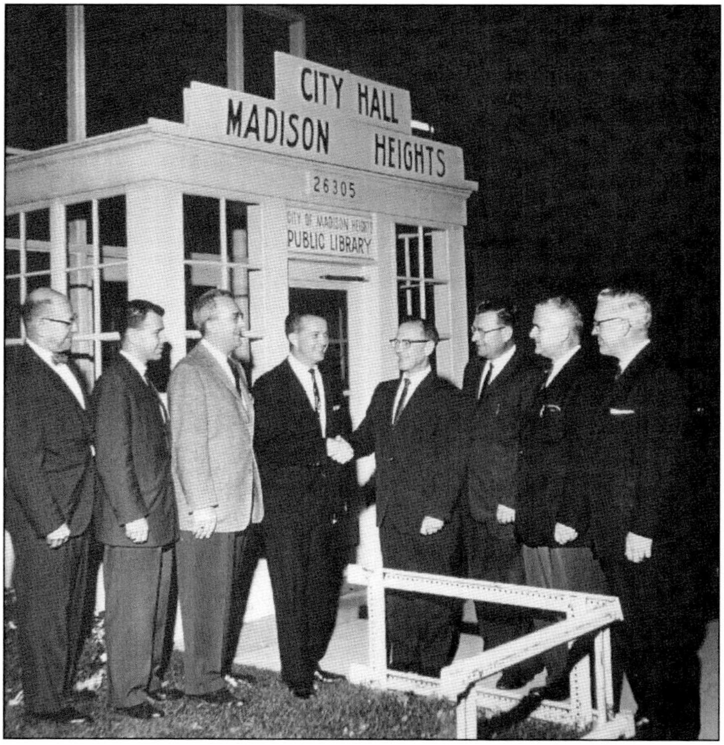

This October 23, 1961, photograph of a street lighting ceremony marks the introduction of city streetlights. Pictured from left to right are George K. Glass, sales department, Detroit Edison; Dean W. Eggart, councilman; Jerome A. Nowacki, councilman; Bill S. Huffman, mayor; Howard Stephenson, assistant vice president and sales manager, Detroit Edison; John B. Michrina, councilman; Richard W. Marshall, city manager; and Harland Ritze, assistant manager, Oakland Sales, Detroit Edison. (Courtesy of City of Madison Heights.)

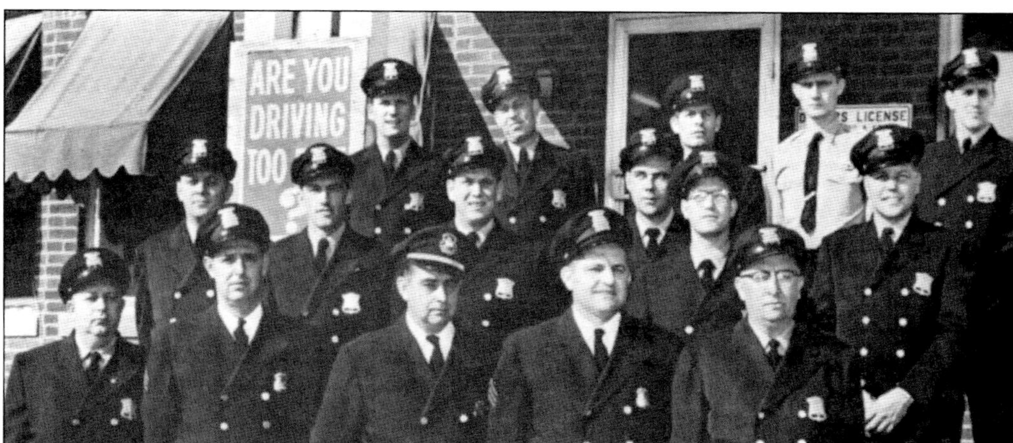

Transitioning to a city from a township brought a paid, expanded police force. Ready for action are, from left to right (first row) H. Todd, Sgt. Joseph Landino, Chief Robert E. Richardson, Sgt. Frank Rutecki, and Paul Myatt; (second row) V. Balabuch, J. Rehse, J. Simpson, Robert Sager, D. Badgley, and Clarence Hill; (third row) William Sloan, Thomas Linville, Russell Pearce, Joseph Dale Whitefield, and R. Pineau. (Courtesy of Madison Heights Metropolitan Club No. 69)

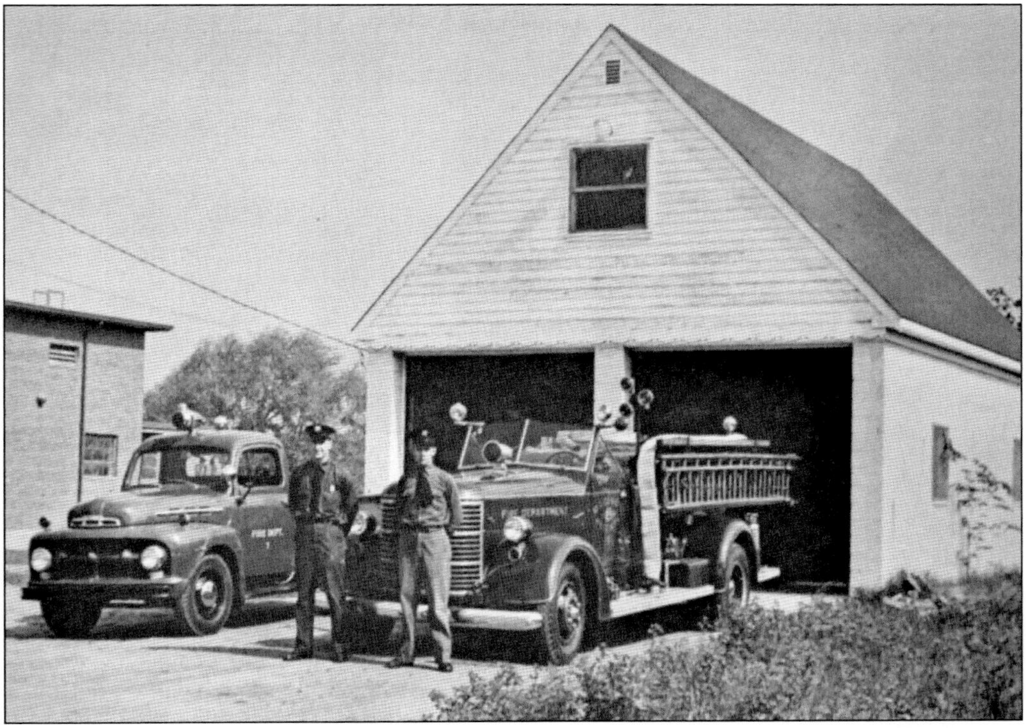

This two-car garage served as the early fire station for the north end of the city, replaced by the station at 13 Mile Road and Brush Street, and then by the new fire station at 31313 Brush. The wood framed garage was originally part of the Thomas Brace farm. Living quarters for the men were on the upstairs floor, complete with a slide-down pole. (Courtesy of City of Madison Heights.)

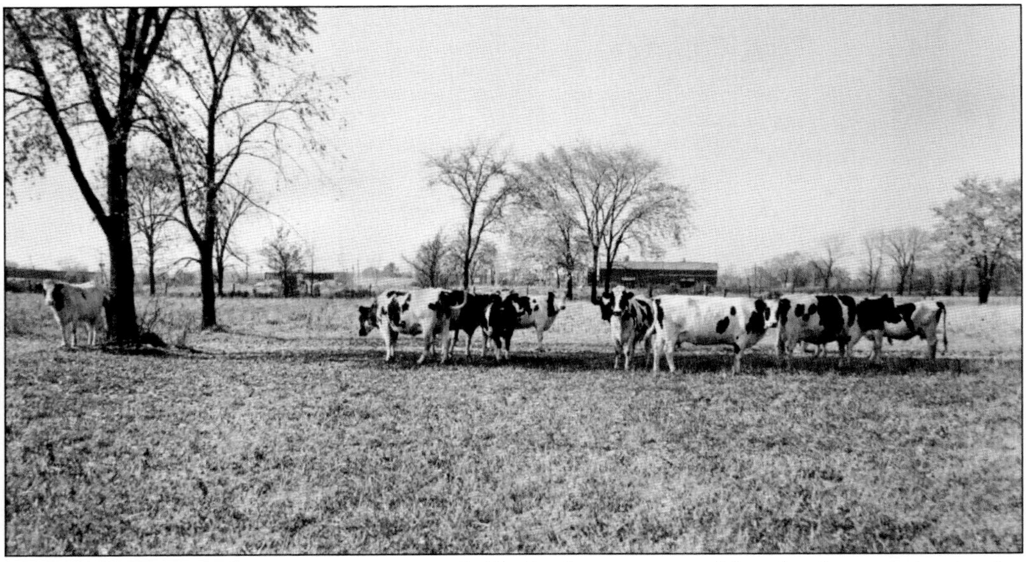

A herd of cows calmly grazes in an open field, the last vestiges of farmland remaining in the changing city landscape. This November 1956 view highlights an area north of 13 Mile Road near Stephenson Highway. In the distance, one can faintly view Commercial Steel Treating, the beginning of the light industrial areas that are common throughout Madison Heights and contribute to the tax base. (Courtesy of Gary Cheek.)

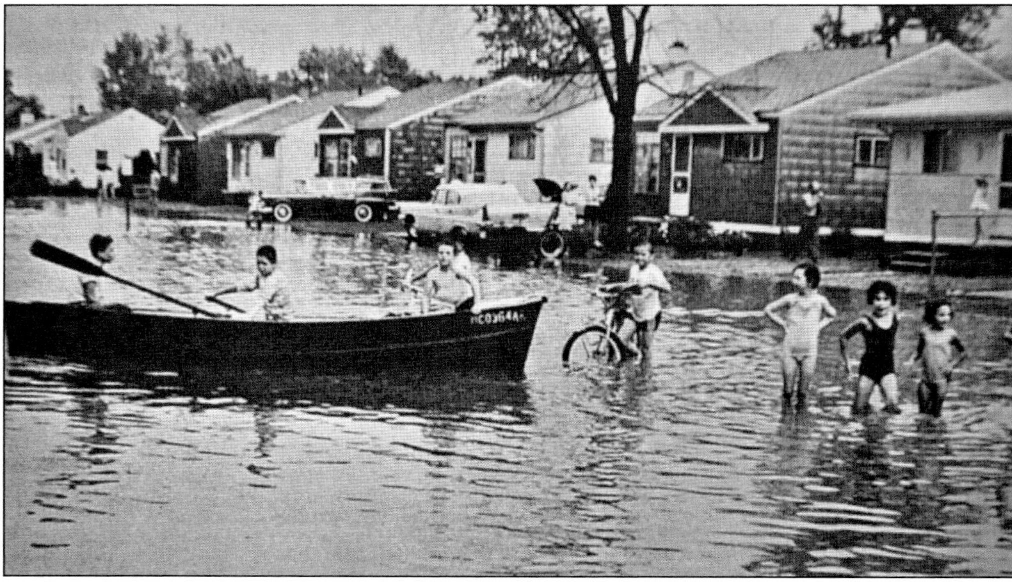

Madison Heights inherited many old problems from the township. These included inadequate and poorly maintained dirt roads. Only a few of the 50 miles of roads were paved. The rest were almost impassable during wet weather. This problem and others were among those the city was determined to remedy. (Courtesy of Madison Heights Historical Commission.)

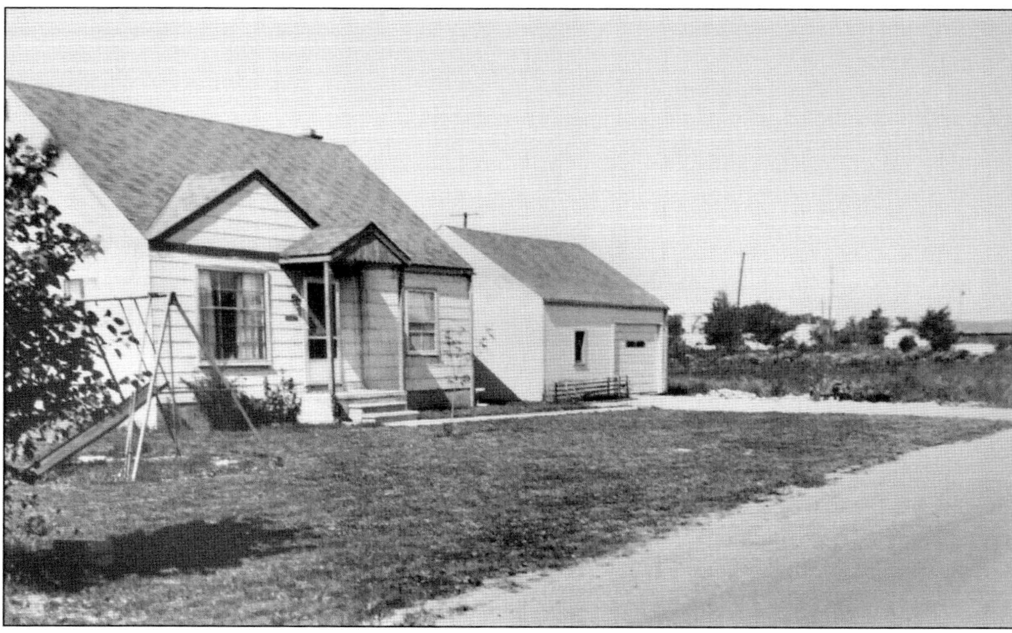

Another family of German immigrants in the early 1900s included Fred and Ida Gosbeth with their four children. Mother Ida passed away in 1983 at the age of 98. Their son Franz and his wife, Hazel, became one of the first families to live on Groveland Street south of 14 Mile Road during the Royal Oak Township days. The rear of their lot faced the early Texaco gas station on John R Road, although grassy fields made up the open spaces surrounding them in the "Northeastern Highway" subdivision. Hazel passed in 2002 and was proud to raise her family in the area. (Courtesy of Jim Carlton.)

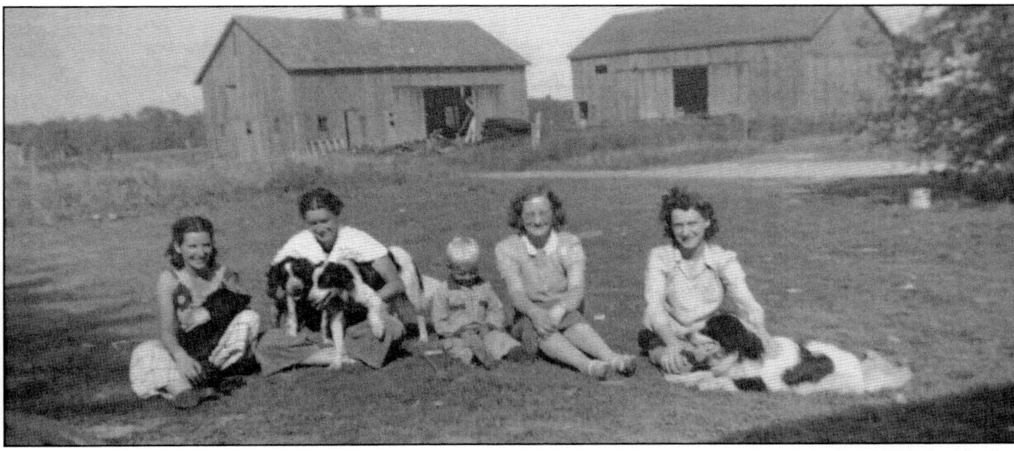

In the 1940s, a group of over 20 families formed the Cooperative Homesteads Inc. on a secluded tract near the northeastern corner of John R and 13 Mile Roads for the purposes of building their own private subdivision. The famed architect Frank Lloyd Wright offered to build the homes in his unique style and sell them, with the co-op members providing the labor. Wright lost interest when the prospective homeowners went to war, and a new architect drew the houses. Once built, homes on five streets were shielded from the rest of the community and became self-sufficient, using their own well water and raising chickens, hogs, and even a few cows. (Courtesy of Madison Heights Historical Commission.)

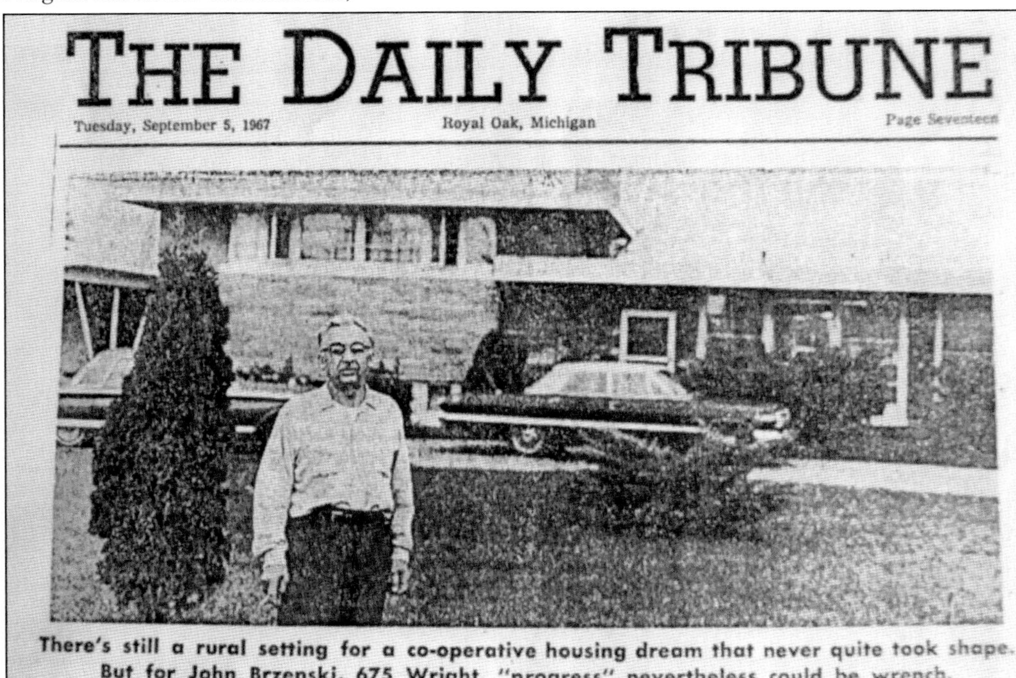

THE DAILY TRIBUNE

Tuesday, September 5, 1967 Royal Oak, Michigan Page Seventeen

There's still a rural setting for a co-operative housing dream that never quite took shape. But for John Brzenski, 675 Wright, "progress" nevertheless could be wrench.

Homesteader John Brzezinski and his family were the first residents in the unique Frank Lloyd Wright–style subdivision. Serving as the group's 15-year president, he related how the area was isolated from the community by a row of trees, a wide field, and single street access. In the 1990s, the homes were caught up in redevelopment issues and, after much debate, were torn down. Developer Stuart Frankel replaced the entire area with 47 condominiums and a Meijer retail/grocery complex that opened in May 2002. (Courtesy of Madison Heights Public Library.)

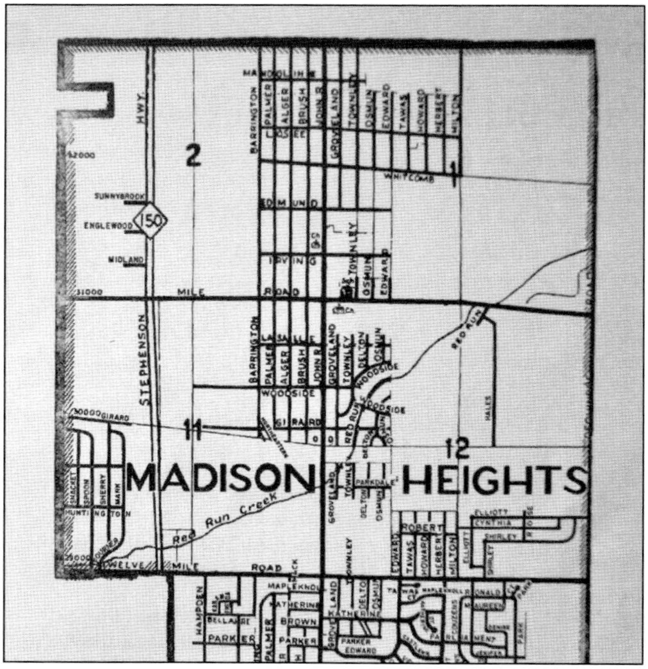

This map from a 1959 program book details the physical landscape of Madison Heights before the Red Run creek was covered. The north section of the city is displayed, with 12 Mile Road running along the bottom of the image, 13 Mile Road in the middle, and 14 Mile Road along the top. I-75 did not exist then. Woodside Avenue is wrapped in a semicircle around the drain area, with an extension of that semicircle going west off John R Road. Many streets and subdivisions on the west are now large commercial developments. (Courtesy of Mary Merkel and Madison Heights Metropolitan Club 69.)

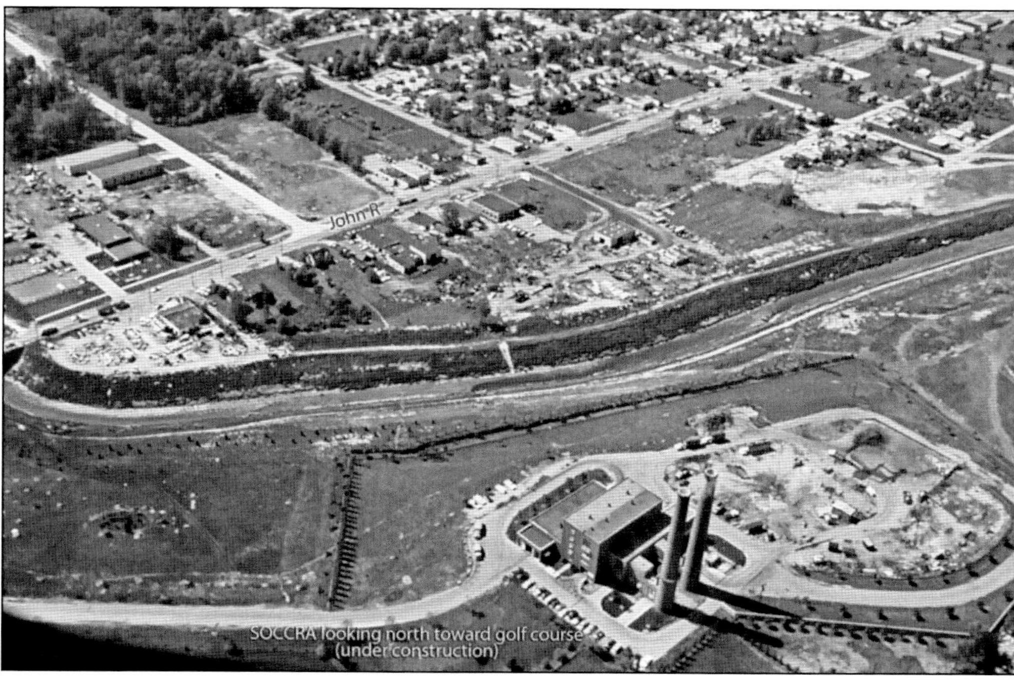

This aerial image from 1970 shows the future location of the Red Oaks Golf Course looking northwest. Near the bottom, the South Oakland County Incinerator Plant with two smokestacks is visible. The bridge on John R Road where vehicles crossed over the open drain is visible on the extreme left. The light-colored road near the printed name John R is newly poured Ajax Drive, which travels between the wooded areas. (Courtesy of the Oakland County Economic Development Department.)

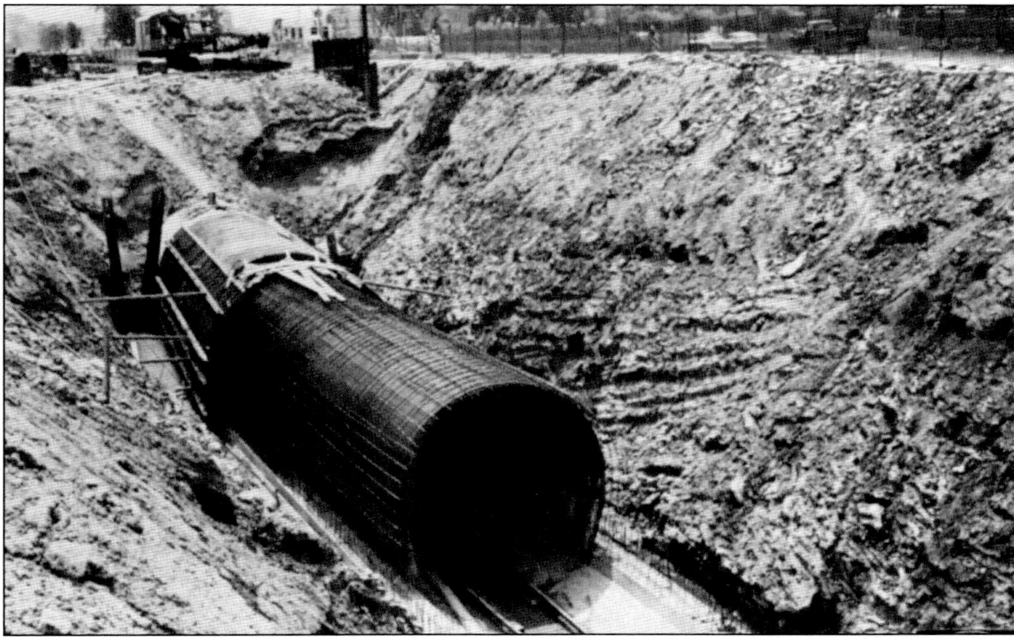

Early development turned Red Run, the small river within the community, into a drain. With no environmental thoughts or laws, Red Run's south branch was buried in the late 1920s, followed by the north branch in the 1960s. Both became part of the storm and sanitary drain systems for the fast-growing northern suburbs. Here the drain is being covered along the Stephenson Highway right-of-way at 12 Mile Road in late June 1962, facing southwest. (Courtesy of City of Madison Heights.)

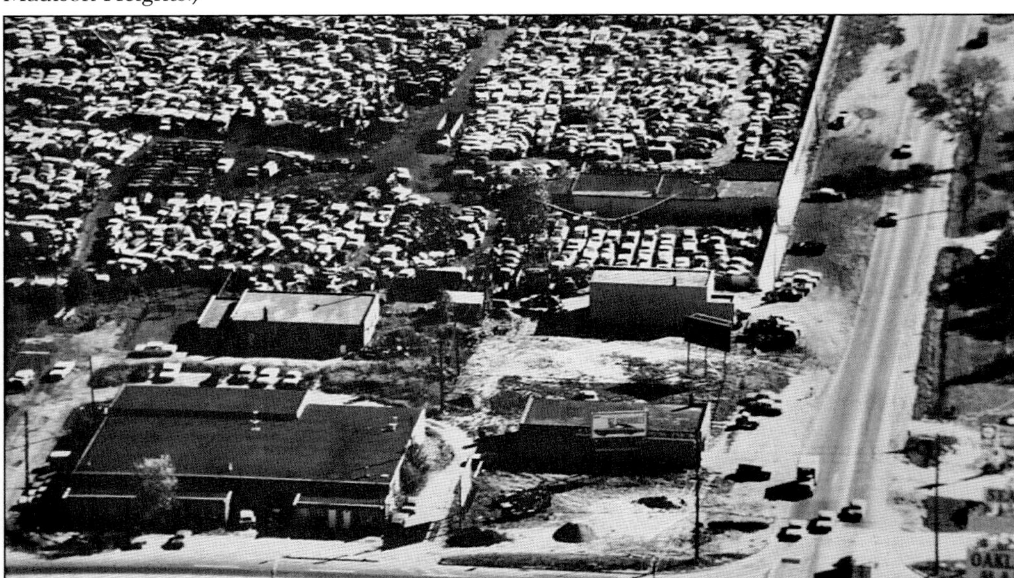

This aerial view of 14 Mile and John R Roads provides a sense of the physical landscape of Madison Heights at the time. John R runs vertically along the right, and 14 Mile runs along the bottom. An Oakland Mall sign and Sears are visible in the lower right corner, with a billboard advertising a 1967 Chevrolet in the lower middle. The image features a large walled junkyard of cars on the east side of John R south of 14 Mile. (Courtesy of Madison Heights Historical Commission.)

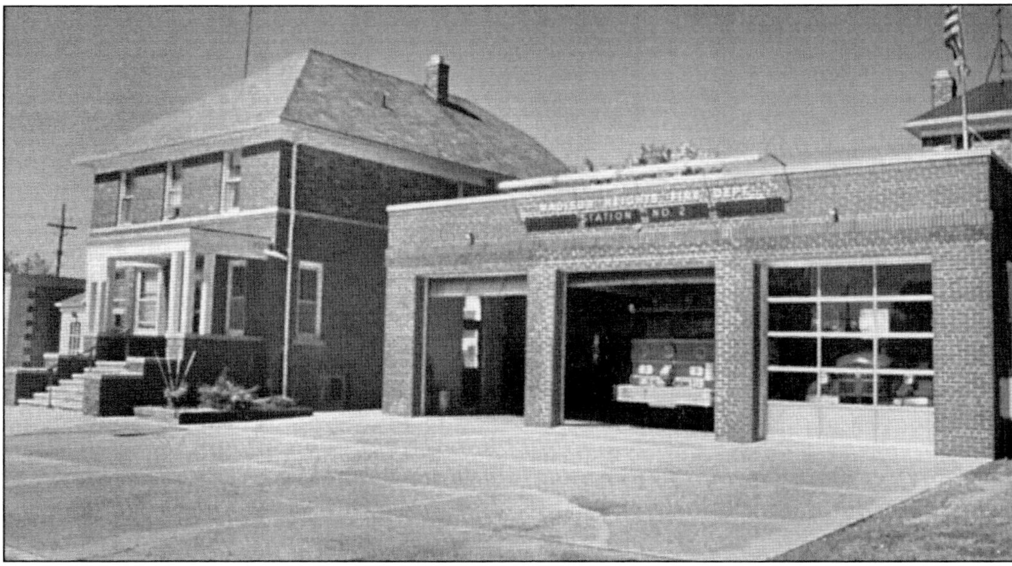

This image features the first south-end fire station. The two-story house to the left of the station housed the city's probation offices and the majority of city services in the early years. A second Station No. 2 for this part of Madison Heights was constructed in 1978 on John R Road, just north of the existing one. Upon completion of Phase 1 of the new south-end station, operations were moved from the old into the new, along with the probation offices. Demolition of the old station and probation offices was necessary to complete the fire complex. (Courtesy of Madison Heights Historical Commission.)

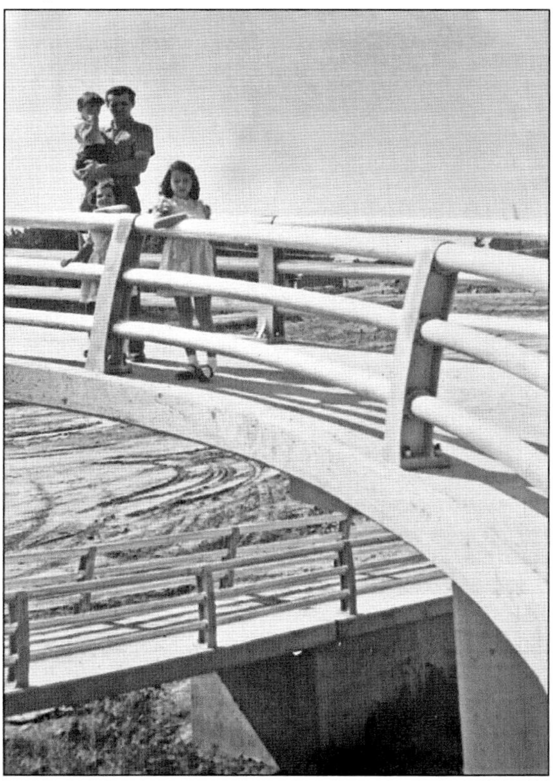

Ralph Merkel and his children watch the construction of I-75 from the newly constructed overpass on Gardenia Avenue in 1963. The freeway was extended south from Pontiac to 11 Mile Road with a connection along 8 Mile Road. Gardenia Avenue is located at 11 1/2 Mile Road. The development of the interstate helped connect Madison Heights to the rest of the country. (Courtesy of Mary Merkel.)

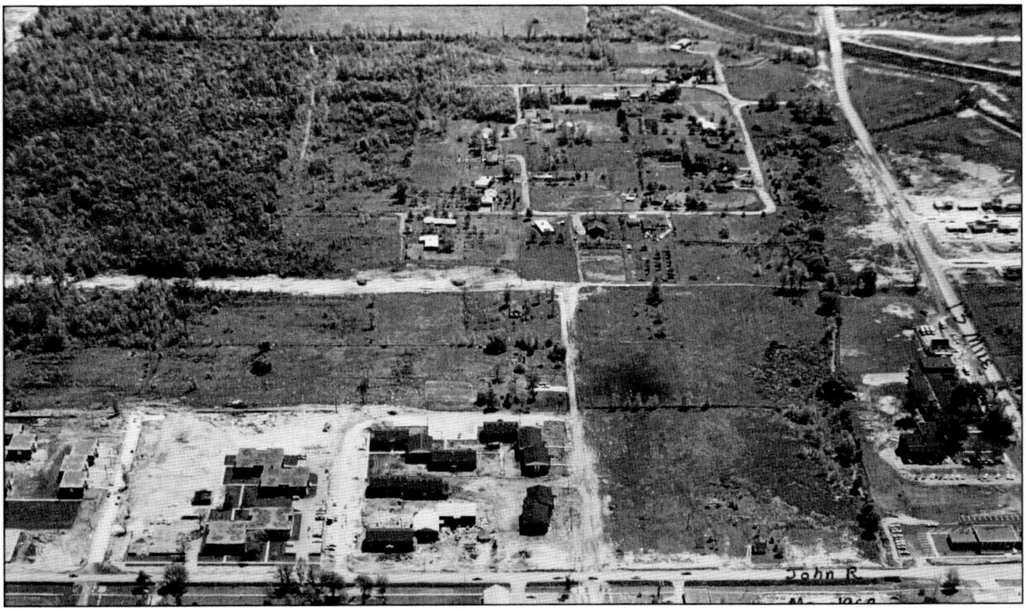

This 1968 aerial view of 13 Mile and John R Roads shows the physical landscape of Madison Heights at the time. The photograph looks east from the intersection. (Photograph by Margene Scott.)

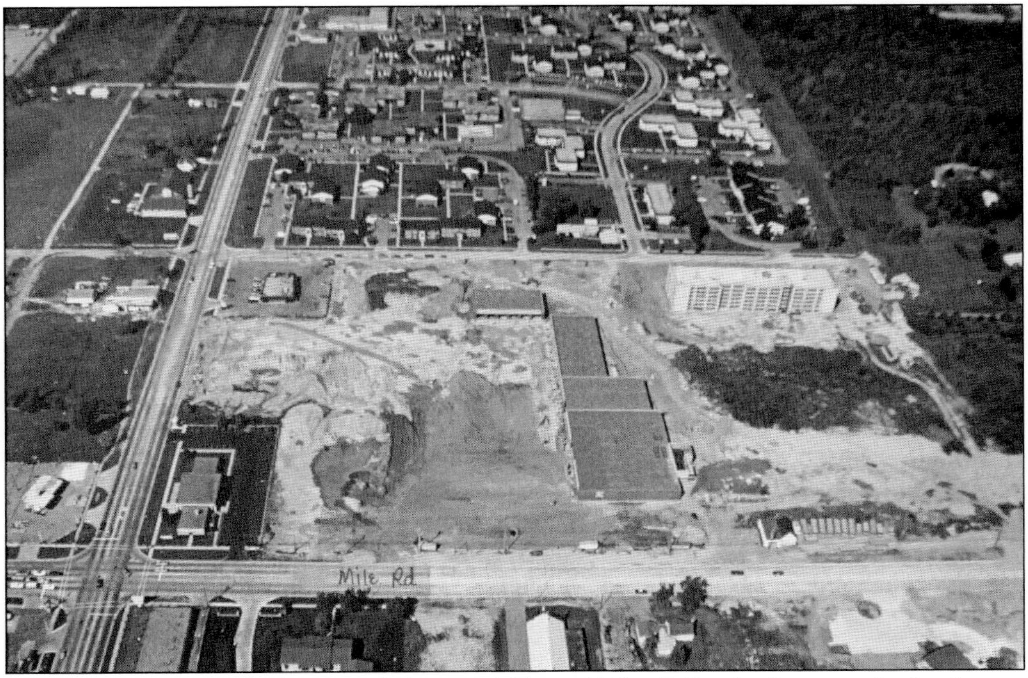

This 1978 aerial view looking north from 13 Mile and John R Roads illustrates the landscape. The shopping center under construction housed a Farmer Jack and smaller stores, all of which are gone now. The site is now home to Sam's Club, with a CVS drugstore on the corner at lower left. The little white building with the dark roof was the original north-end fire station, part of the Thomas Brace farm. In the middle right is the just-built first senior co-op, on Irving Avenue. The wooded area at upper right is just north of the Frank Lloyd Wright subdivision, which is now Meijer. (Photograph by Margene Scott.)

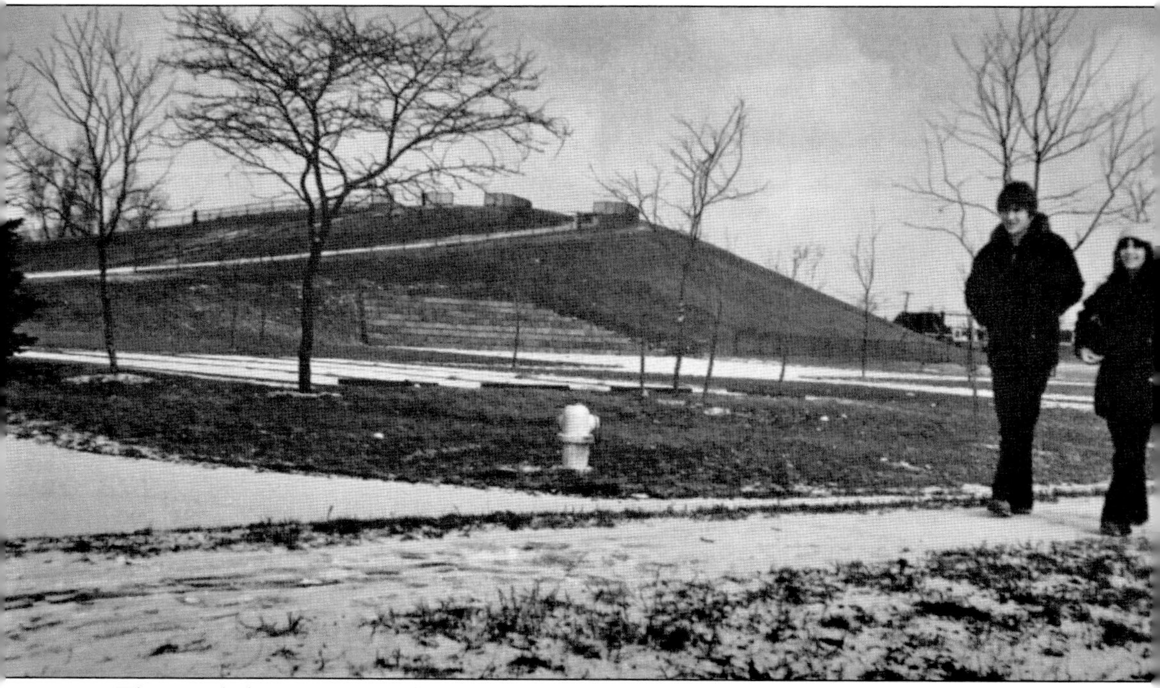

This south-facing view of the sled hill illustrates the larger scope of the hill and includes the city amphitheater that was used for small events. The photograph, taken in the late 1970s, was included in the 1980 city calendar. The new 2005 fire station would be constructed to the east of the hill. (Photograph by Margene Scott.)

Three

City Departments

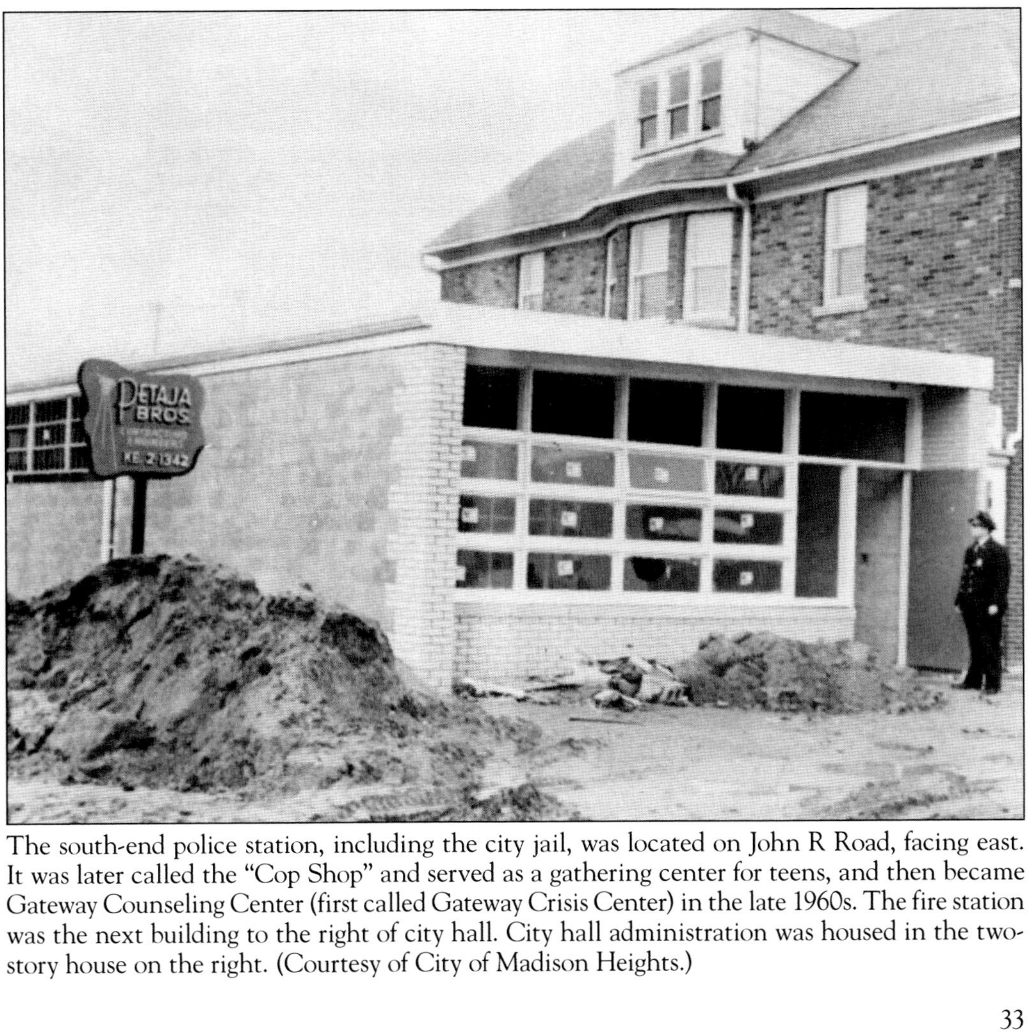

The south-end police station, including the city jail, was located on John R Road, facing east. It was later called the "Cop Shop" and served as a gathering center for teens, and then became Gateway Counseling Center (first called Gateway Crisis Center) in the late 1960s. The fire station was the next building to the right of city hall. City hall administration was housed in the two-story house on the right. (Courtesy of City of Madison Heights.)

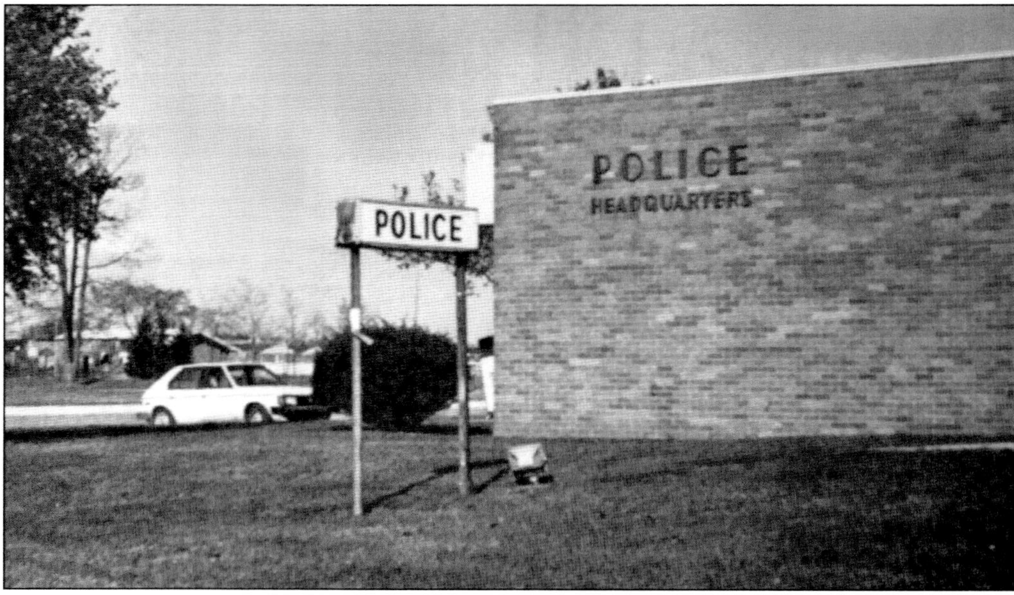

Police headquarters was located at 200 West 13 Mile Road after moving out of the large home on John R Road south of Greig Avenue and before moving to its current location at 280 West 13 Mile. The Jaycee Park Shelter, which is hidden by the new station, is clearly visible. (Photograph by Margene Scott.)

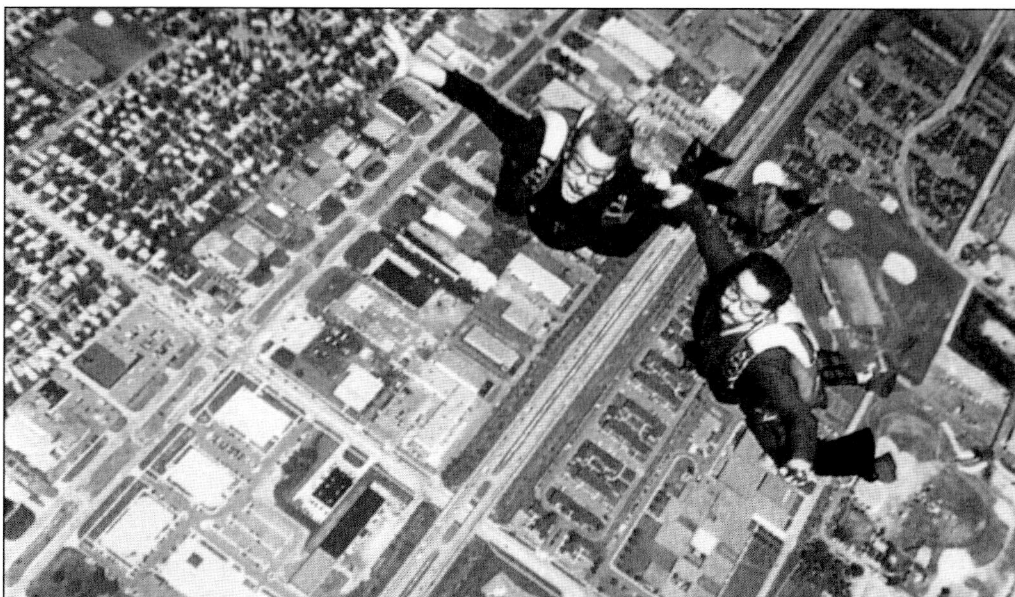
Men posing as Batman and the Joker make a dramatic entrance at a Say No To Drugs Day rally by skydiving to the sled hill where this event was held, as elementary-aged children await their arrival. The characters in any given year would lead the crowd in reciting the word "No" repeatedly, with an emphasis on the dangers of taking drugs. It was believed that presenting this program to this age group would serve as a significant influence, particularly ahead of middle school. Each child was given a T-shirt with the year and the school name printed on it along with the event logo. (Courtesy of City of Madison Heights.)

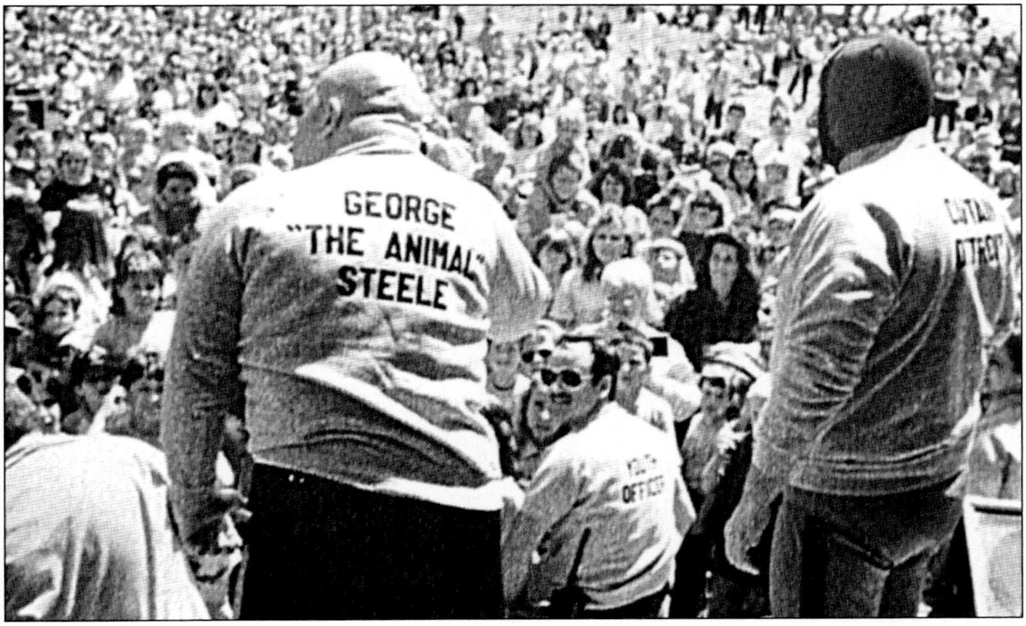

The police department held the annual event in June in the 1980s and 1990s. Children received lunch with the program promoting the slogan. Noteworthy guests included Ronald McDonald, Santa Claus, former governor of Michigan the Hon. John Engler, and professional athletes such as George "The Animal" Steele (pictured) and Lions football players Lomas Brown and Ken Dallafior. Captain Detroit is also seen here, along with officer Larry Gibson, who helped coordinate the program. (Courtesy of the *Daily Tribune*.)

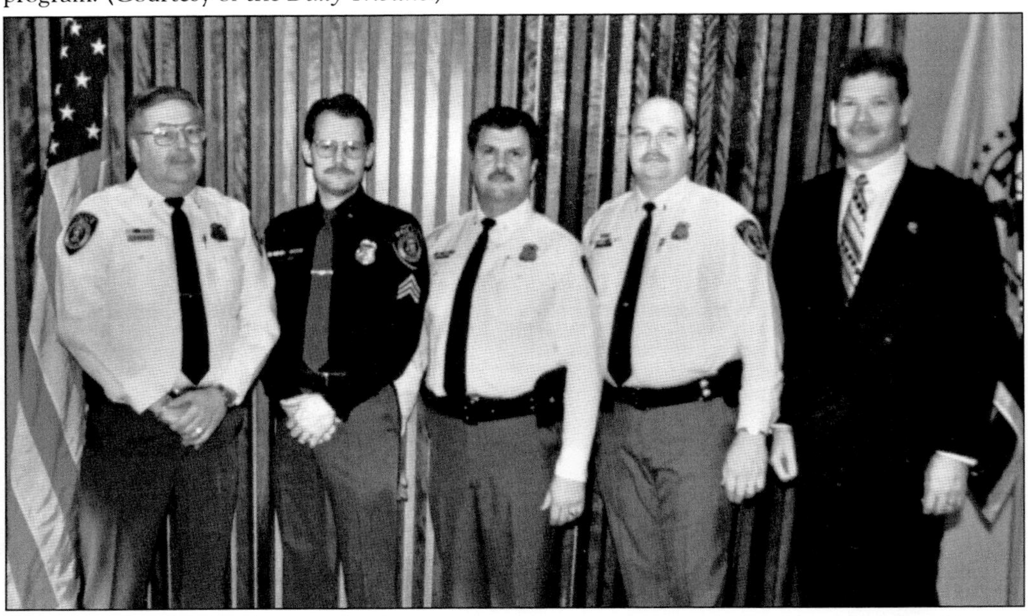

City manager Jon R. Austin, the longest serving city manager in Madison Heights history, congratulates four police officers on their promotions on January 15, 1996. From left to right are new police chief James Keary, Sgt. Kevin Sagan, deputy police chief Mike Harries, and Lt. Bob Blickensdorf. All four served as police chief later in their careers with the Madison Heights Police Department. (Courtesy of City of Madison Heights.)

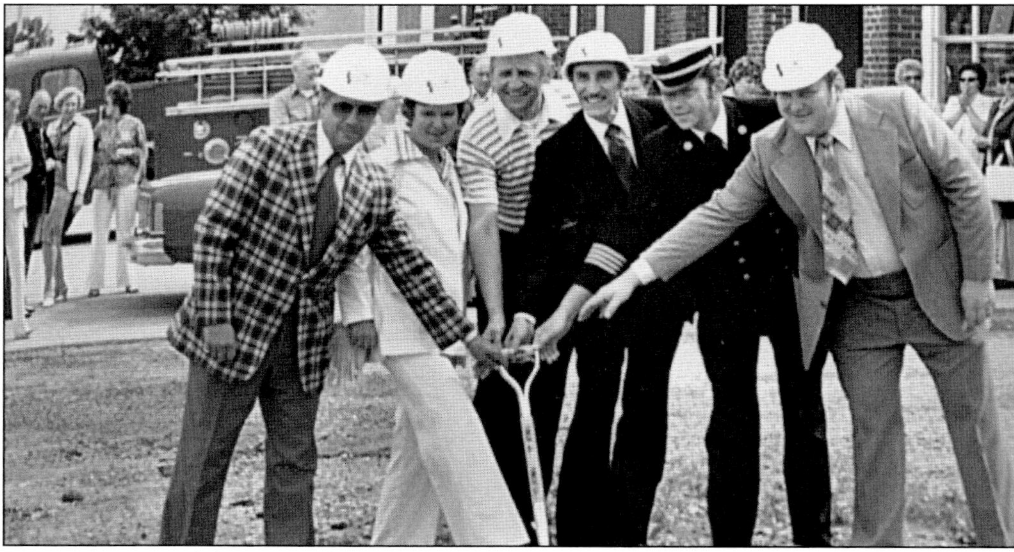

Representatives of the city and contractor Cronk and Tocco Inc. held a formal ground-breaking ceremony on Wednesday, June 14, 1978, for the new south-end fire station at the construction site, adjacent to the existing south-end station on John R Road south of 11 Mile Road. Participating in the ground-breaking were, from left to right, John Tocco; Betty Huffman, wife of state senator Bill S. Huffman; Councilman Walter N. Giszczak; Mayor George W. Suarez; fire chief Donald Hoskins; and Councilman Gary M. Geralds. The old station was demolished after the contractor completed enough of the new building to enable fire equipment to be moved in. (Photograph by Margene Scott.)

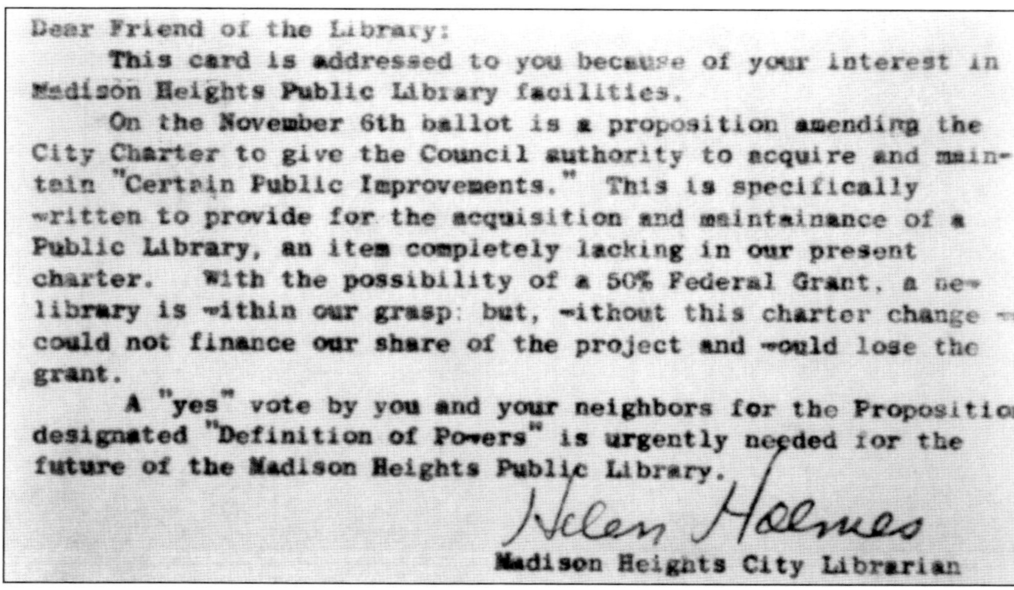

Dear Friend of the Library:

This card is addressed to you because of your interest in Madison Heights Public Library facilities.

On the November 6th ballot is a proposition amending the City Charter to give the Council authority to acquire and maintain "Certain Public Improvements." This is specifically written to provide for the acquisition and maintainance of a Public Library, an item completely lacking in our present charter. With the possibility of a 50% Federal Grant, a new library is within our grasp; but, without this charter change we could not finance our share of the project and would lose the grant.

A "yes" vote by you and your neighbors for the Proposition designated "Definition of Powers" is urgently needed for the future of the Madison Heights Public Library.

Helen Holmes

Madison Heights City Librarian

The city's public library was housed in the basement of the former city hall before moving to its current location in the city's civic center complex on 13 Mile Road. Residents had to pass a proposition amending the city charter to give the council authority to provide for the acquisition and maintenance of a public library, an item lacking in the existing charter. A library was within the city's grasp with a 50-percent federal grant, but without the charter amendment, the city would be unable to finance its portion of the project. (Courtesy of Madison Heights Public Library.)

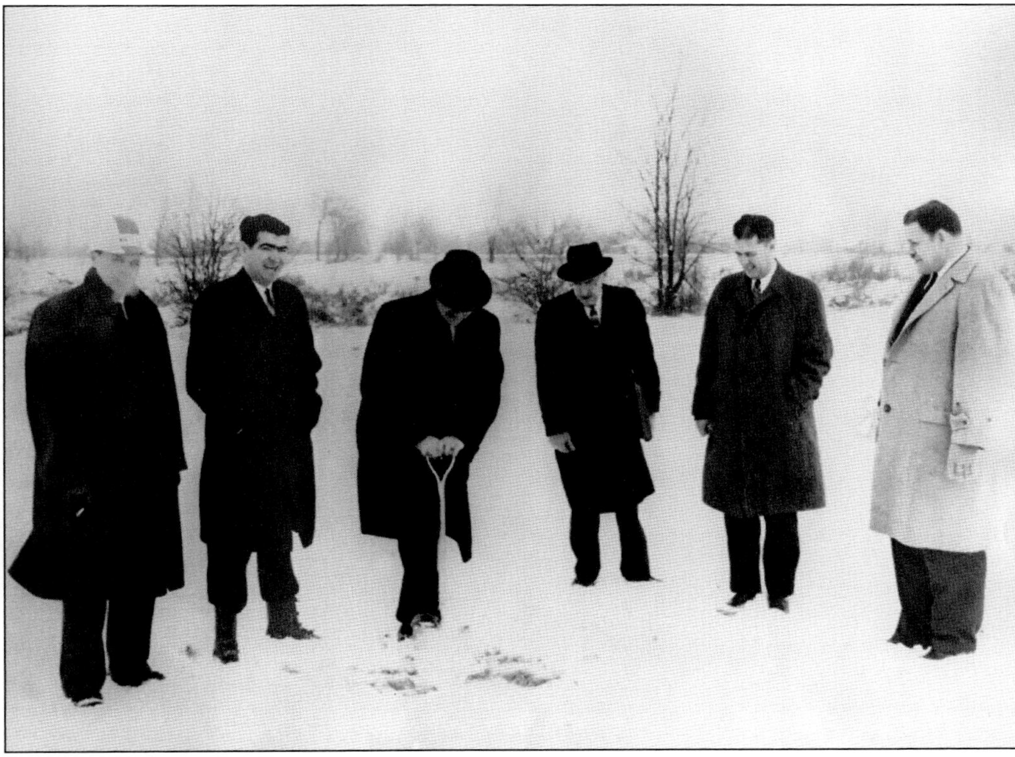

The new library's 13,000-book collection was augmented during the move by a three-year loan of 10,000 books from the state library. Richard Marshall, city manager, breaks ground for the new building about 1962, as, from left to right, Bernard F. Kronk of K&C Associates; Desmond P. Hamill of Ralls, Hamill, Becker, Architects; H. Eugene Field, city attorney; O.H. Johnson, housing and home finance agency; and Martin D. Payne, municipal building authority and building inspector, look on. (Courtesy of City of Madison Heights.)

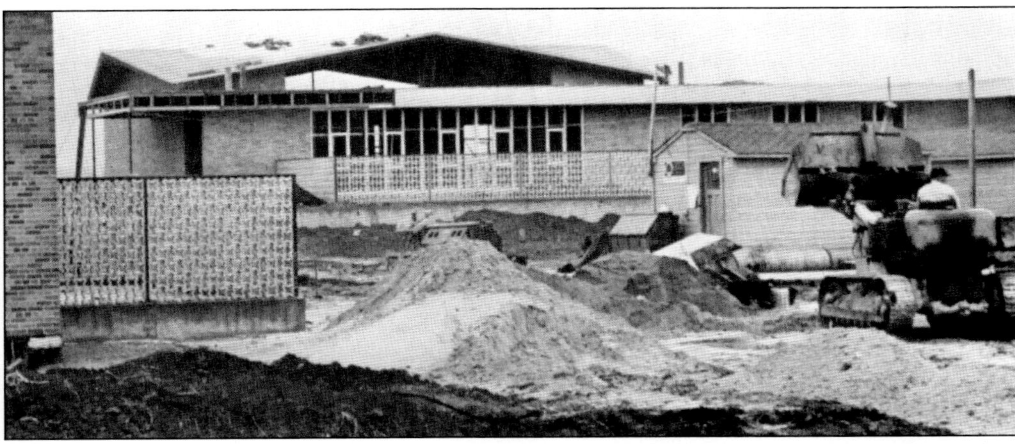

Construction is underway in 1963 on the new library and city hall (pictured). The new library had over 15,000 square feet of floor space. Before the move, a librarian and four part-time assistants kept the library open 50 hours per week. Following the move, Margaret (Marge) St. Amour, library director from 1964 to 1979, worked with a part-time adult staff of five, a full-time staff of two, and 11 college and high school students and kept the library open 61 hours, 15 minutes a week. (Courtesy of City of Madison Heights.)

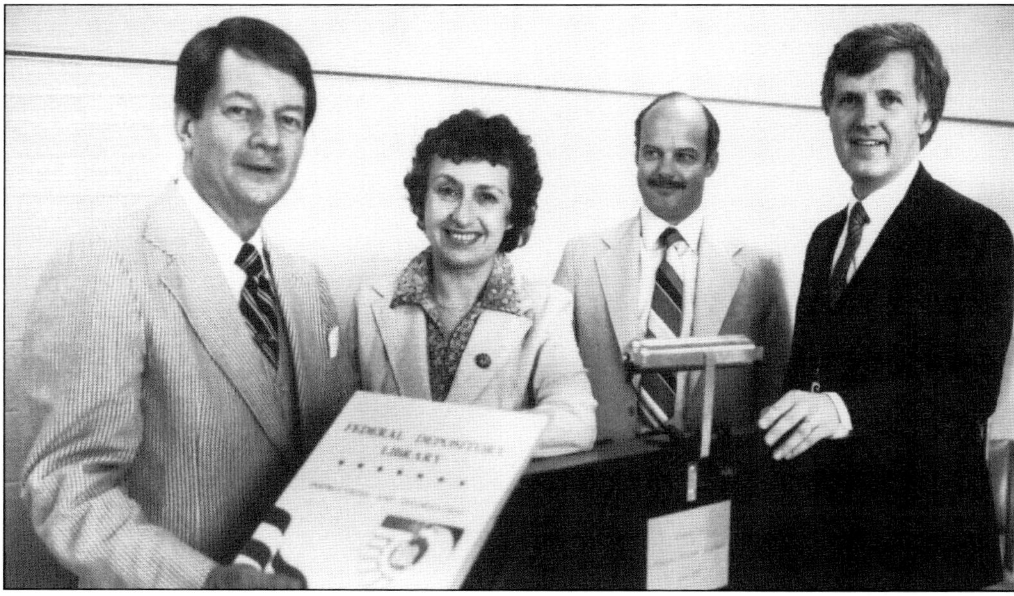

The public library became a Federal Documents Depository Library on June 15, 1982. The library was a selective depository, which meant that depository library staff was able to select a percentage of available material. City librarian A. Michael Deller (right) served as library director from 1979 to 1986. He also served as director of the Livonia Civic Center Library and as the director of The Library Network (TLN), the library cooperative to which Madison Heights belongs, after his tenure with the City of Madison Heights. (Photograph by Margene Scott.)

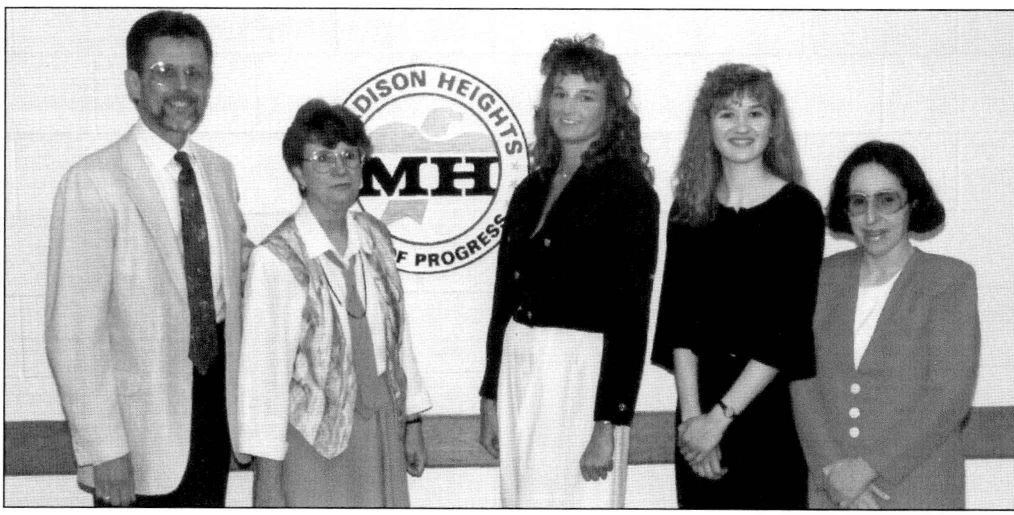

A 1993 edition of the city employee newsletter included a "Spotlight on the Library" column. Included in this photograph are, from left to right, William Miles, library director; Norma Dick, youth services librarian; Jennifer Stephens, library assistant; Andrea Mrozek, circulation assistant; and Roslyn Yerman, head reference librarian. Miles served as library director from 1986 to 1995, after which he assumed the position of Madison Heights Department of Public Services deputy superintendent until his retirement in April 2011, with a year as deputy community development director from June 1999 until June 2000. Roslyn Yerman served as head reference librarian from 1987 to 1995. She assumed the position of interim library director in May 1995, and in December of that year she became library director, a position she holds to the present day. (Photograph by Margene Scott.)

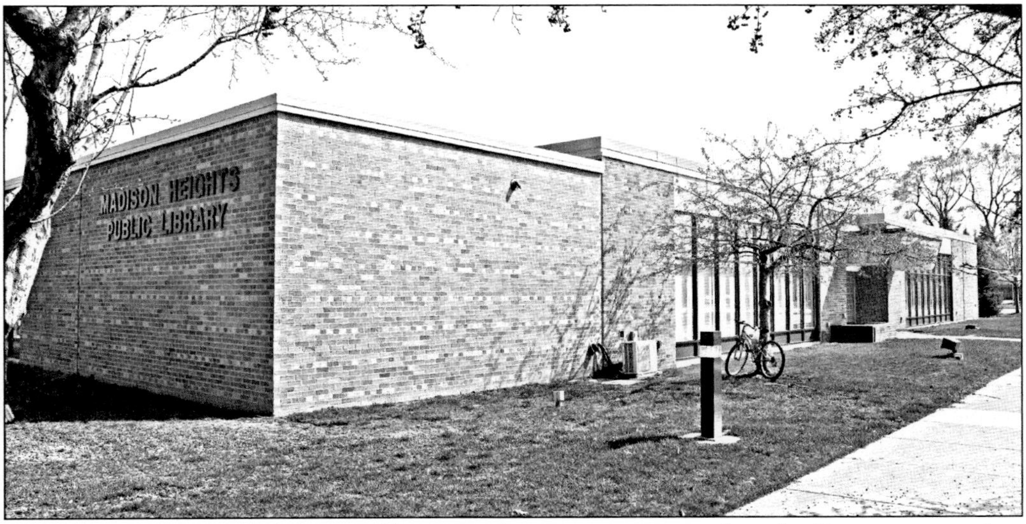

With the construction of the new library in the civic center complex, the library remained in much the same state for over 40 years. The library advisory board was established in 2000 and worked with city and library staff in conjunction with Ehresman and Associates to complete a conceptual building design. In May 2002, an option was identified for recommendation to the city council that included a renovation and expansion to be funded by budget money held during this time and supplemented with additional funds. (Photograph by Margene Scott.)

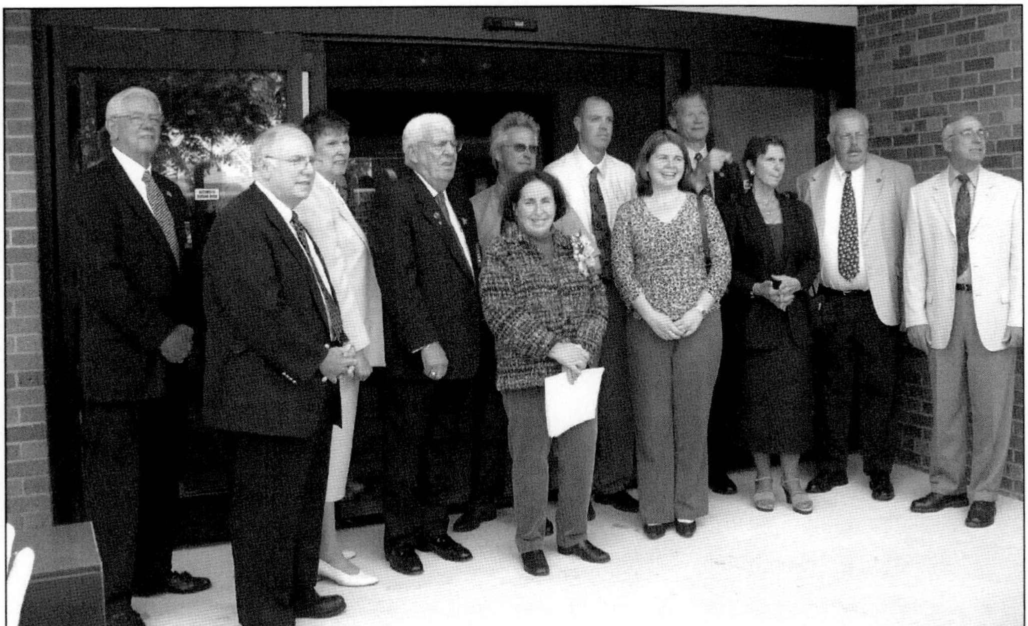

The library closed to the public in December 2006 for seven months. The grand reopening was held on July 23, 2007. Posing for a photograph after the ribbon-cutting are, from left to right, (first row) city councilman Richard Clark, city councilman Robert Corbett, city councilwoman Marilyn Russell, Mayor Edward Swanson, library director Roslyn Yerman, architect Elizabeth Muzyk, Mayor pro tem Toni Shad, Oakland County commissioner Gary McGillivray, and architect Dale Ehresman; (second row) contractor Richard Cedroni, architect Marc Chamberlin, and city manager Jon R. Austin. (Photograph by Sue Yerman.)

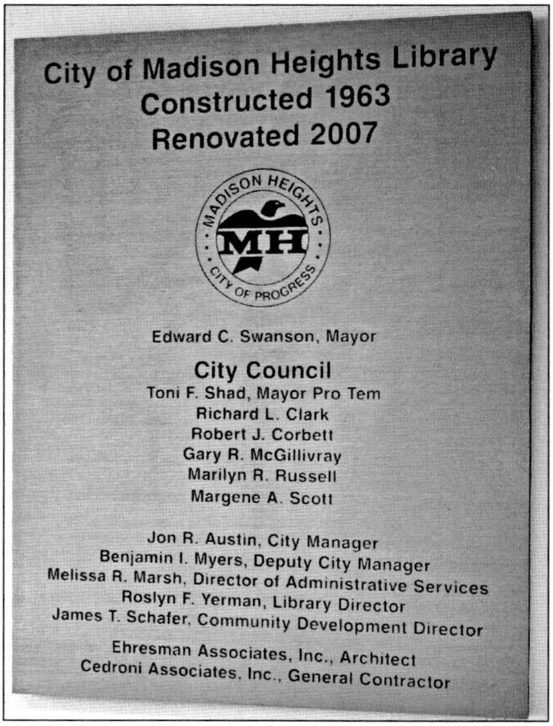

The dedication plaque represents the culmination of cooperation between city and library staff and some of the library's southeast Oakland County neighbors. Library staff packed up and unpacked the building around the renovation, with building contents stored in other city buildings. Full-time staff found temporary city homes, and part time staff worked at neighboring libraries to allow the city to maintain reciprocity through TLN, a practice that had begun with Royal Oak. (Photograph by Margene Scott.)

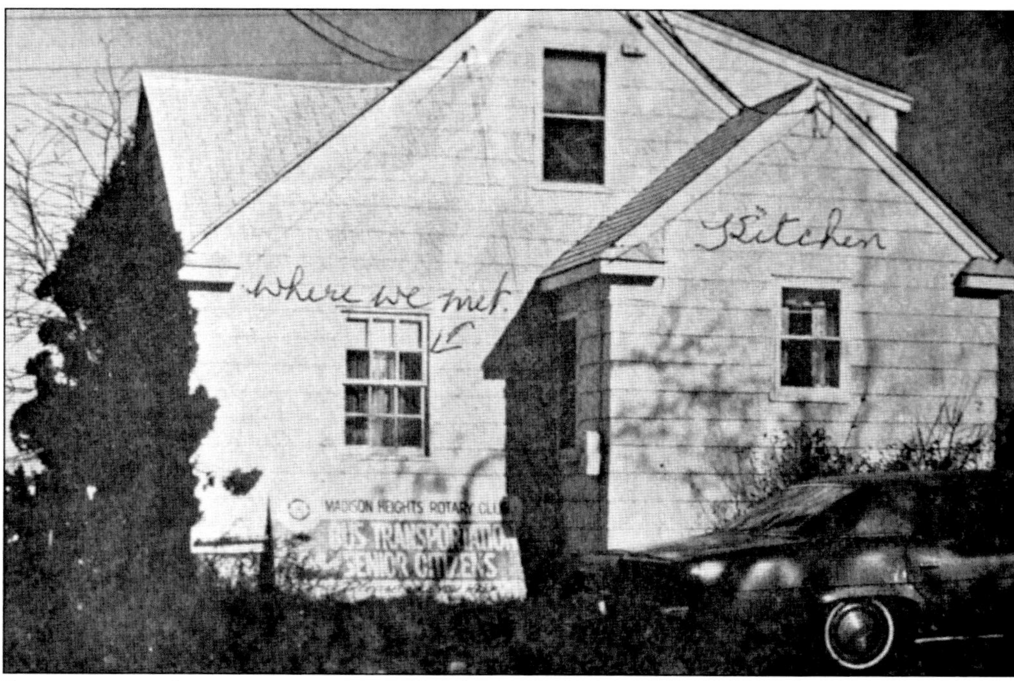

Senior services began as just a recreational program in a small white house that served as the activity center until 1975. It culminated in a 9,000-square-foot building to meet the needs of the senior population. In 1976, the Rotary Club purchased a bus that it donated to the city for the specific purpose of senior transportation. Known as the "Rotary Wheel" van, it was retired in 1982. (Courtesy of City of Madison Heights.)

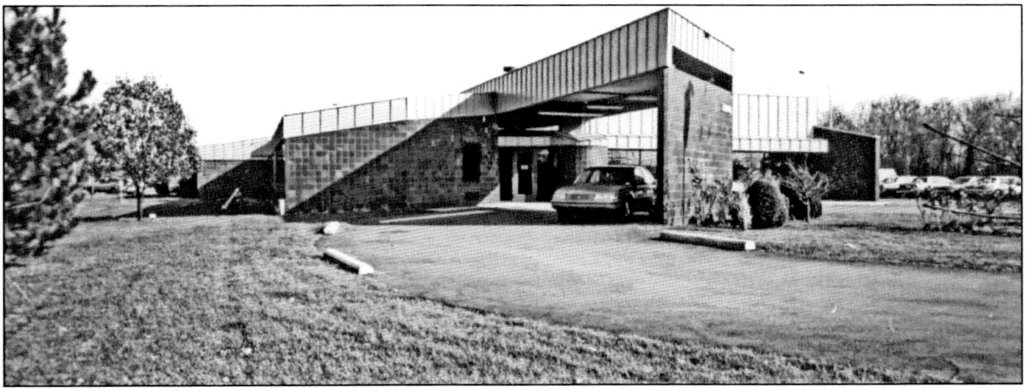

The new senior center was constructed in 1976 at 29448 John R Road, accompanied by new services such as the meals program in 1983 and transportation for seniors. In 1984, an innovative home chore program was introduced that provided basic maintenance tasks at minimal cost, allowing seniors to remain independent. A 4,500-square-foot addition was made to the building in April 1986. (Courtesy of City of Madison Heights.)

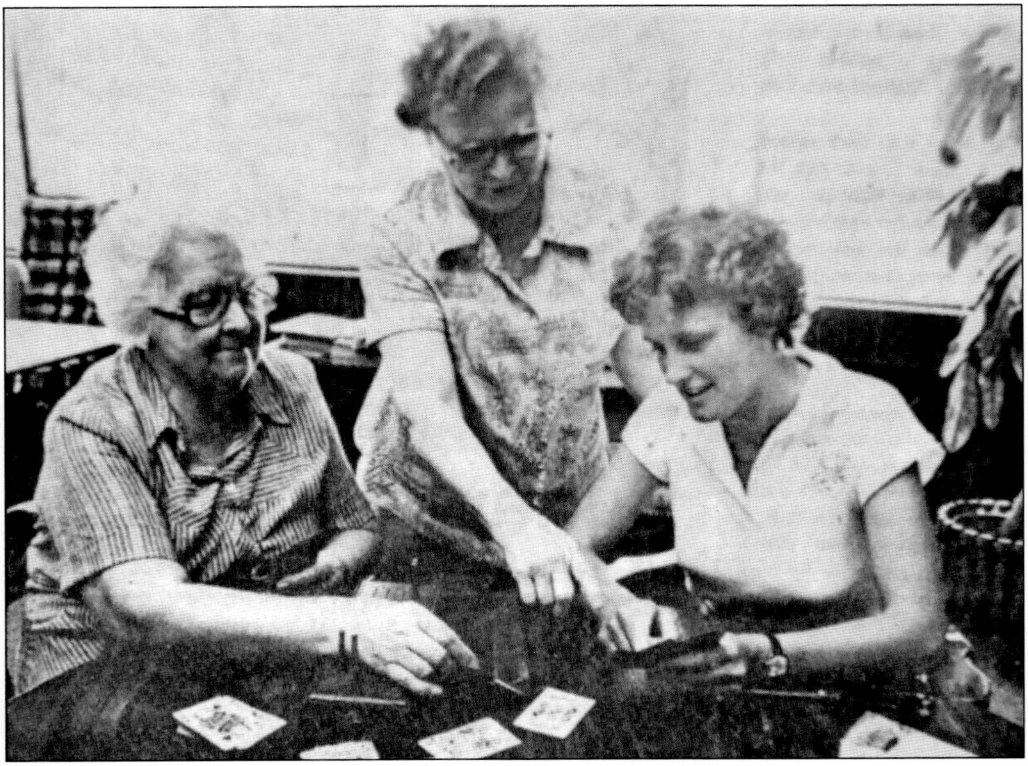

The new senior citizen center coordinator, Jenny Crawford Martin, discusses cribbage pointers with Alice White and Nette Lamke in this July 1979 photograph. Hired on May 21, 1979, at 23, Jenny's youthful appearance further accentuated the generation gap that outsiders initially perceived. It was quickly dispelled, however, with her confidence and concern. Jenny's supervisory position was new to the center, and she sought to address the physical and emotional needs of the seniors. (Photograph by Margene Scott.)

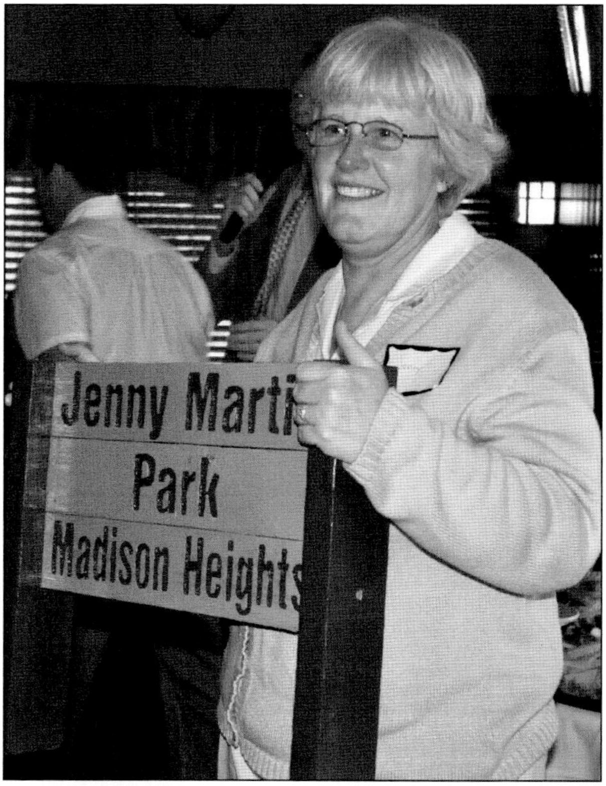

Jenny Crawford Martin retired on May 26, 2011, after serving city residents for more than 32 years. Jenny was promoted to recreation and senior center supervisor in July 1984, offering programs that reflected current trends and the needs of city residents. Jenny was involved with the senior building addition in 1985 and the development of the nature center in 1989, among other programs. (Photograph by Margene Scott.)

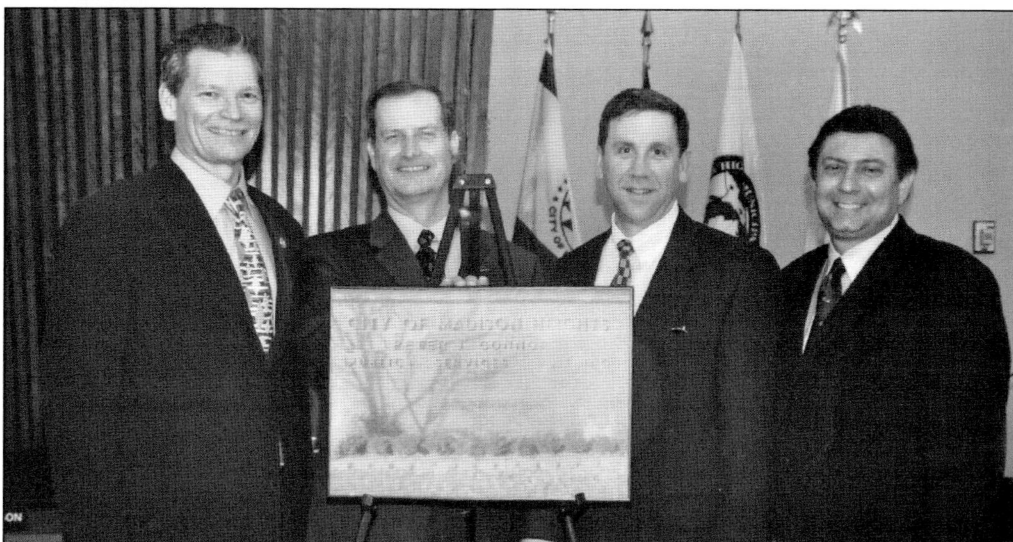

From left to right, city manager Jon R. Austin, deputy city manager Pete Connors, assistant city manager Benjamin I. Myers, and city attorney Larry Sherman smile after the announcement of the renaming of the Madison Heights Department of Public Services building after the retiring deputy city manager. Pete Connors worked for the City of Madison Heights from February 1981 to February 2006, and this presentation was made on February 27, 2006. City manager Jon R. Austin has also since retired, with Benjamin I. Myers replacing him as city manager, and Larry Sherman is still on board as city attorney. (Photograph by Margene Scott.)

Four

MAYORS

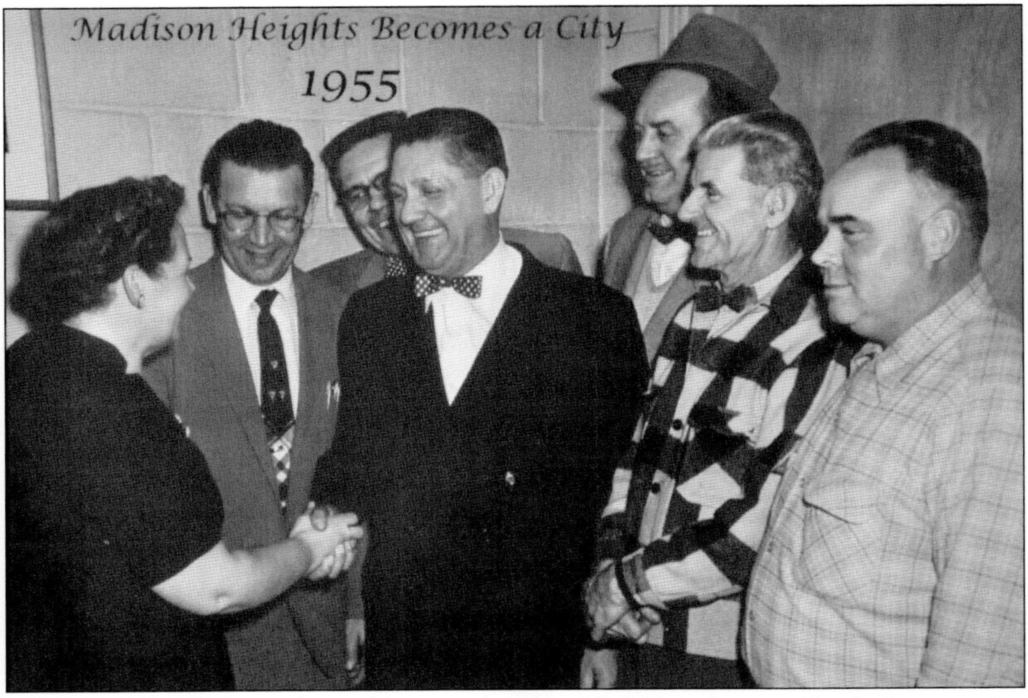

On January 17, 1955, the residents of the east side of Royal Oak Township voted for the incorporation of the City of Madison Heights and elected nine commissioners to draft a charter for the new city. The draft charter was presented to the citizens at a June 6 election and was defeated. A revised charter was presented to the citizens on December 6, 1955, and approved, creating the 10th city government in South Oakland County. (Courtesy of City of Madison Heights.)

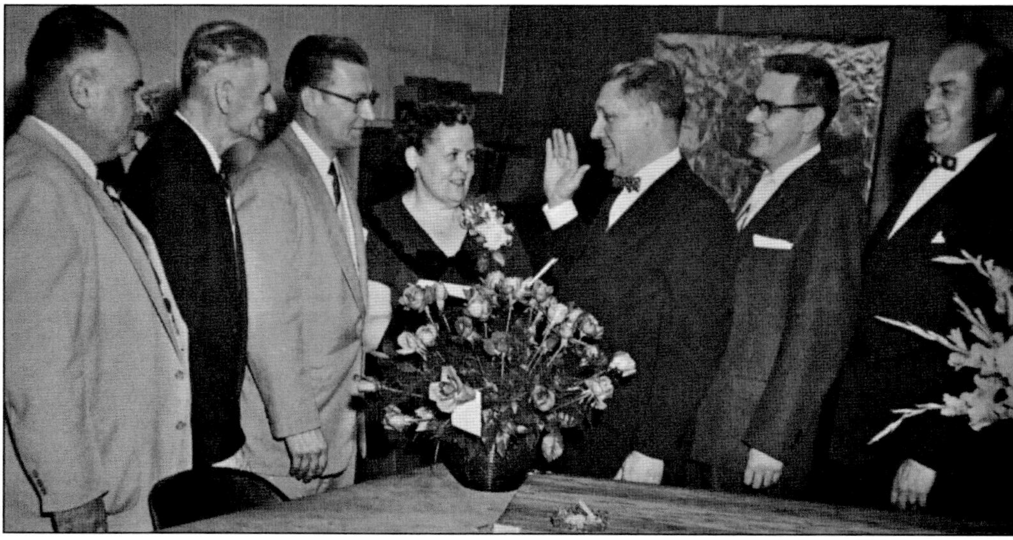

The first mayor and city council complete the oath of office. From left to right are Darrell K. Davis, George Sargeant, John B. Michrina, Virginia M. Solberg, Mayor Lloyd H. Ferguson, Theodore Krenn, and Charles B. Edwards Jr. The council constituted the legislature, and Virginia Solberg became de facto mayor (mayor pro tem) with the largest number of council votes. (Courtesy of City of Madison Heights.)

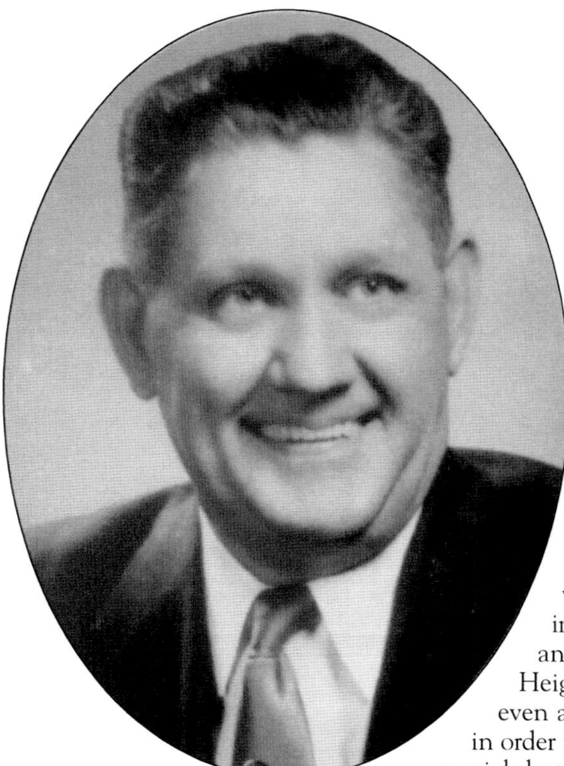

Lloyd Ferguson served as mayor from December 1955 to April 1958. As the first mayor, he led a council that oversaw a flurry of activity to form a city administration and nurture the infant city's development. Significant improvements were made to roads, sewers, and utility infrastructure. A new city jail was constructed, and a new home was found for the Madison Heights Department of Public Works. Voters even approved the first charter revision in 1956 in order to allow the city to borrow money without special elections. (Courtesy of City of Madison Heights.)

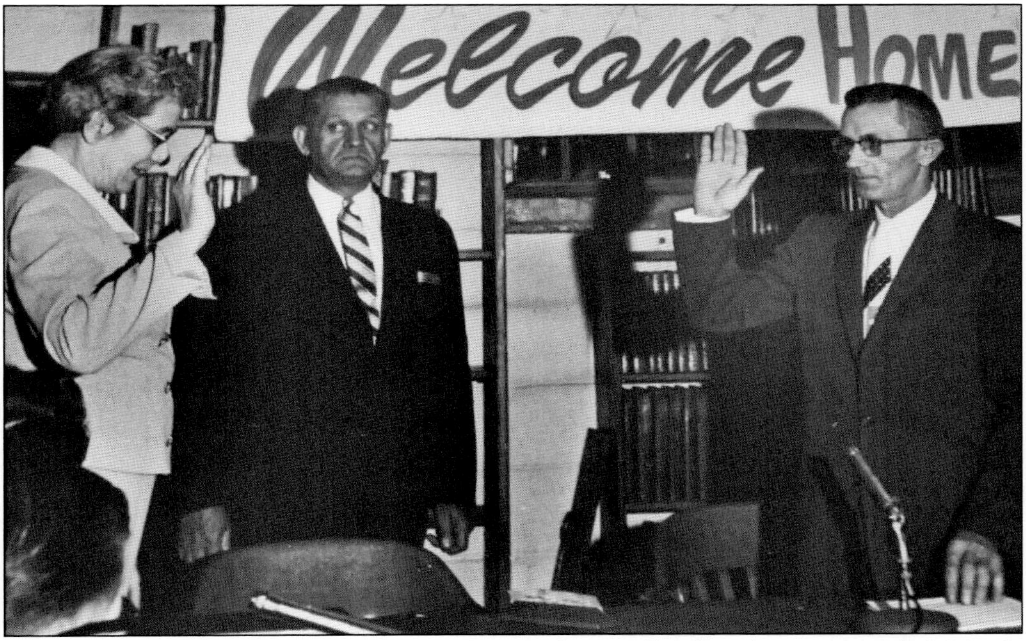

In the second election, the first mayor and council were all defeated. Here, city clerk Myrtle Chamberlain swears in the newly elected mayor, George Horkey, in front of his "Welcome Home" sign. Horkey had previously served as Royal Oak Township supervisor for more than 17 years but opposed incorporation. Defeated mayor Lloyd Ferguson observes the proceedings. (Courtesy of Marietta Horkey Walden and George Horkey Jr.)

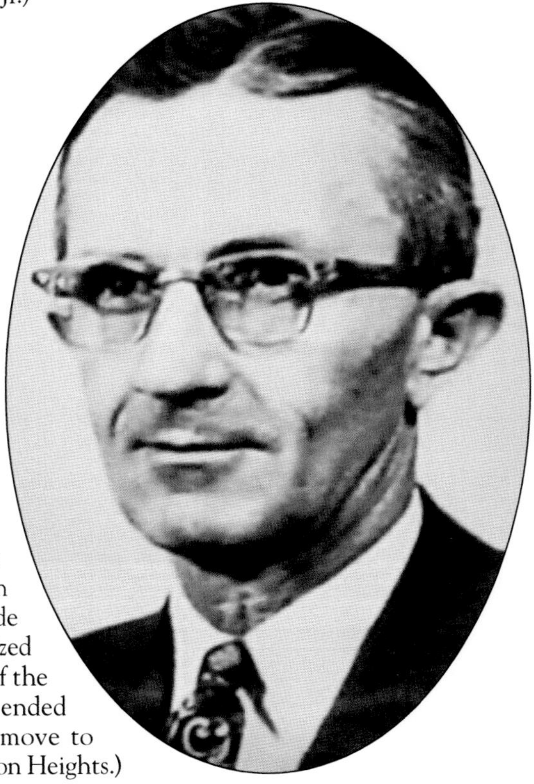

George Horkey served as mayor from April 1958 to August 1959. He presided over a particularly turbulent period in the city's political history, leading a coalition of opposition candidates, five of whom saw election by wide margins. The Friends of the Library were organized to spur the city council to get the library out of the basement of city hall. Mayor Horkey's term ended when he resigned on August 21, 1959, to move to Dundee, Michigan. (Courtesy of City of Madison Heights.)

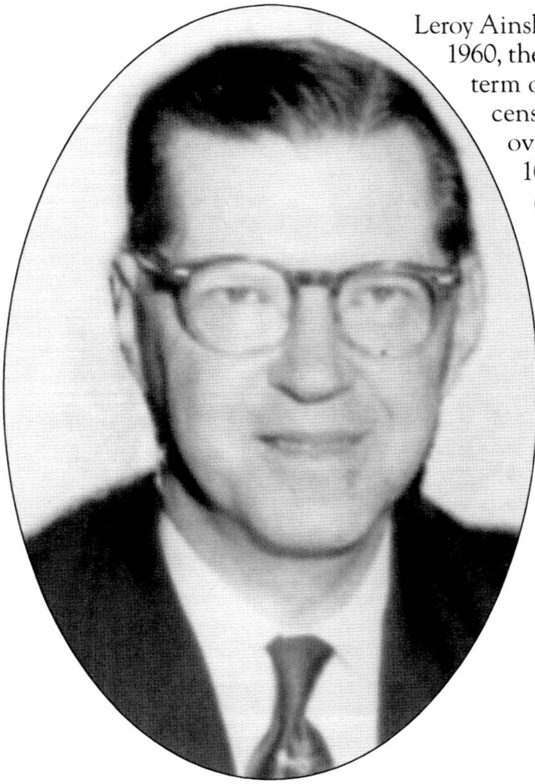

Leroy Ainsley served as mayor from October 1959 to April 1960, the city's shortest-serving mayor, finishing out the term of Mayor Horkey. During his tenure, the 1960 census was taken, which revealed a huge increase over the Royal Oak Township area count of 10 years earlier. The city was able to enjoy a diversion from some of the political unrest. In February 1960, the city saw a record number of candidates for election. Leroy Ainsley lost in his bid for mayor to Theodore Krenn. (Courtesy of City of Madison Heights.)

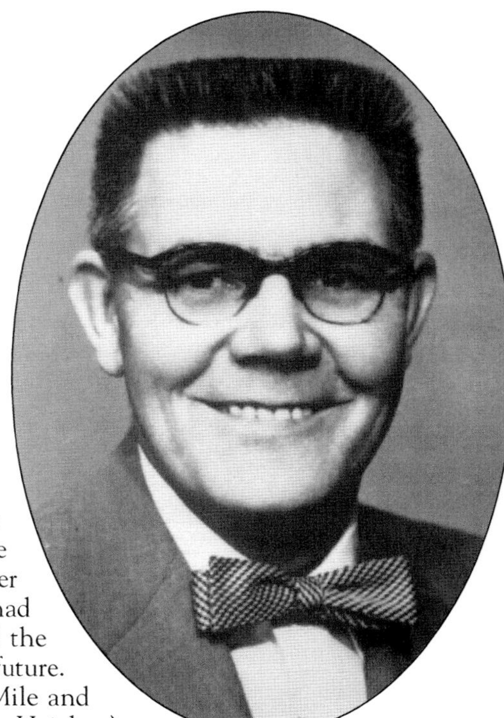

Theodore Krenn was mayor from April 1960 to April 1961. He was among the city's founding fathers, serving on the Charter Commission and the first city council prior to being elected mayor. During his term, a traffic violations bureau was created, and a council resolution opposed Detroit's proposal to assess an income tax on nonresidents who worked in Detroit. Over 60 percent of land was occupied. Residents had a median age of 22 years, which emphasized the importance of additional schools in the near future. The center of town was expected to be 12 Mile and John R Roads. (Courtesy of City of Madison Heights.)

Bill Huffman served as mayor from April 1961 to April 1963. He presided over a period of significant transformation for the city government's infrastructure. During his tenure, the city acquired the 30-acre civic center site, opened a new fire department headquarters, and broke ground on the city hall and library, which remain hubs of the local government. Mayor Huffman ultimately moved on to become a state representative and then state senator. (Courtesy of City of Madison Heights.)

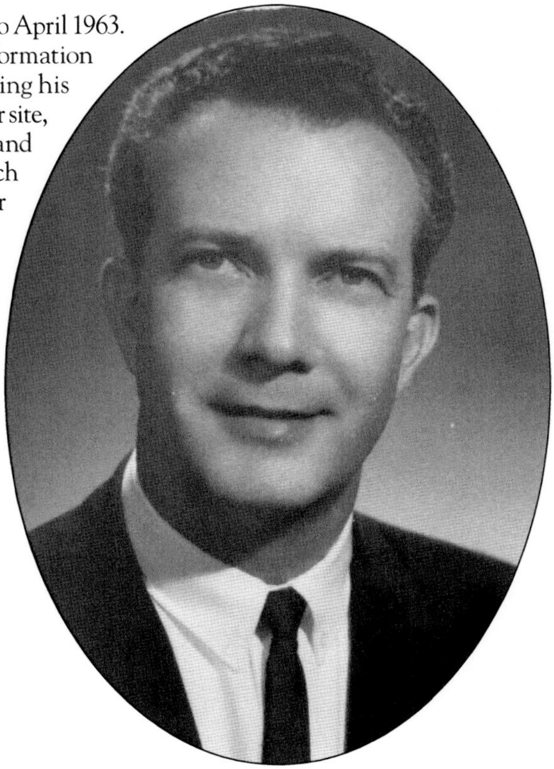

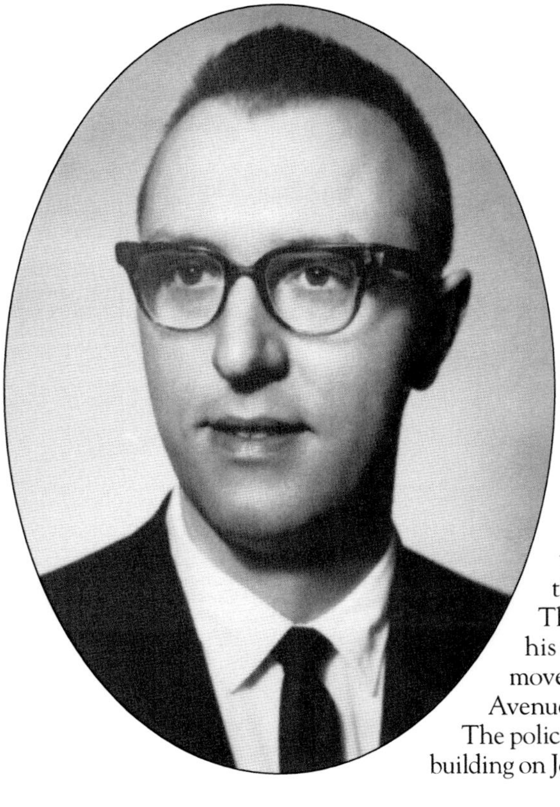

Herbert A. Smith served as mayor from April 1963 to April 1967. His tenure was an active one for completing major projects related to land use, including final approval for the first large-scale revision of the city's master plan and zoning laws since incorporation. The 12 Towns Drain project was completed in 1965, allowing control over the flow of sewage through the Red Run Drain. The city hall and library were completed under his watch in 1964. The recreation department moved from the community center at Gardenia Avenue and John R Road to the city hall basement. The police department relocated to the former city hall building on John R. (Courtesy of City of Madison Heights.)

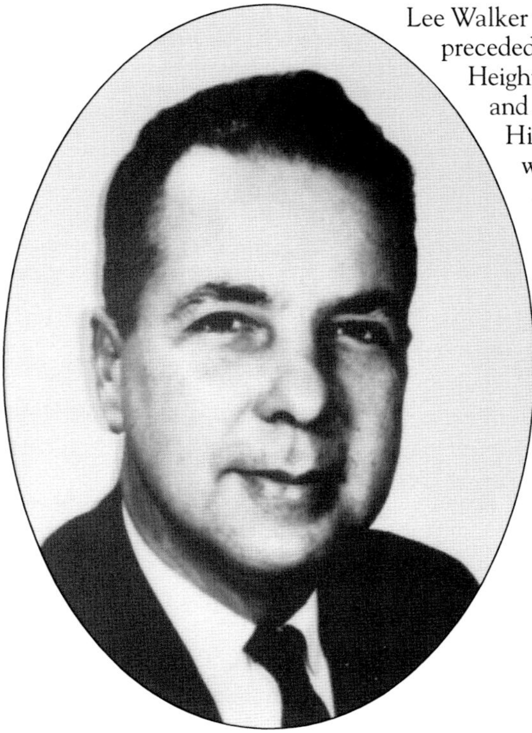

Lee Walker served as mayor from April 1967 to April 1969, preceded by a council term. During his tenure, Madison Heights made preparations for I-696 freeway expansion and entered into a contract with the Michigan State Highway Department to help homeowners who would be displaced. Mayor Walker's term saw significant light industrial development in the former northern farm parcels. He also played a role in rejuvenating the Friends of the Library. In February 1969, the police department moved to a new location at 200 West 13 Mile Road. In 1968, the fire department became a member of the Oakway Fire Mutual Aid Association. (Courtesy of City of Madison Heights.)

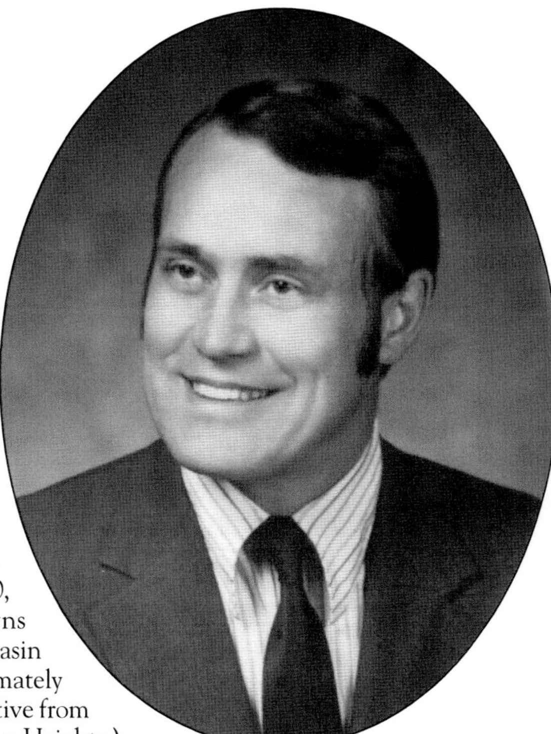

Monte R. Geralds served as mayor from April 1969 to August 1972 after serving on the council since 1965. He proposed a parental responsibility law that gained national publicity. During his terms of office, the busing of school children for purposes of integration became a very controversial issue, and Mayor Geralds urged mayors and councils to resist calls by vocal residents for adoption of city ordinances prohibiting school busing. He warned that such ordinances could be used as evidence against communities in the courts. In 1970, Geralds oversaw the building of the 12 Towns Retention Treatment Facility and retention basin in the former Red Run Drain. Geralds ultimately served as Madison Heights' state representative from 1975 to 1978. (Courtesy of City of Madison Heights.)

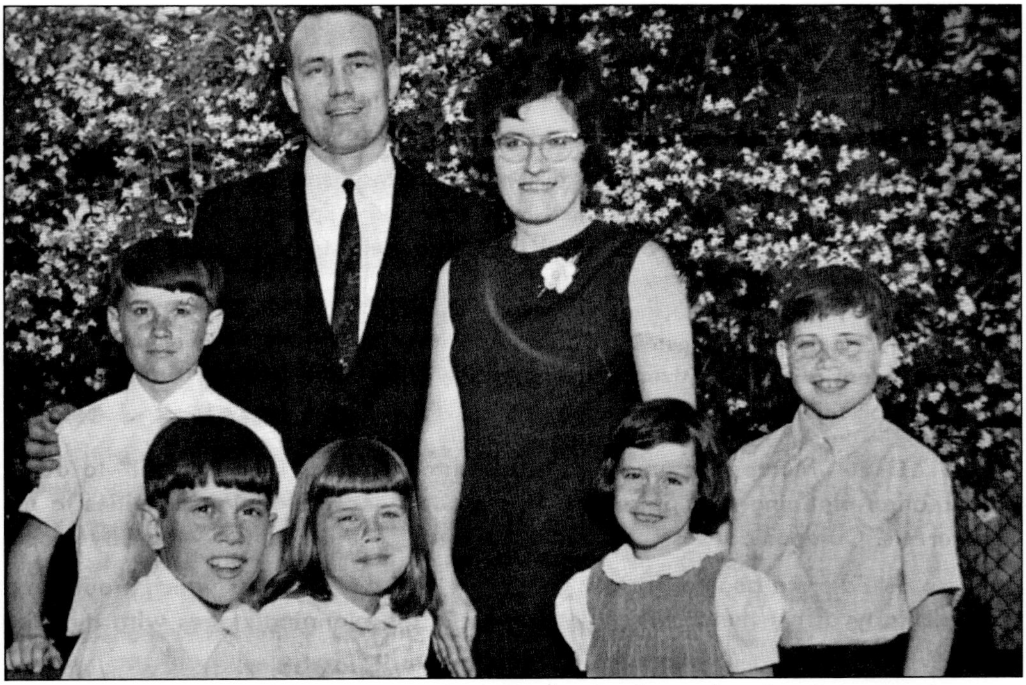

The Geralds family is well known in Madison Heights for their political and civic involvement. This family photograph was used as part of Monte Geralds's mayoral election efforts in early 1969 and shows Monte and his wife, Barbara, and their children, from left to right, Jeff, age 12; Cam, age 10; Cindy, age 8; Laurie, age 7; and Scott, age 9. The family's community involvement includes Scouting, wrestling, and the Greater Federation of Women's Clubs Madison Heights Intermediate Women's Club. The Geralds family was recognized by the Community Round Table in 2011 with the prestigious Volunteer of the Year award. (Courtesy of Monte Geralds.)

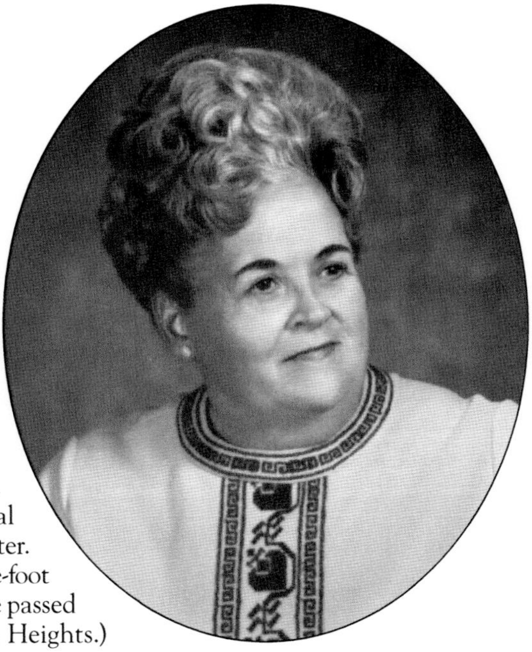

Virginia Solberg served as mayor from September 1972 to April 1977, and served on the council at various points before and after becoming the city's first and only female mayor. In 1974, the fire department began upgrading the Emergency Medical Services. During her term, the council set aside Federal Revenue Sharing Funds for the new senior center. In 1976, the seniors moved into the 5,000-square-foot facility, which remains in operation today. She passed away in 1982. (Courtesy of City of Madison Heights.)

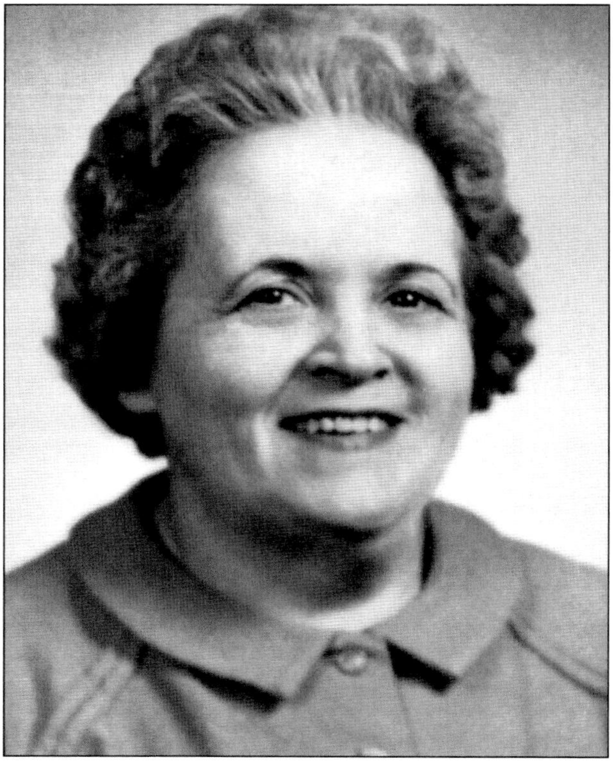

Virginia Solberg was active in civic and community organizations, with a particular involvement with seniors. She helped raise funds for the senior center, and a senior citizen apartment complex, Solberg Towers, was built in the 1970s during her tenure as mayor. Virginia Solberg and her husband, Arthur, owned an eating establishment on the corner of Dequindre Road and Greig Street. Their home was next door and remains in that location today. (Courtesy of Madison Heights Public Library.)

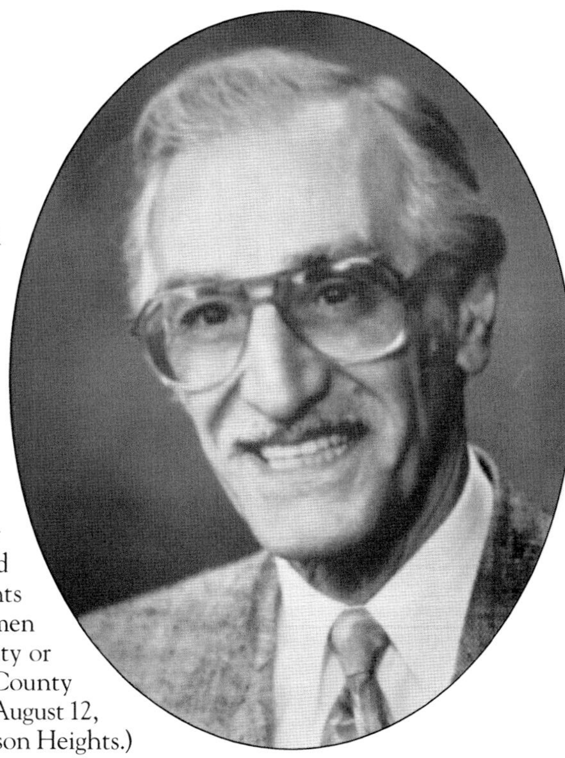

George Suarez served as mayor from April 1977 to November 1998, preceded by four years on city council. He holds the record for longest serving mayor. While mayor, he was a strong advocate of senior and youth programs and sought to maintain political stability. In 1981, cable television allowed the live broadcast of council meetings. During a period of turmoil, city manager Ernest Fisher was fired on live television, and city clerk Dorothy Lents took over as city manager. This led to the successful recall in Madison Heights and Oakland County of the three councilmen who led the opposition, the first in the city or the county. Suarez was elected Oakland County commissioner in 1998 and died in office on August 12, 2008, at age 82. (Courtesy of City of Madison Heights.)

George W. Suarez poses with his family—wife Linda, son Justin, and daughter Sara—in this 1981 photograph taken in his home on Mapleknoll during a photo session for a mayoral reelection campaign. (Photograph by Margene Scott.)

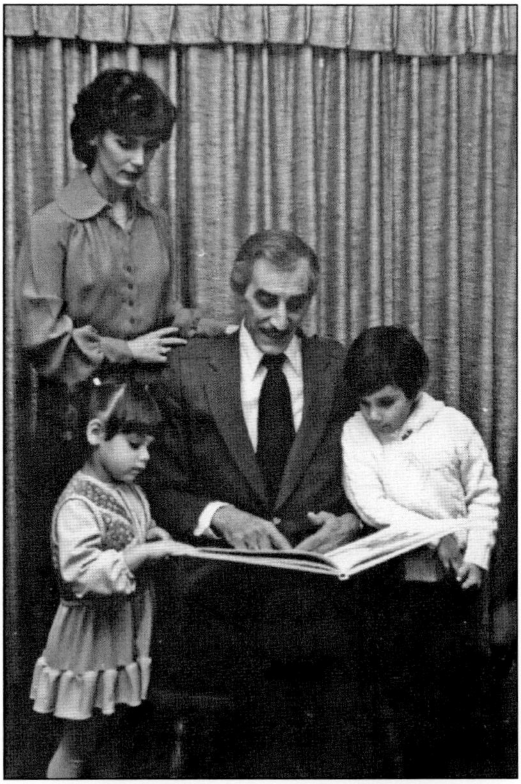

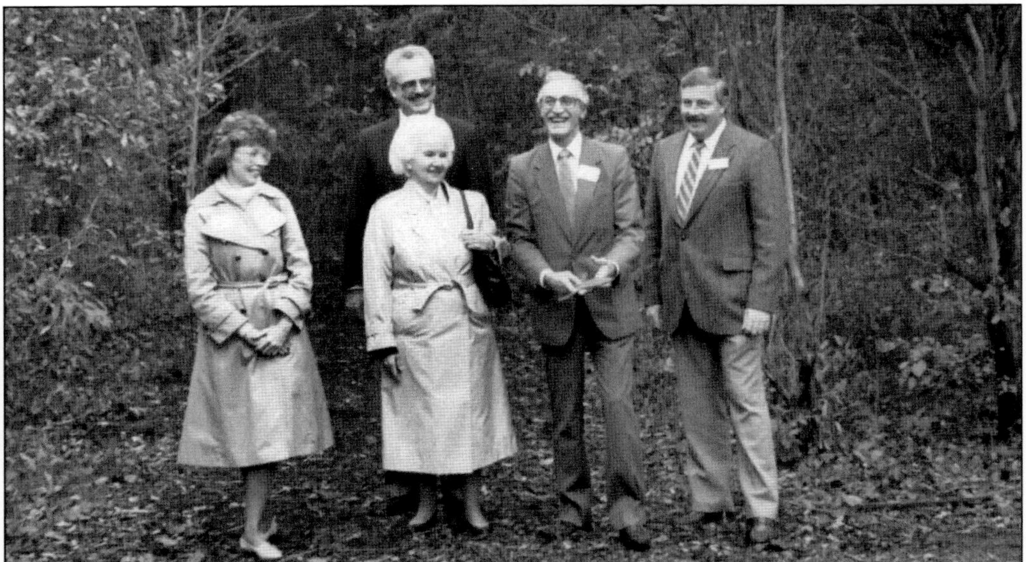

One of Mayor Suarez's most defining accomplishments was his work to preserve what is known today as the George W. Suarez Friendship Woods and to develop a nature center within those woods, which instantly became one of Madison Heights' most popular destinations. The day of the ribbon-cutting for those woods is pictured with, from left to right, Councilwoman Susan Kraimer, Councilwoman Elva Mills, Councilman Lindell Ross, Mayor George W. Suarez, and Councilman Gary McGillivray. (Photograph by Margene Scott.)

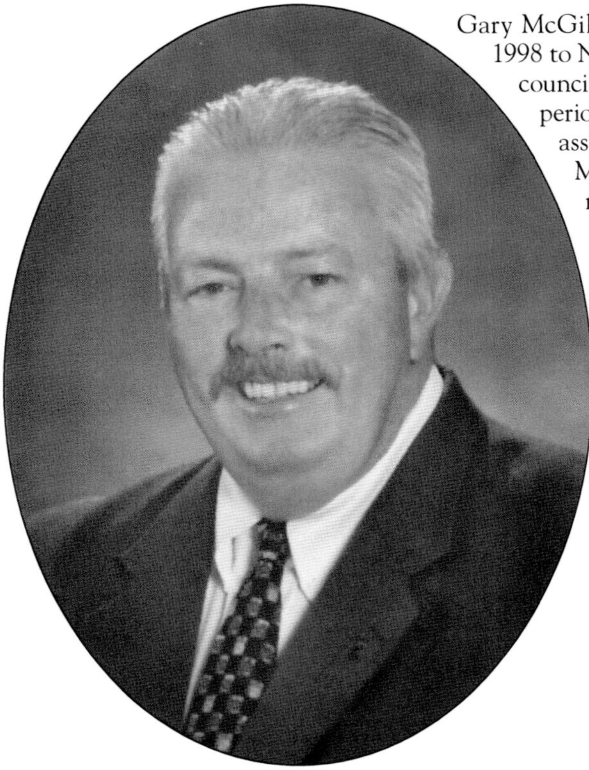

Gary McGillivray served as mayor from November 1998 to November 1999, preceded by 15 years as a councilman. He served as acting mayor for a brief period and became mayor when George Suarez assumed his county commissioner position. Mayor McGillivray advocated for careful monitoring of the budget. He supported the community's parks and recreation programs and was instrumental in the development of the new Little Baseball complex. McGillivray began on city council in 1981 and was elected as an Oakland County commissioner in November 2008, a position he still holds. (Courtesy of City of Madison Heights.)

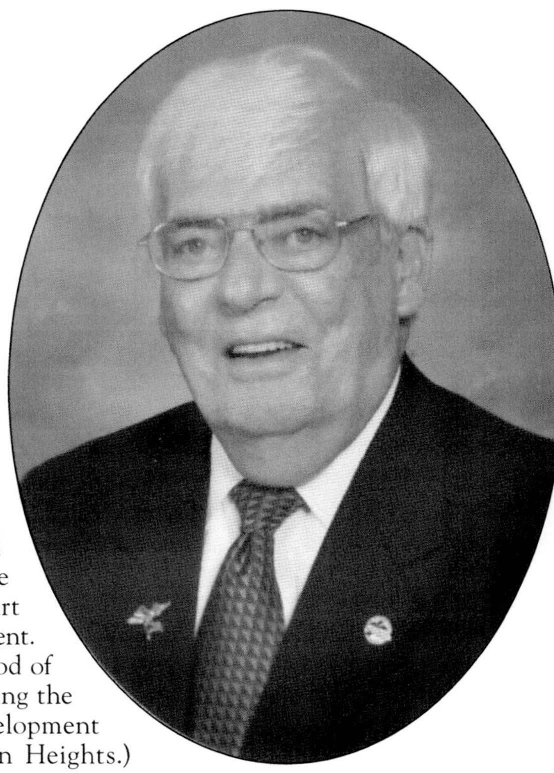

Edward C. Swanson began serving as mayor in November 1999 and serves to the present day as the city's second-longest serving mayor. He has advocated for citizen involvement in local government, especially through board and commission involvement. His tenure has seen the expansion of the district court and a new, greatly expanded fire department. Mayor Swanson has presided over a period of extensive economic development, including the hiring of the city's first economic development director. (Courtesy of City of Madison Heights.)

Five

Businesses

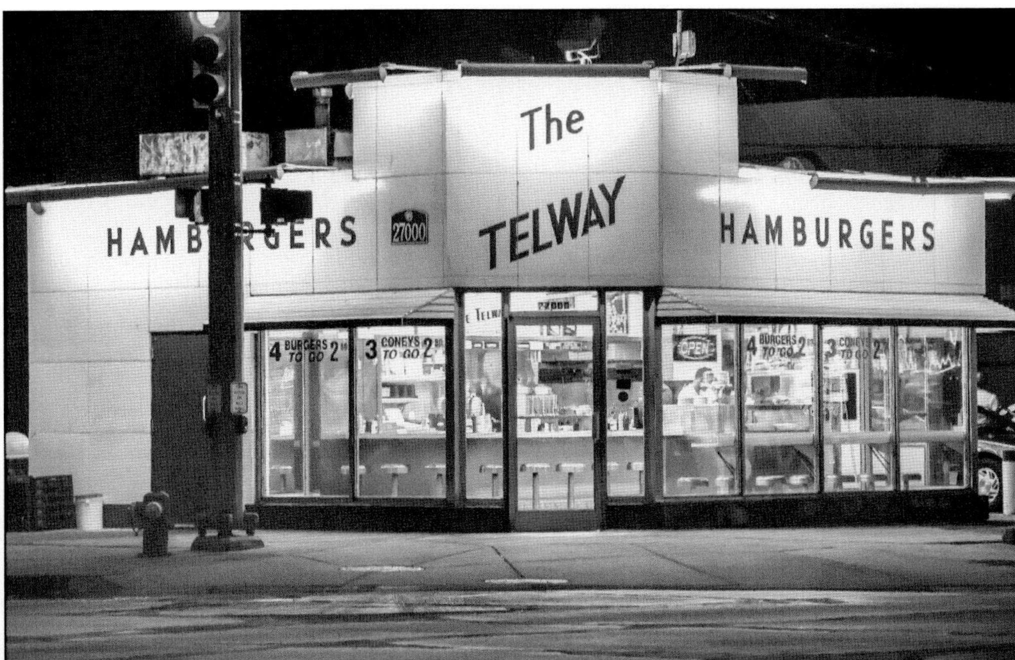

The little white tile monument known as The Telway has been a landmark in Madison Heights for over half a century. Located on the corner of 11 Mile and John R Roads, the restaurant is famous for its fresh sliders (bite-size burgers). The restaurant is family operated, with current owner Alan Owens having worked in the business since he was 11. He took over from his father, who still keeps his hand in. The Telway is known for the people, the tasty burgers, and its retro atmosphere and remains a staple in the city, even while things around it have changed. (Photograph by Chris Betea.)

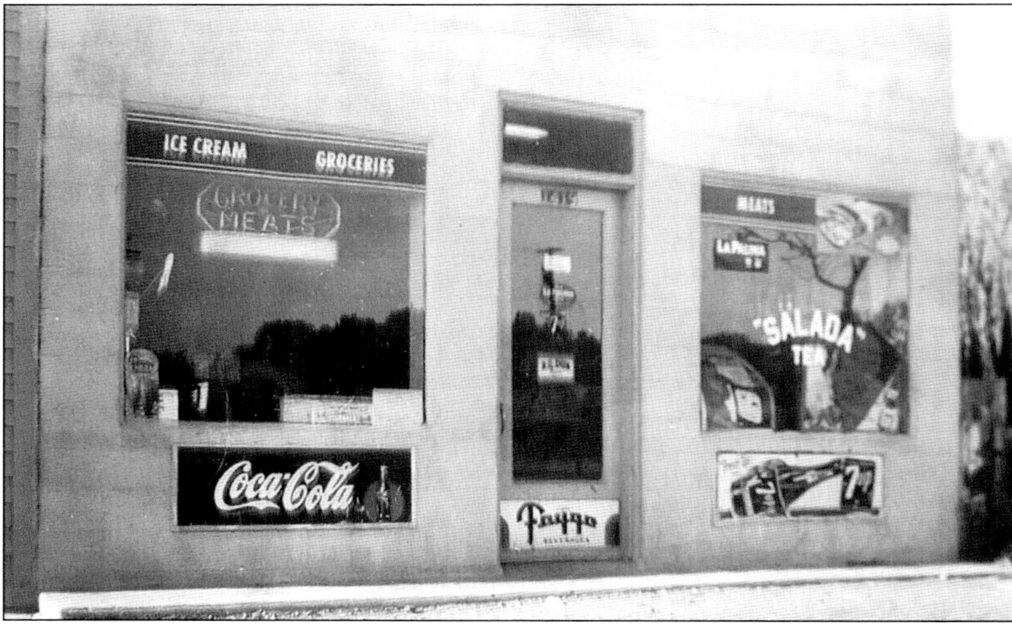

Paul and Katherine Bilovus opened a very small store in front of their house with only a few things on the shelves. The store was located at 1415 East 11 Mile Road in Madison Heights. Life was a struggle, but things eventually got better, and they built a store next to their home, located at 1419 East 11 Mile. The store with the wood front and "Groceries" sign was to the left of the cinder-block storefront. (Courtesy of Gerri Hall.)

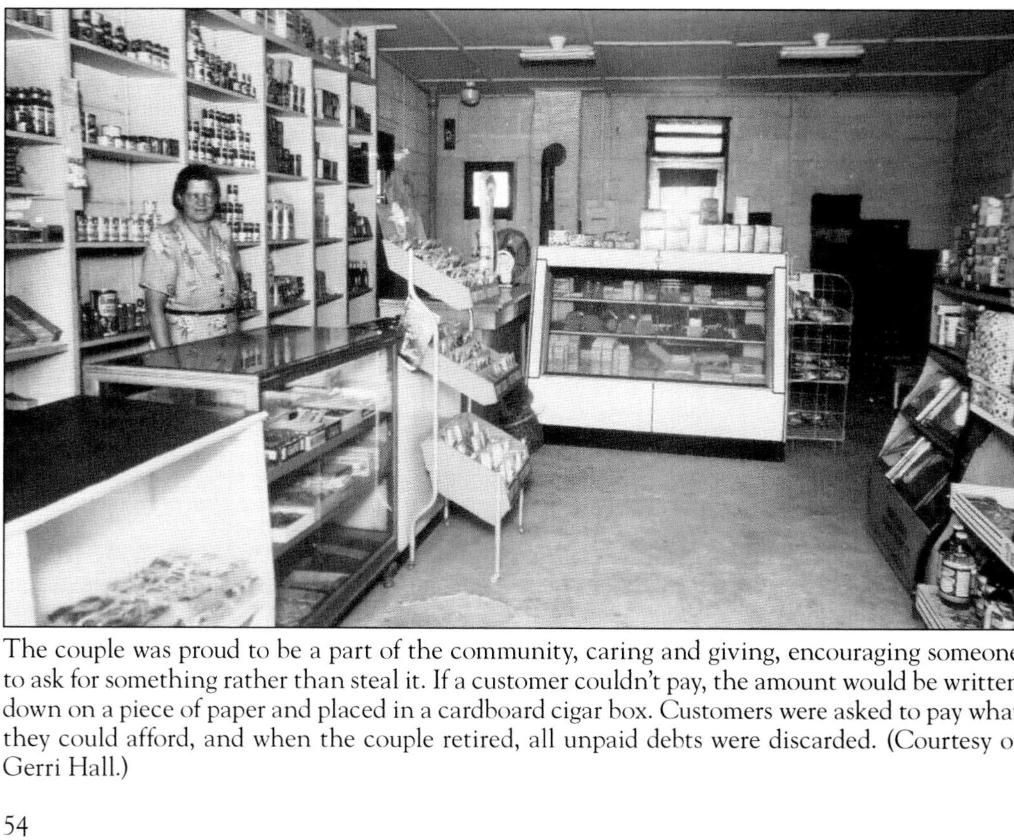

The couple was proud to be a part of the community, caring and giving, encouraging someone to ask for something rather than steal it. If a customer couldn't pay, the amount would be written down on a piece of paper and placed in a cardboard cigar box. Customers were asked to pay what they could afford, and when the couple retired, all unpaid debts were discarded. (Courtesy of Gerri Hall.)

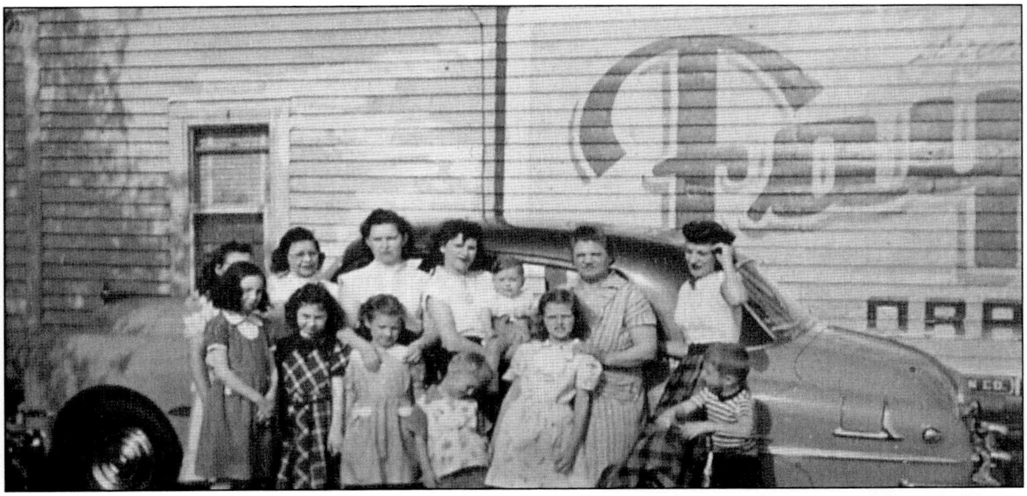

Bilovus Grocery was open from 1938 to 1957. The couple were the proud parents of four children: Geraldine, Jeanette, Richard, and Paul Jr. Paul Bilovus was born in the Ukraine. His brother Joseph preceded him to the United States and helped him immigrate. He married Katherine Skop, the daughter of Austrian and Polish immigrants, on June 11, 1938. (Courtesy of Gerri Hall.)

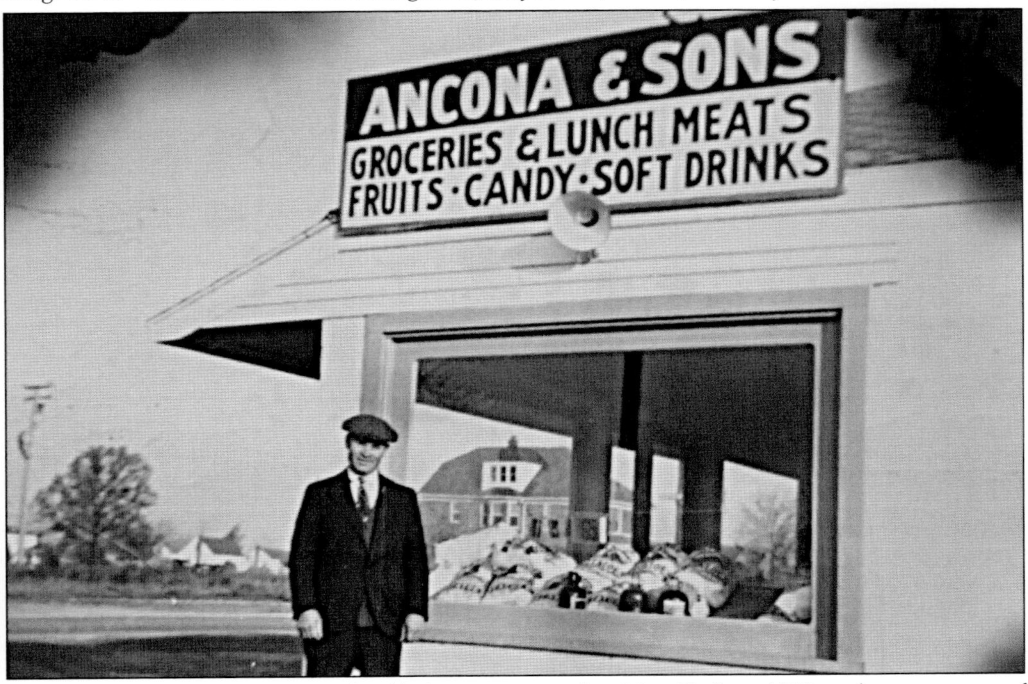

Born in Italy in 1887, Giacomo (Jack) Ancona arrived in New York in 1912 at the young age of 24. Moving to the Detroit area, he learned the grocery store business while working as a butcher. In the 1940s, Jack opened his popular Ancona's market at 26122 John R Road in a strategic location near the Cowan corner of the first city hall–police/fire station–library. At one point, their restaurant opened just north of the market, specializing in Italian dishes. Beginning in the 1950s, Giacomo's sons Samuel, Joseph, Anthony, and Giacomo Jr., and even son-in-law Leo Ciaramitaro, were involved with the business, renamed Ancona & Sons. Upon Jack's retirement, the Ancona sons renamed it Ancona Brothers Market. The store was sold in 1982 and is now Amori's party store. (Courtesy of MaryAnn (Ancona) Gemignani.)

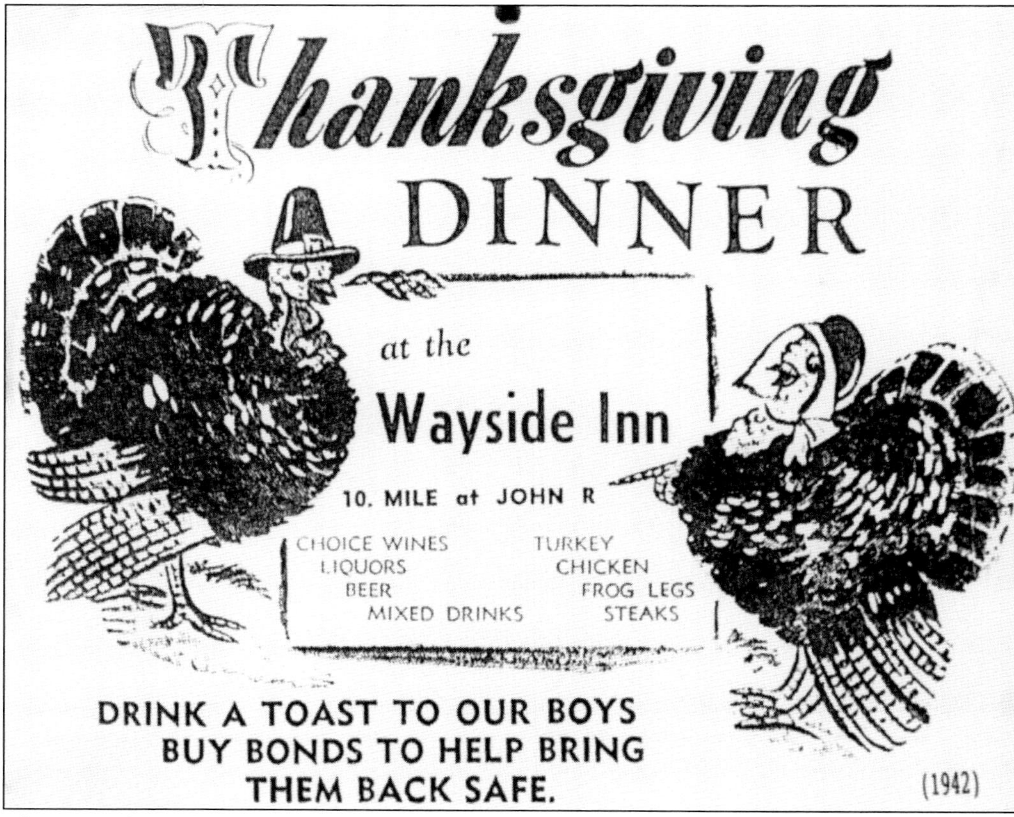

The Wayside Bar has been a fixture in Madison Heights since it was opened by Eugene Busco in 1935. It served as a gathering place for the locals, as many didn't have cars. Entire families could be found in the bar on weekend nights, and many young people would enjoy the dance floor. Johnny Johnson ran the bar at the time, remembers longtime resident Joy Davids, who recalled that after working (and drinking) all day, Johnson would need help closing up and getting home. (Courtesy of Madison Heights Historical Commission.)

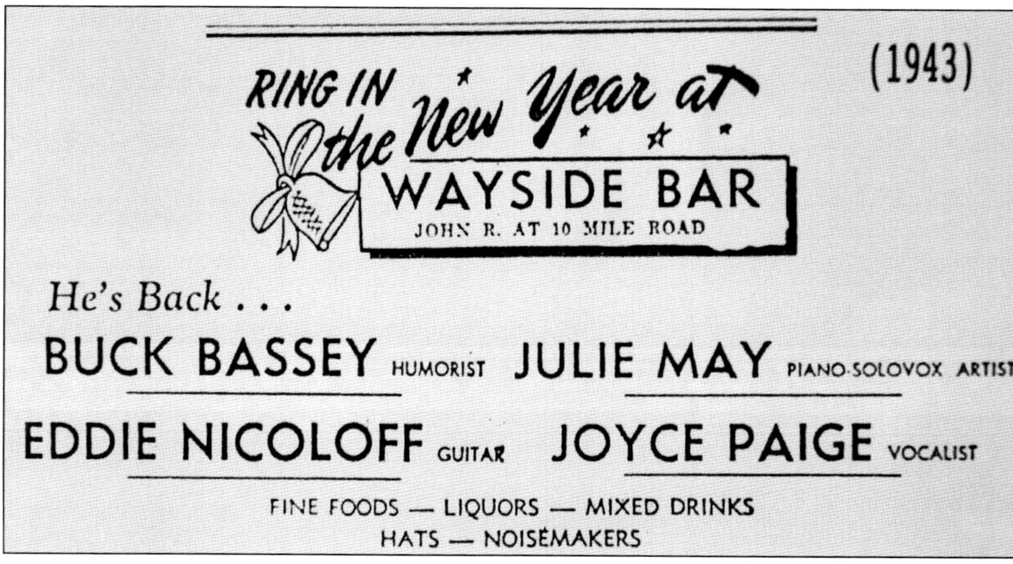

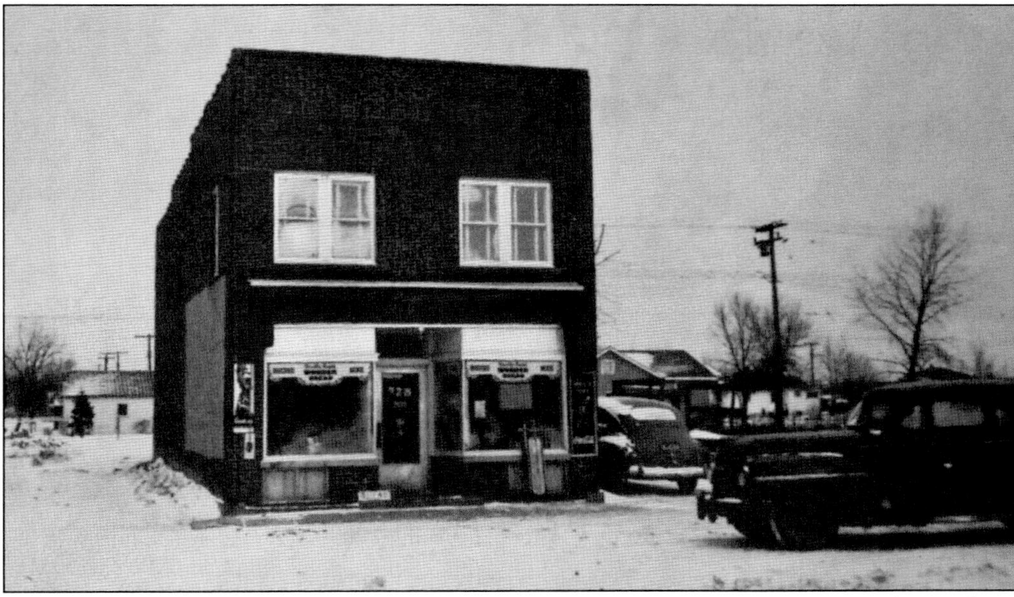

In 1946, Clarence Rainey bought the old Kroger store building at 728 West 11 Mile Road and opened a neighborhood grocery, with his family living in the upstairs flat. The little neighborhood stores offered credit, and bills could be paid monthly or bimonthly. Such stores were forced out by the big box stores, and Rainey closed the grocery around 1969, when Chatham opened on Stephenson Highway and 11 Mile. The space was remodeled into Madison Beauty Shop in 1958. (Courtesy of the Rainey family.)

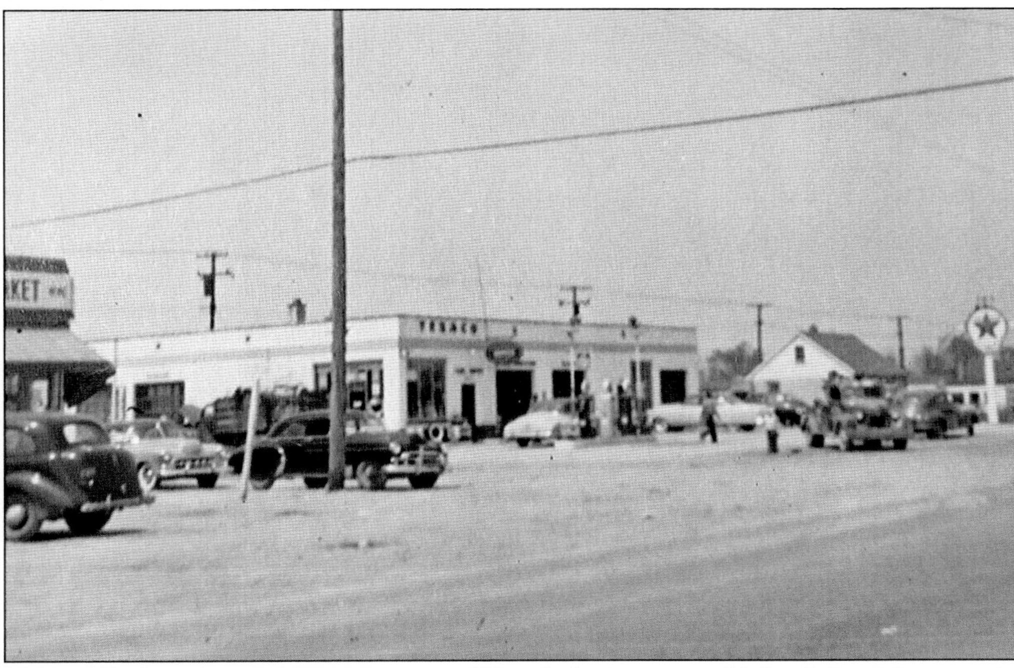

This northwest view of the intersection of Woodside Avenue and John R Road features the Texaco gas station on west John R between 13 and 14 Mile Roads during the late 1940s. The image features cars representative of that period as well. Woodside Market, partially visible on the left, is still there today. (Courtesy of Mary Merkel.)

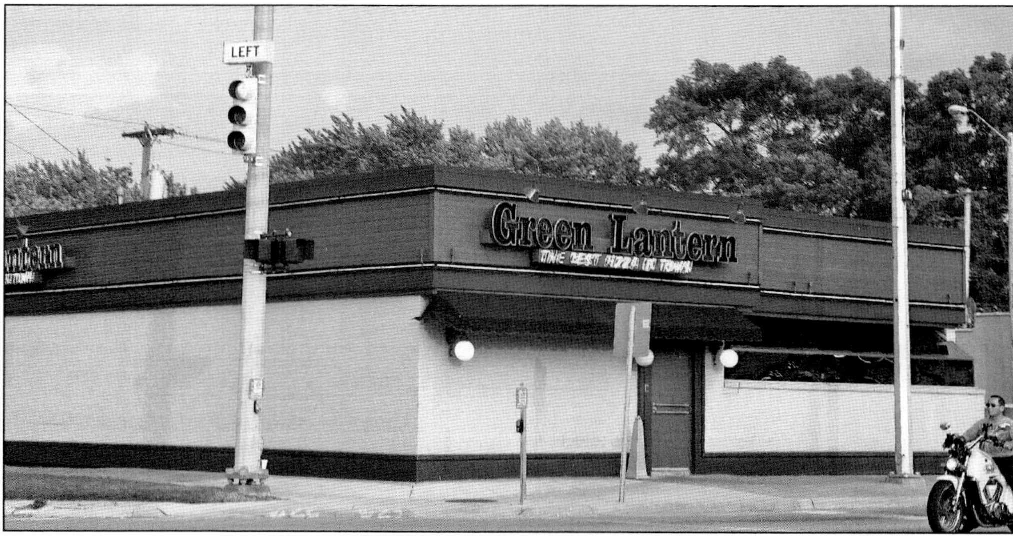

The Green Lantern has long served as the neighborhood establishment at the corner of 12 Mile and John R Roads, opening in 1936. Originally, it was an old farmhouse with a central potbellied stove. Thomas and Irene Vettraino bought the farmhouse, along with its green lantern, in 1954. In 1961, fire nearly destroyed it, and the current building was erected around the old. A second major overhaul followed. Tom and Irene passed along their pizza recipe to daughter Marlene, the present owner. She managed the restaurant with her husband John Spreitzer until his death in 1993. The pizza built the business and remains its specialty. The Green Lantern Restaurant boasts "the Best Pizza in Town," which has won numerous awards. (Photograph by Margene Scott.)

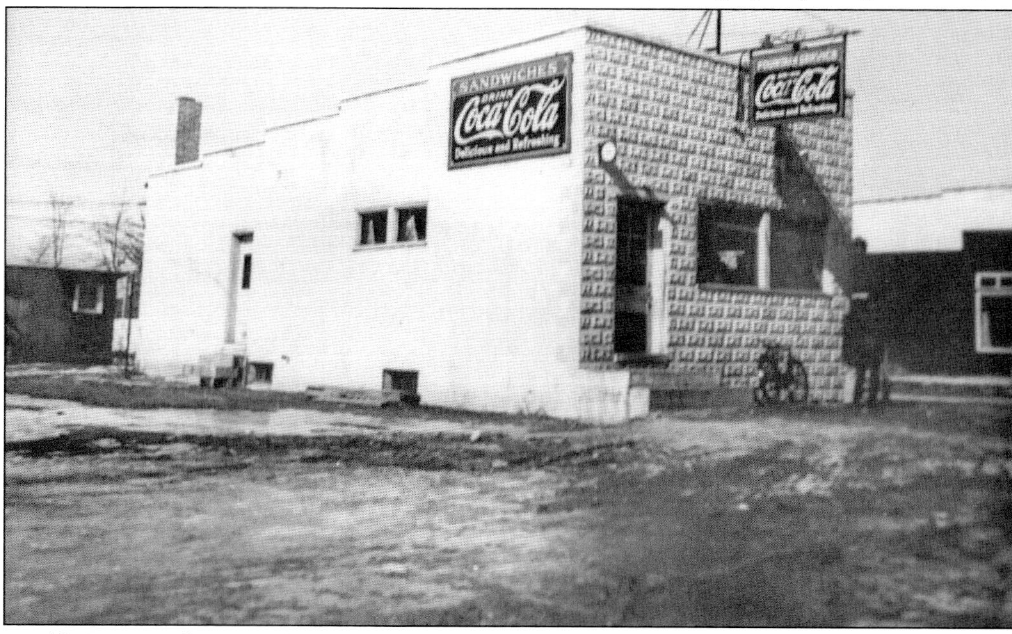

Panfilo Bucciarelli married the love of his life, Antonina Colaniro, in 1927, came to Royal Oak Township, and built a small corner restaurant on John R Road. His wife, "Mrs. B," managed the business. Their clientele featured students, given their location across from the old Madison High School, and the business was also known as a hangout for the political crowd. (Courtesy of Teresa Bucciarelli Hoskins and the late Angelina Bucciarelli Joyce.)

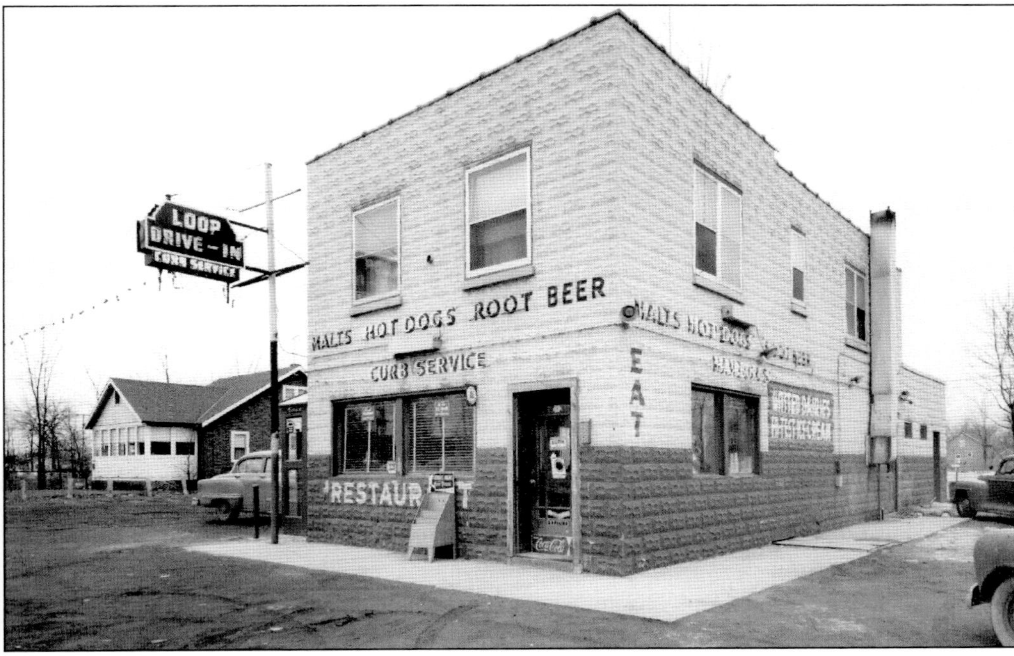

The Bucciarellis' house was located on the south side of the restaurant. A drive-through was added in the 1950s, and thus the name became the Loop. Later the original building was removed, although the deep basement still exists. It is now the Star Family Dining Restaurant. (Courtesy of Teresa Bucciarelli Hoskins and the late Angelina Bucciarelli Joyce.)

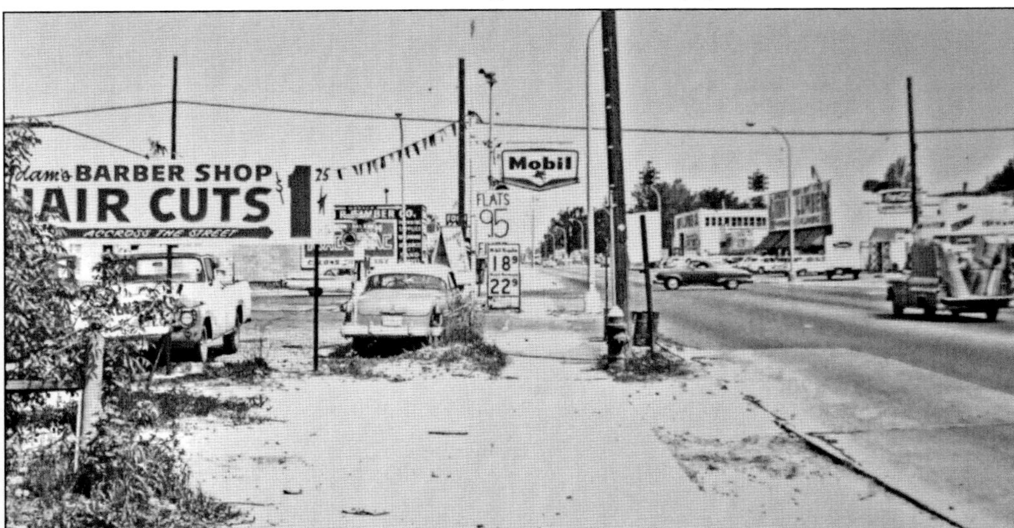

John R Lumber was one of the city's longest-running and most well-known businesses. It was owned by brothers Donald and Will Katz, which explains the use of cats in their logo and advertisements. The business opened in 1939. John R Lumber is pictured here on the right, with the store coming first, followed by the lumber storage area in the next building north. Another warehouse and lumber storage area is pictured across the street on the left side. The business's unofficial slogan was "If we don't have it, you don't need it," as John R Lumber was known to have everything. It has been likened to the big box stores of today—huge and full of stuff. (Courtesy of Madison Heights Historical Commission.)

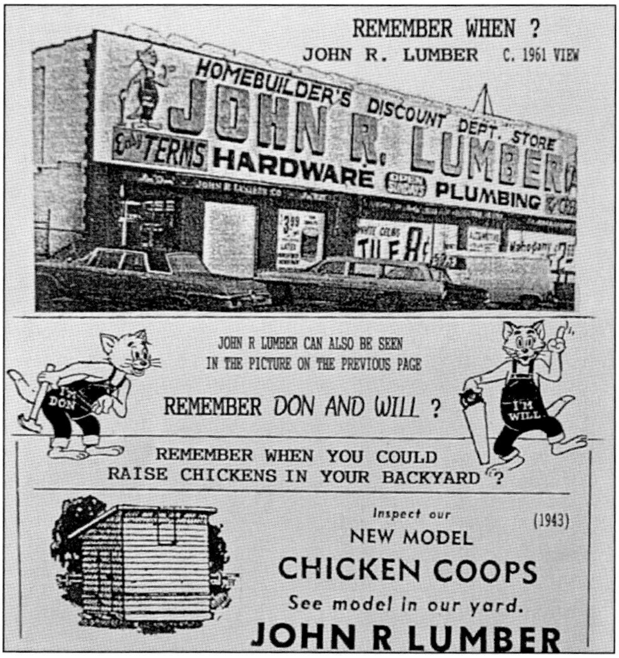

This 1961 advertisement for John R Lumber is noteworthy for its reminiscence on raising chickens in one's own backyard with its invitation to inspect its new-model chicken coops, given that the city now allows the same, after a good deal of discussion. Also of note was the practice of giving out free popcorn, which prompted at least one young man to pretend that his father was elsewhere in the store when asked. The business was a precursor to today's big box stores. (Courtesy of Madison Heights Historical Commission.)

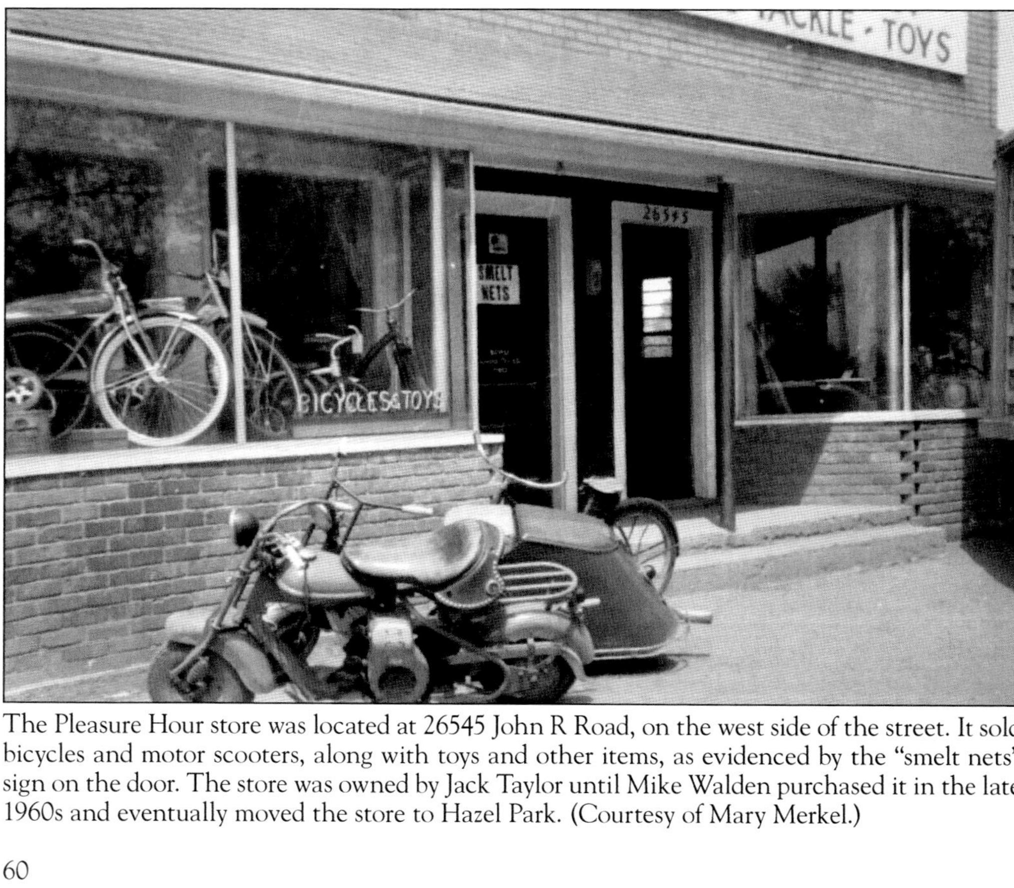

The Pleasure Hour store was located at 26545 John R Road, on the west side of the street. It sold bicycles and motor scooters, along with toys and other items, as evidenced by the "smelt nets" sign on the door. The store was owned by Jack Taylor until Mike Walden purchased it in the late 1960s and eventually moved the store to Hazel Park. (Courtesy of Mary Merkel.)

Jack Taylor stands outside of his business, the Pleasure Hour store, at 26545 John R Road. The store later became Mike Walden's Continental Bike Shop and underwent at least one additional change in ownership. Some city residents continued to patronize the store in Hazel Park, as it remained within bicycling distance. (Courtesy of Mary Merkel.)

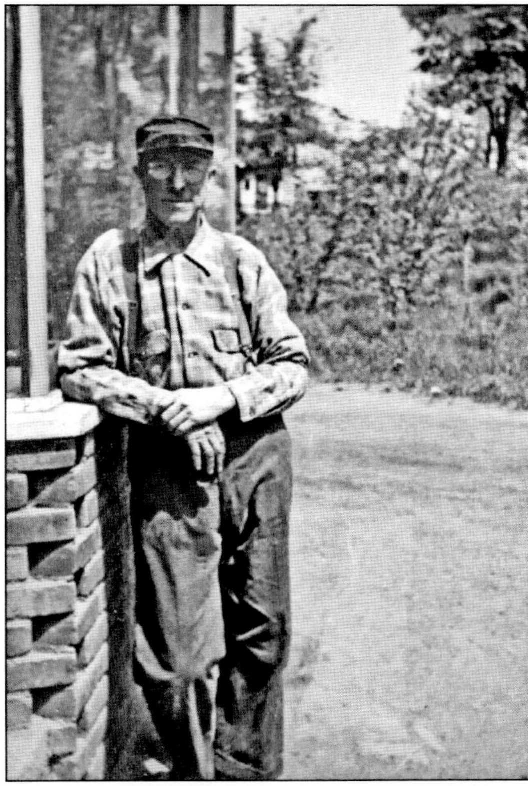

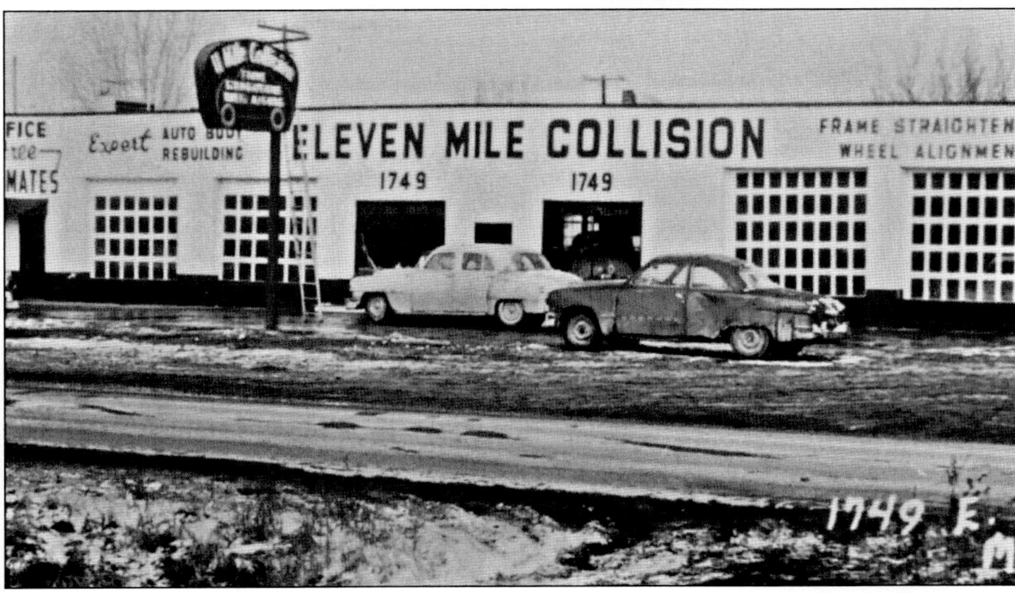

The repair shop Eleven Mile Collision is seen at its original location at 1749 East 11 Mile Road. The business moved from the north side of 11 Mile to its current south-side location at 1750 and has been in business since 1945. The business is independently owned and operated by the Krstich family. Milo Krstich first opened Northeast Truck & Trailer Repair, then purchased 11 Mile Truck Frame & Axle in 1980 and merged the two companies together. Milo has since left ownership of the business to his three sons. (Courtesy of the Krstich family.)

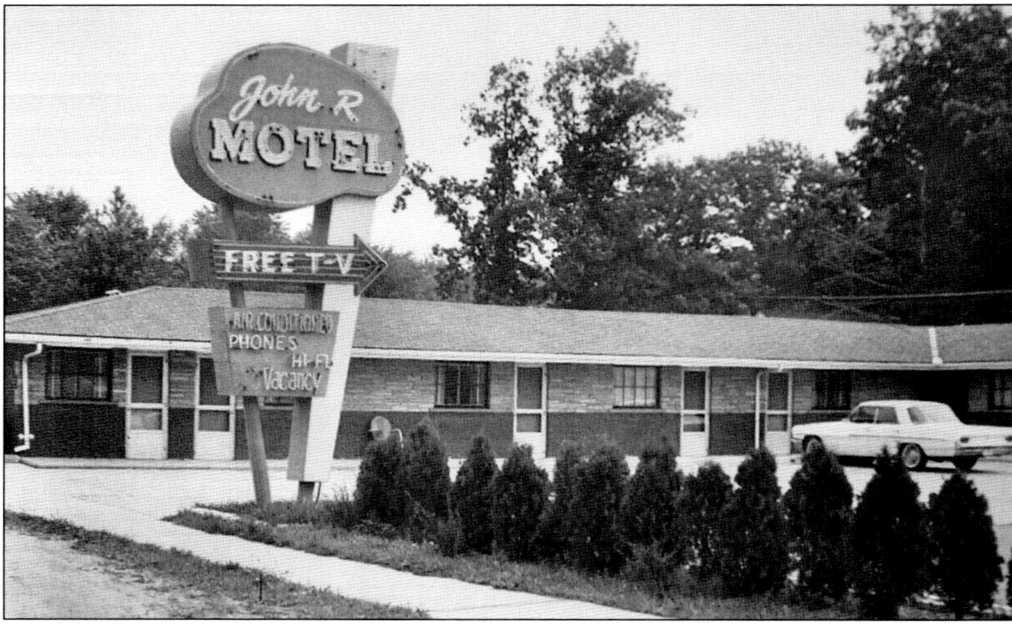

The John R Motel, located at 27746 John R Road, is believed to be the city's first hotel or motel. It also had the distinction of being the only one then that rented by the hour. Established in the early 1960s, a second floor was added at some point later. The motel has undergone new management over the years, and is currently under new management again. (Courtesy of City of Madison Heights.)

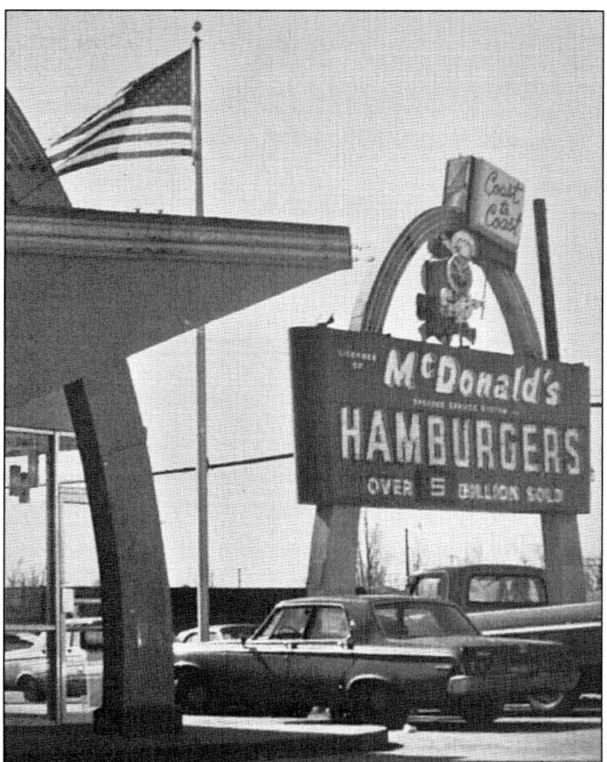

Madison Heights is home to two McDonald's restaurants, but its first has a unique claim to fame. Located on John R Road, south of 12 Mile Road, the restaurant boasted the "ancient" McDonald's restaurant arch sign, which had been sought by the Henry Ford Museum in a nationwide search. The rare find is unique for its single arch and "Speedee" figure, which McDonald's dropped in 1962. On December 11, 1986, the sign was lowered and readied for a trip to its new home. The Madison Heights sign is now part of the Automobile in American Life exhibit on display at The Henry Ford Museum. (Courtesy of Lamphere School District.)

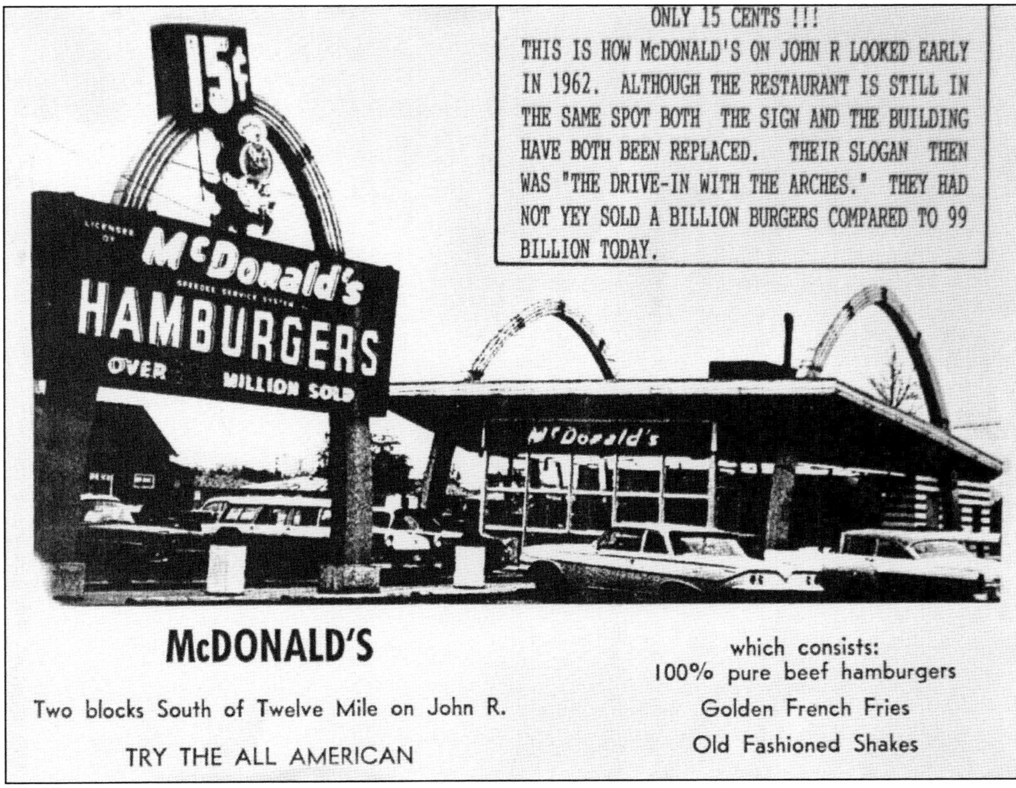

This 2004 calendar waxes nostalgic about how the John R Road McDonald's looked early in 1962. The restaurant is still in the same location, although both the sign and the building have been replaced. (Courtesy of Madison Heights Historical Commission.)

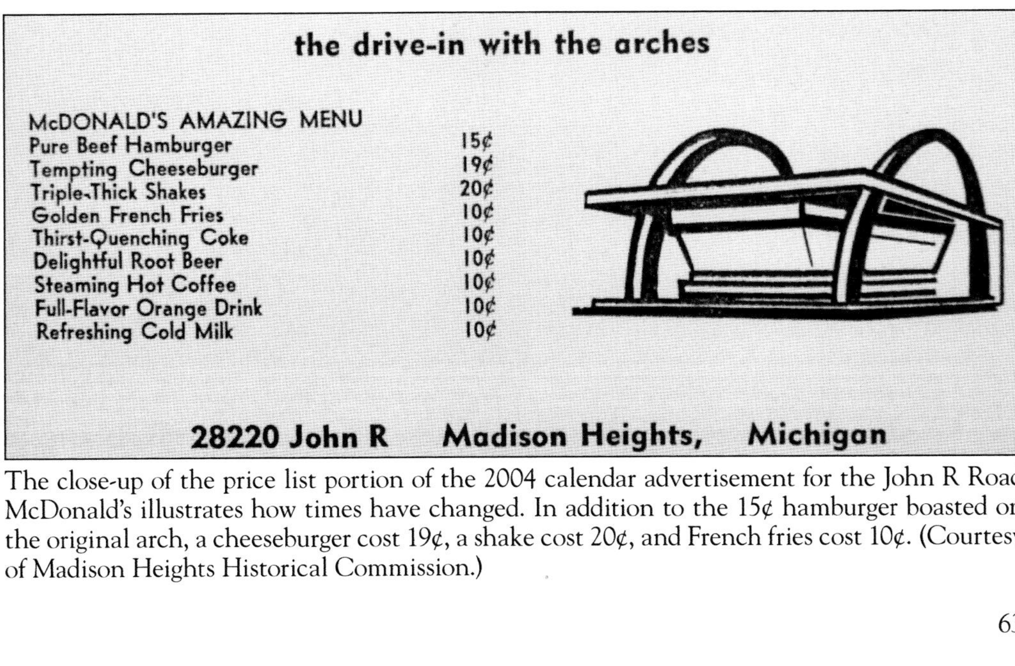

The close-up of the price list portion of the 2004 calendar advertisement for the John R Road McDonald's illustrates how times have changed. In addition to the 15¢ hamburger boasted on the original arch, a cheeseburger cost 19¢, a shake cost 20¢, and French fries cost 10¢. (Courtesy of Madison Heights Historical Commission.)

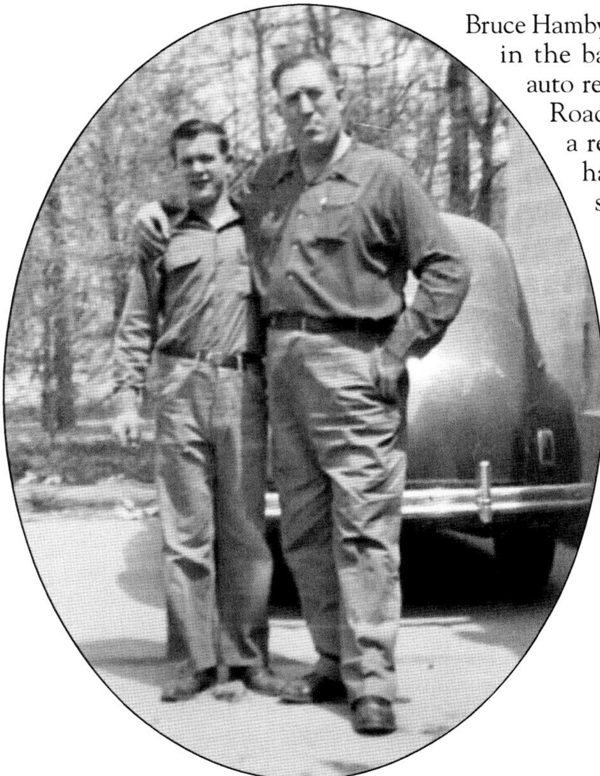

Bruce Hamby (left) and Bill Pierce (right) are pictured in the backyard of the home behind Pierce's auto repair business on the corner of John R Road and Greig Avenue. Hamby remains a resident of Madison Heights, where he has lived since childhood. Jim Mitchell served as a mechanic and was friends with numerous city residents. He met his wife, Annie Rye Mitchell, at the business. (Courtesy of Annie Rye Mitchell.)

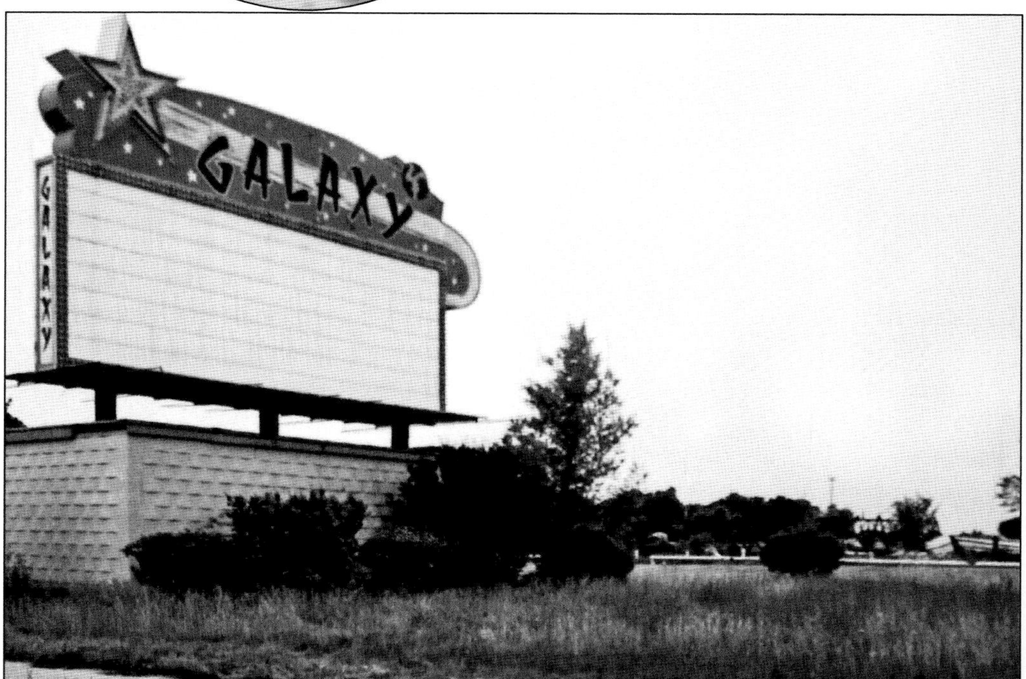

The popular Galaxy Drive-in, at 25257 Dequindre Road, opened on August 22, 1963, and closed in 1986. The screen and building have since been demolished and replaced by an office building, and more recently by the Madison Tech Center. (Photograph by Margene Scott.)

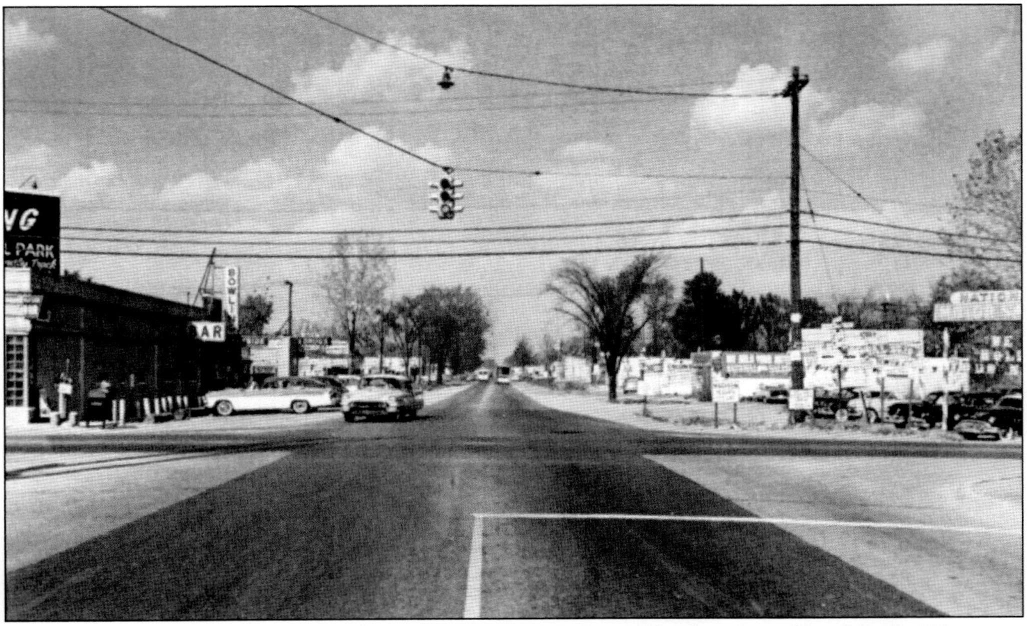

This 1950s image shows the southern gateway to Madison Heights from Hazel Park. The view shows the intersection of John R Road looking north, with 10 Mile Road crossing from left to right. Considered one of the first businesses, the Wayside Bar and bowling alley is seen on the left. (Courtesy of City of Madison Heights.)

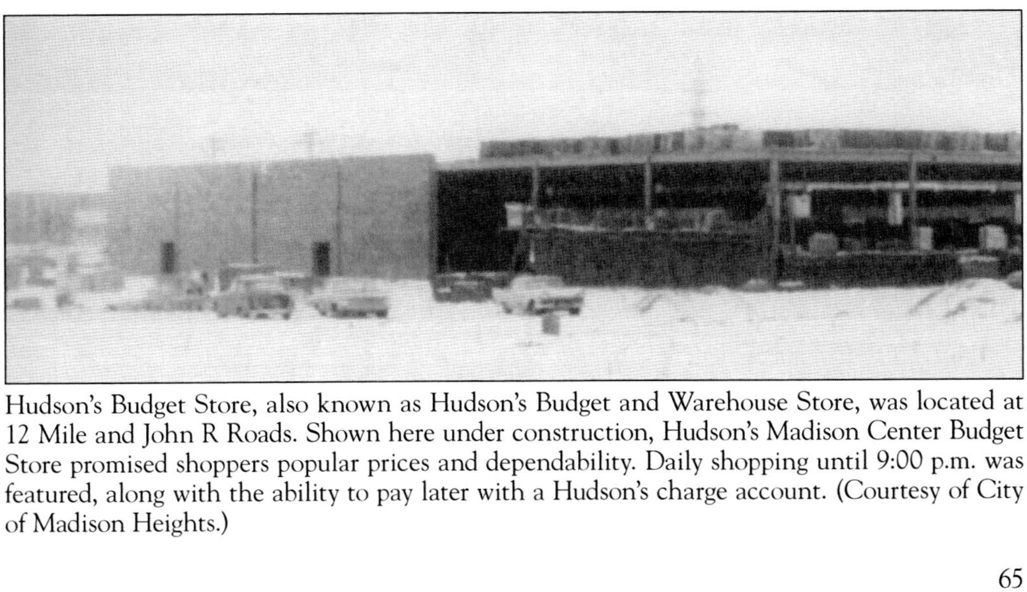

Hudson's Budget Store, also known as Hudson's Budget and Warehouse Store, was located at 12 Mile and John R Roads. Shown here under construction, Hudson's Madison Center Budget Store promised shoppers popular prices and dependability. Daily shopping until 9:00 p.m. was featured, along with the ability to pay later with a Hudson's charge account. (Courtesy of City of Madison Heights.)

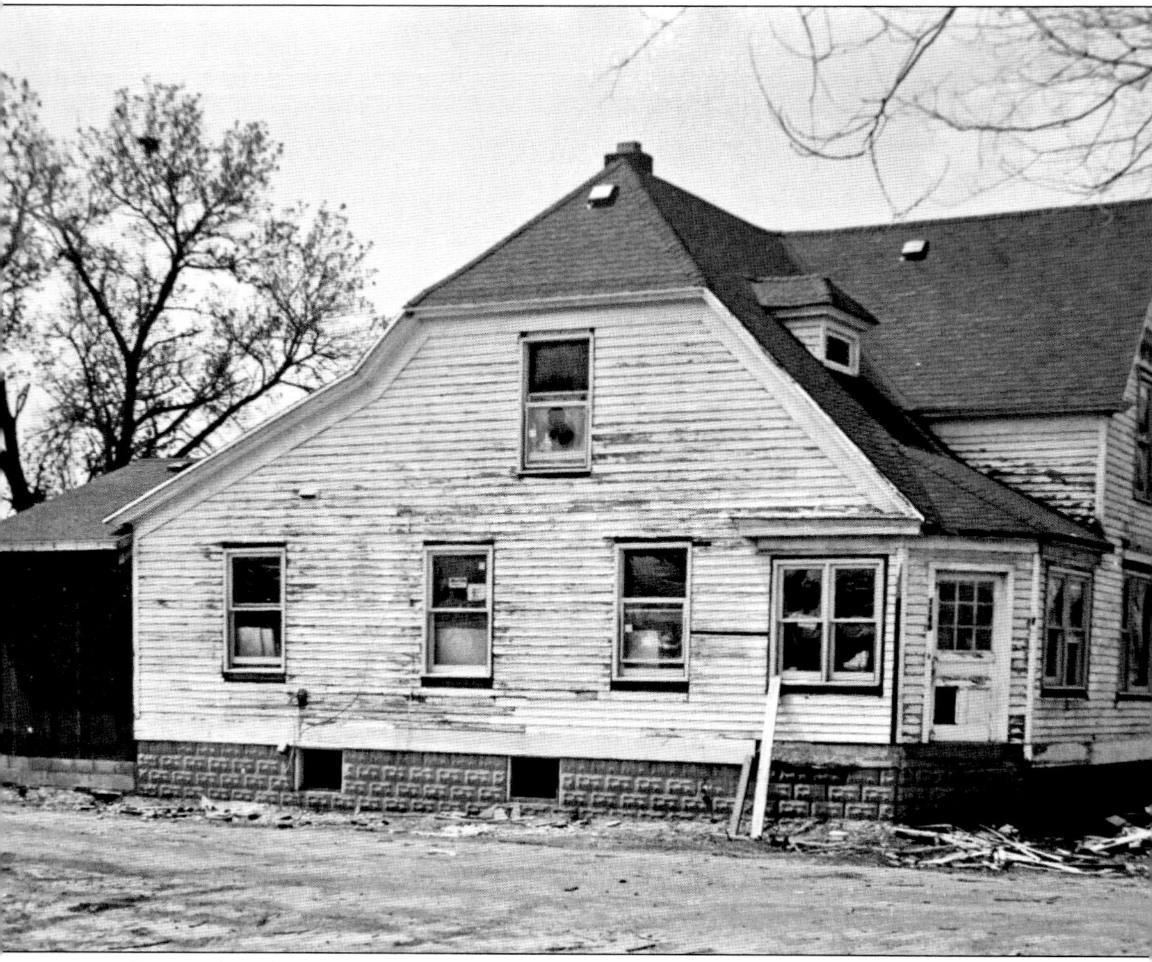

The Kutchey family lived in the city's second oldest house, built in 1891 by their parents. As there were multiple oak trees on the property, the lumber to construct the home was hand milled on site. After the family moved out, the house deteriorated and was condemned by the city. An idealistic realtor, Larry Campbell, took a leap of faith and purchased the home in 1979, although vandals smashed out his 46 new historically accurate windows. (Courtesy of Larry Campbell.)

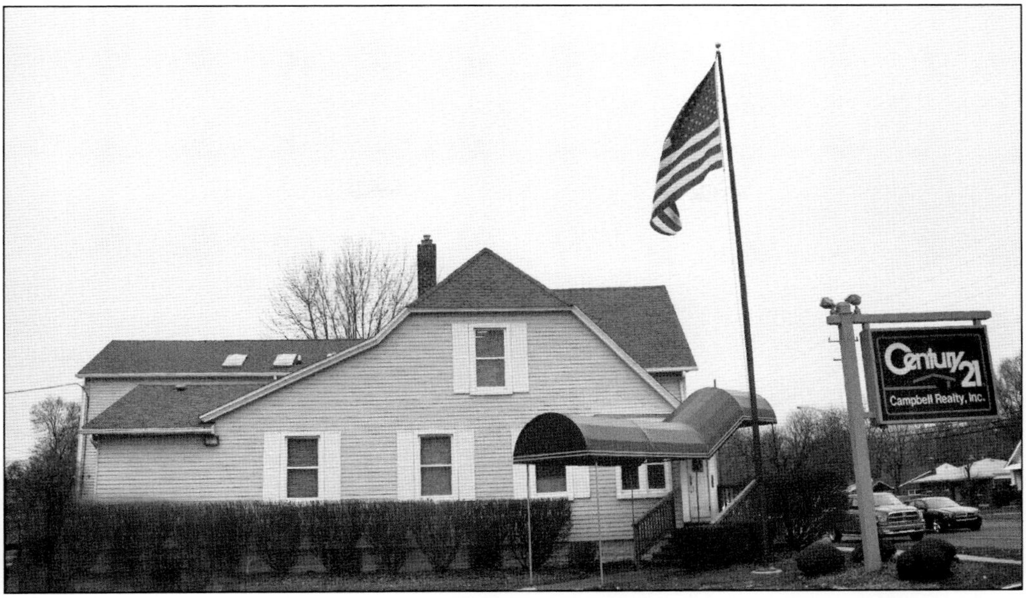

It was Larry Campbell's dream to restore the historically significant farmhouse and to renovate the building into an updated office for his realtors and his mother and partner Evelyn McDonald. After an investment of $350,000 and 15 years of work, he expanded the building at 1186 East 12 Mile Road to more than double its original size, winning praise and admiration from his neighbors and the city. (Photograph by Margene Scott.)

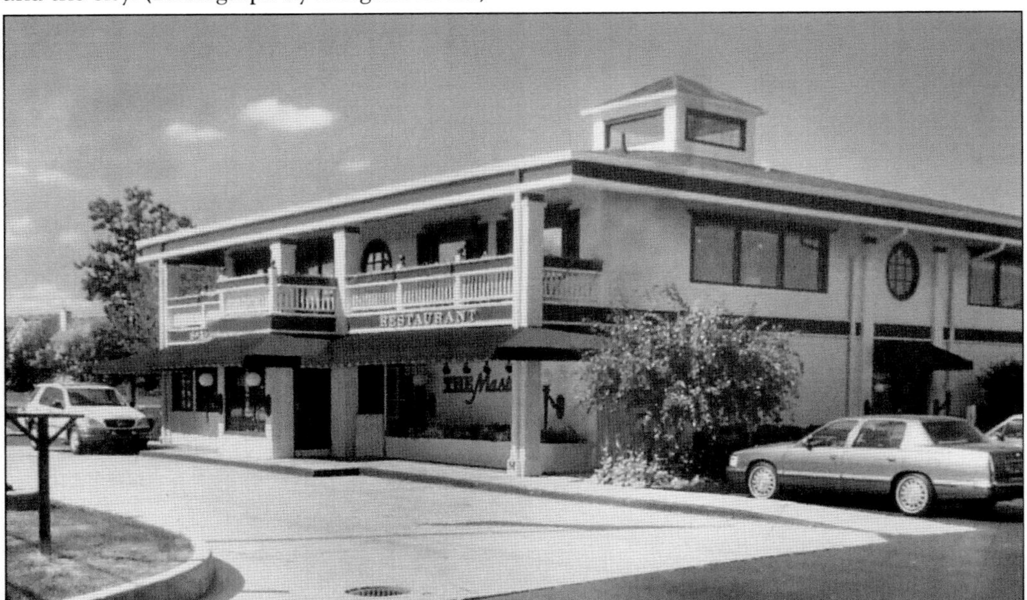

In 1983, golf advocate and local businessman Bob Puskas built the popular Masters Restaurant near the northwest corner of 13 Mile and Dequindre Roads. The decor was reminiscent of the Masters Tournament in Augusta, Georgia. Ten years later, Harry, wife Koula, and brother Nick Andreopoulous purchased the business, and they continue to run the successful gathering place, which supports the community. Sports memorabilia and famous golfer photographs adorn the walls, and the menu features golf-themed dishes. (Courtesy of Masters Restaurant.)

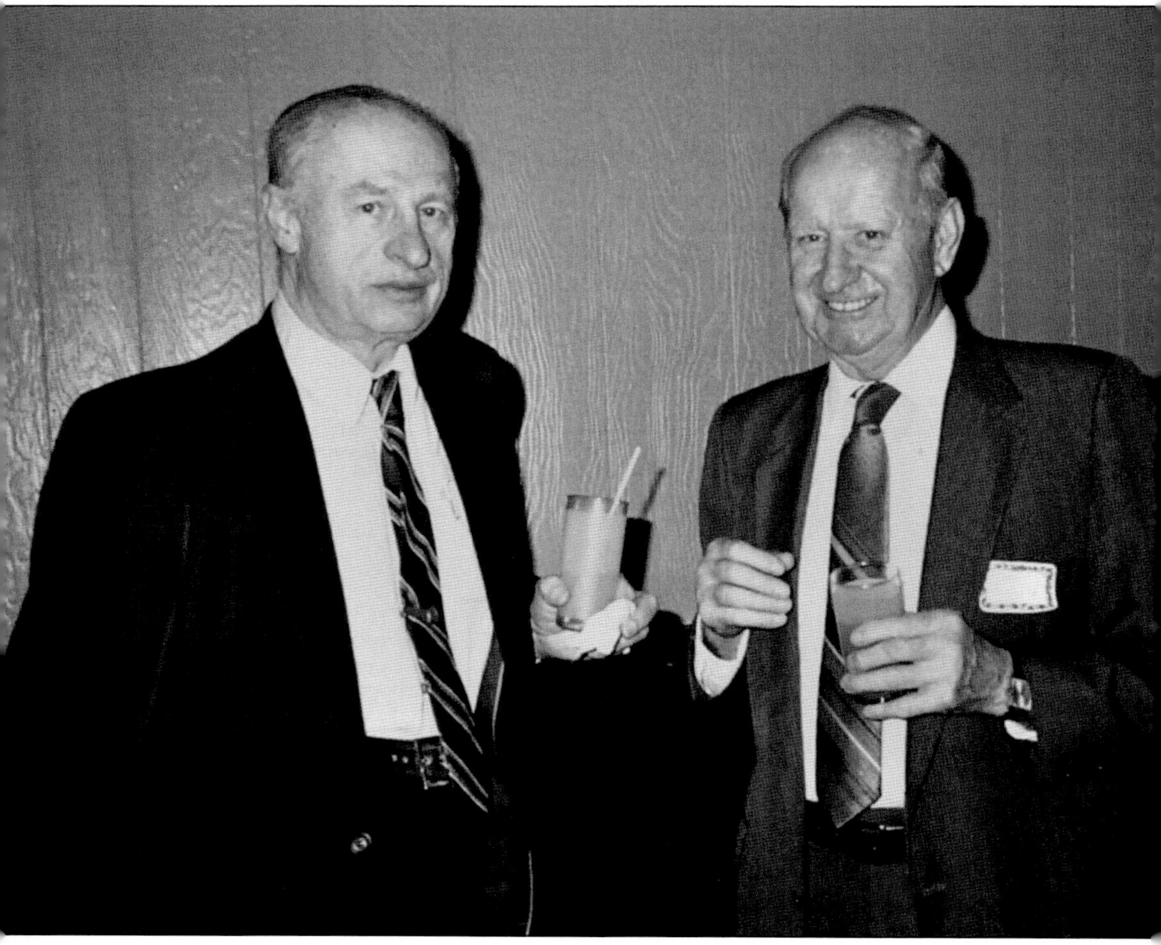

Former assistant city manager Aubrey Green (left) enjoys a drink with Bernie Travnikar, who served on the board of directors for Madison National Bank and was its community affairs representative. He served on multiple city boards and commissions and was instrumental in bringing civil service to Madison Heights, spending his own money to put it on the ballot. He was also a charter member of the chamber of commerce. (Courtesy of Margene Scott.)

Six

SCHOOLS

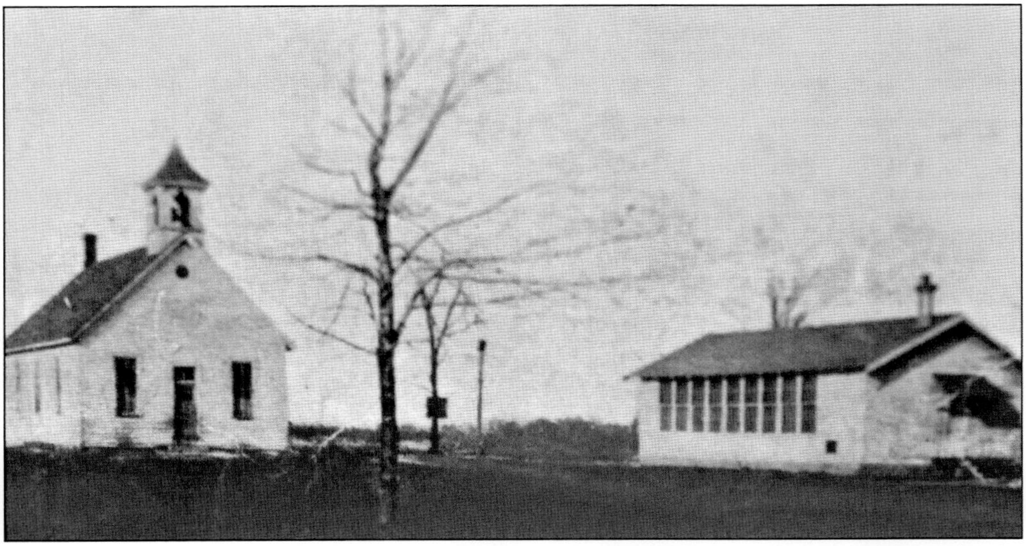

Madison Heights' first home was built in 1834 on 13 Mile Road west of Dequindre Road. The population remained sparse, with a handful of farms dotting the landscape at various mile road tracts of land. In 1840, School District No. 4 was established on that growing portion of eastern Royal Oak Township with 21 students. A log building was constructed near the southeast corner of the current John R and 13 Mile Roads. In 1888, a new one-room schoolhouse was erected, shown on the left. By 1925, the little structure was hopelessly overcrowded, and a second one-story building (on the right) was added to accommodate the upper grades. (Courtesy of George Horkey Jr.)

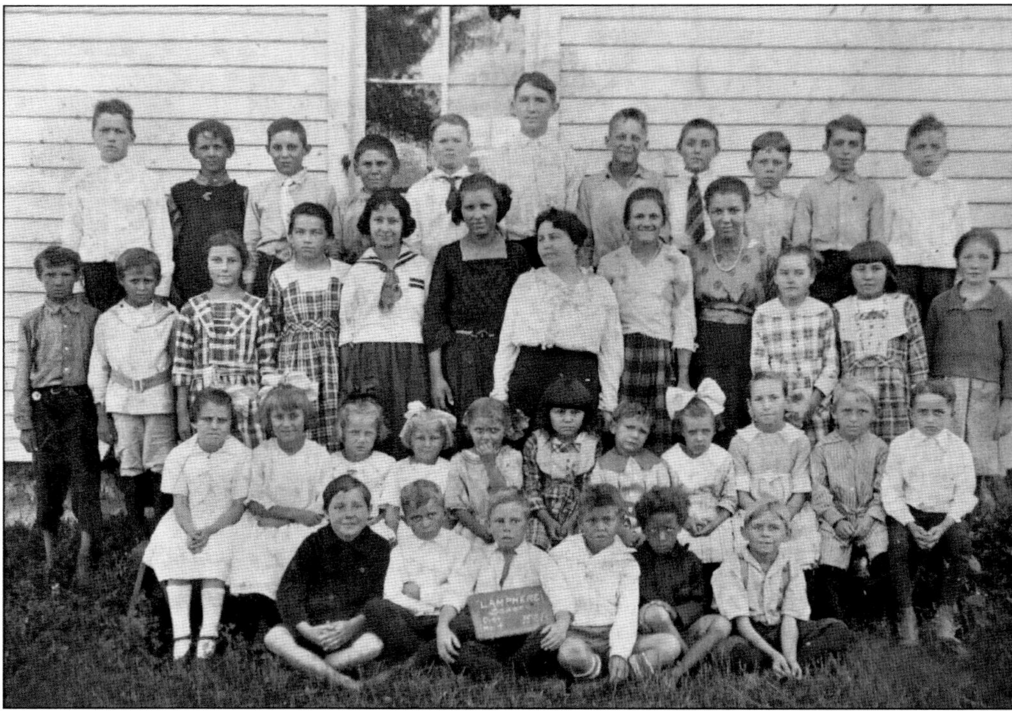

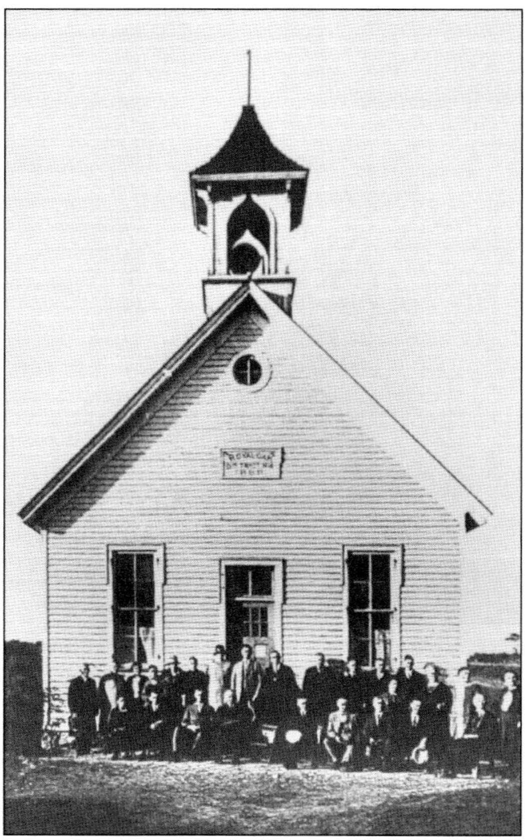

Primary-grade students crowded into the 24-foot-by-40-foot white wooden-frame school in what was then Royal Oak Township District 4 in 1921. The building was erected in 1888 with help from the residents and $1,000 in bonds. Students made their way on country roads from surrounding distant farms, often trudging through deep snow. Among these students were many pioneer farm family names such as Kutchey, Horkey, Nemecheck, Mageehan, Blakley, Halmich and the teacher Luella Macon in the middle. Raymond Kutchey, the tallest boy in the top row, admits to having the errant baseball that traveled through the glazed glass window above him. (Courtesy of the Kutchey family.)

Just before the 1888 one-room schoolhouse was torn down, all the alumni met together in 1928, and commemorative photographs were taken. Former students reminisced about getting to school in deep snow by walking along the tops of fence rails. An old stove was used to build a wood fire every morning, and water in their bucket would freeze into a block of ice. (Courtesy of Lamphere Schools.)

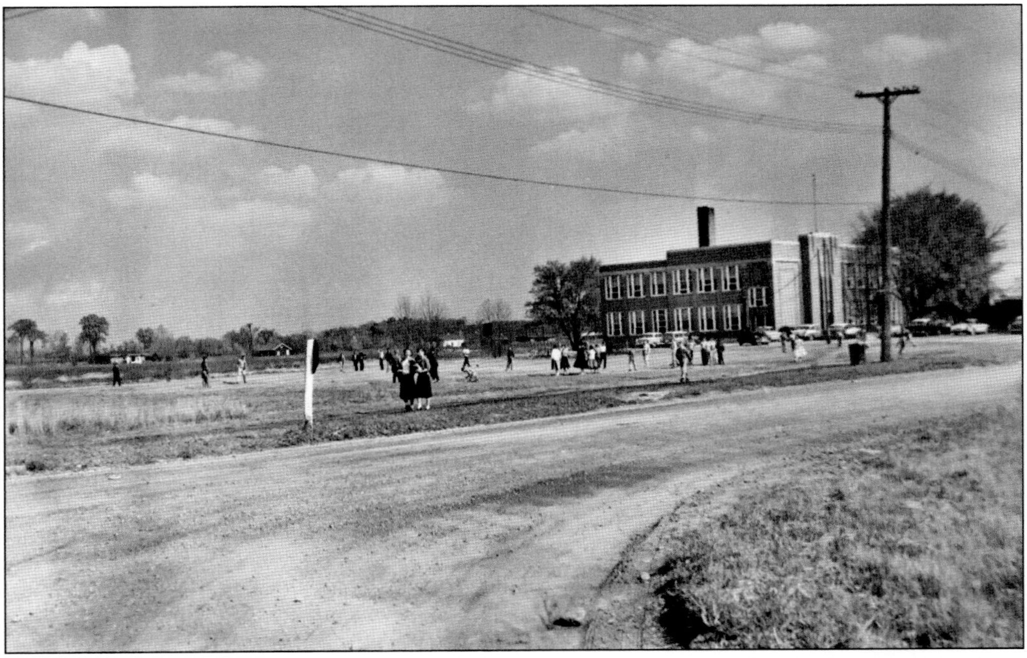

When Madison Heights became a city in 1955, large expanses of open land still existed. Looking northeast from the unpaved two-lane 13 Mile Road, east of John R Road, a baseball game played by local students at the Lamphere School can be glimpsed. The two-story structure, built in 1928, was flanked by the newer Hiller School addition on the east (right) side and the growing group of homes in the Frank Lloyd Wright co-op subdivision to the north (middle left). (Courtesy of Gary Cheek.)

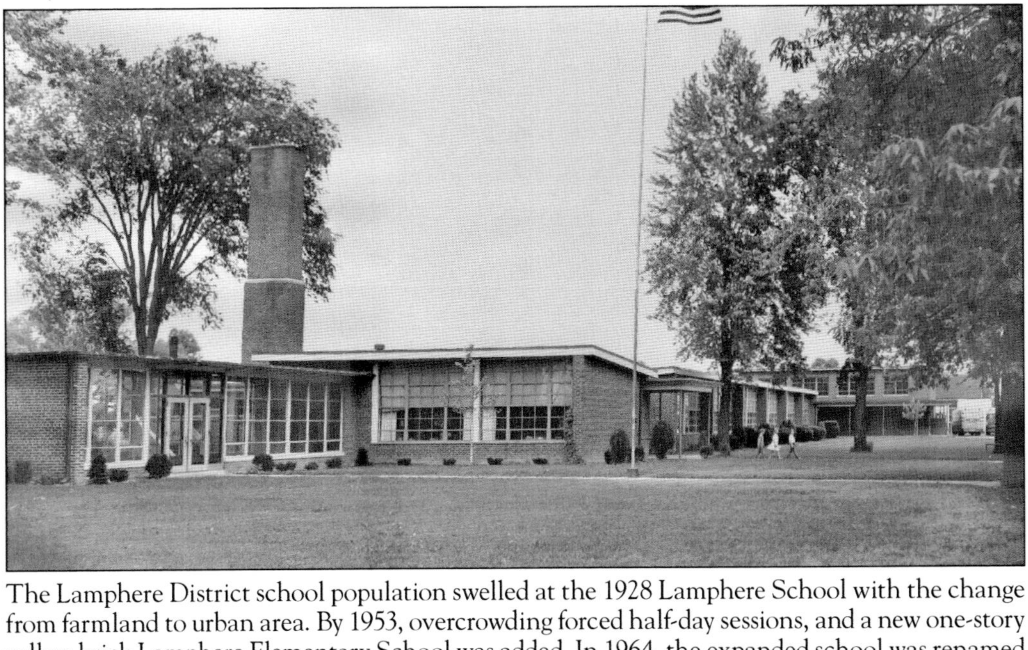

The Lamphere District school population swelled at the 1928 Lamphere School with the change from farmland to urban area. By 1953, overcrowding forced half-day sessions, and a new one-story yellow brick Lamphere Elementary School was added. In 1964, the expanded school was renamed for Frederick Hiller, a longtime member of the district and board. More schools were added, reaching a maximum of 10 in 1969. (Courtesy of Lamphere Schools.)

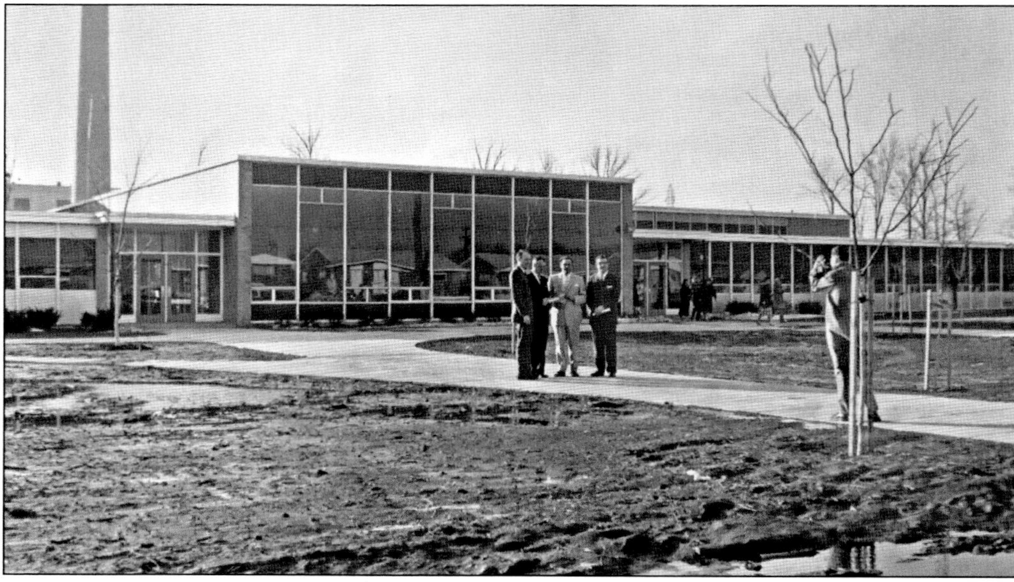

School officials gather for the September 1957 dedication of the newly built junior-senior high school at 29615 Tawas Street. The ceremony opening the first Lamphere District high school included participation by numerous school officials. The school was later used as a middle school and renamed for John Page, Lamphere District School Board treasurer. (Courtesy of Lamphere Schools.)

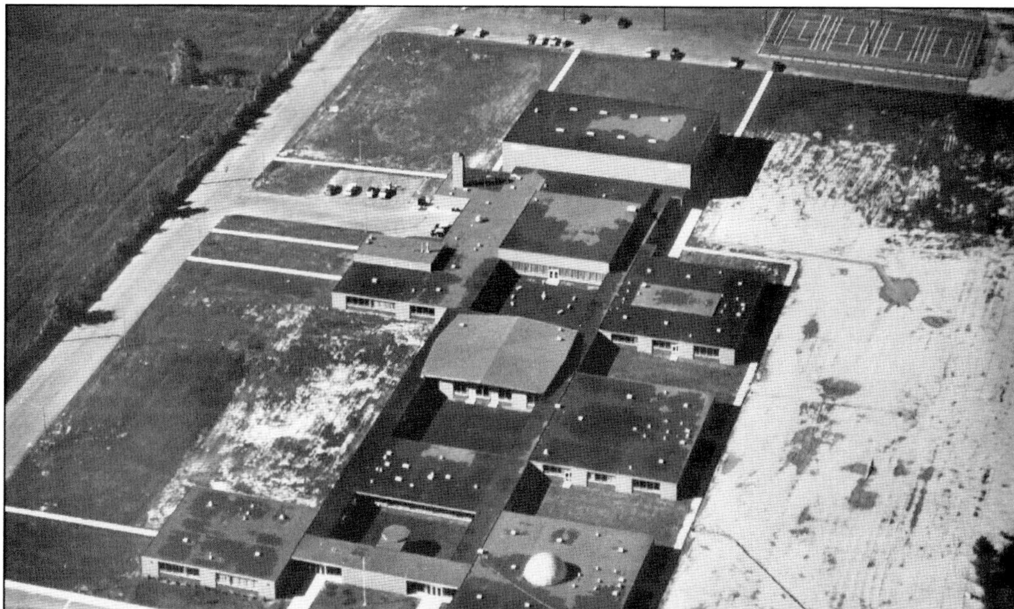

A 1961 aerial view of the new Lamphere High School shows rural farmland on its still-undeveloped west side. A modern six-wing design provided for the new team teaching approach, with each quad devoted to a specific field of study. The athletic wing is visible near the top with a large field to the north dedicated to outdoor sports. Space for a proposed auditorium was allotted at the upper right. After the formal dedication on February 25, 1962, the old high school on Tawas Street was renamed John Page Middle School for seventh- and eighth-grade classes. (Courtesy of Lamphere Schools.)

In the early 1960s, the Lamphere District Council PTA was formed. Staff and parents from all Lamphere schools put on a yearly talent variety program raising proceeds for the scholarship fund through the council PTA. The fun-filled popular event was masterfully directed by teachers Virginia Lambert and Vera Bennett. Practicing their skit in 1978 for "Razz-Ma-Tazz and All that Jazz" are, from left to right, parent performers Donna McQuade, Pauline Jacobs, Rosemarie Tye, school board member Alton Brown, and Cindy Payne. (Courtesy of the *Daily Tribune*.)

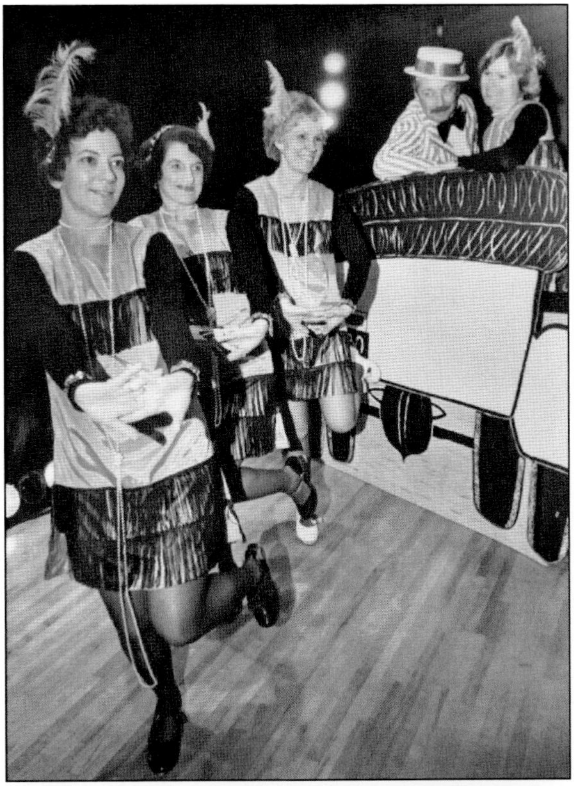

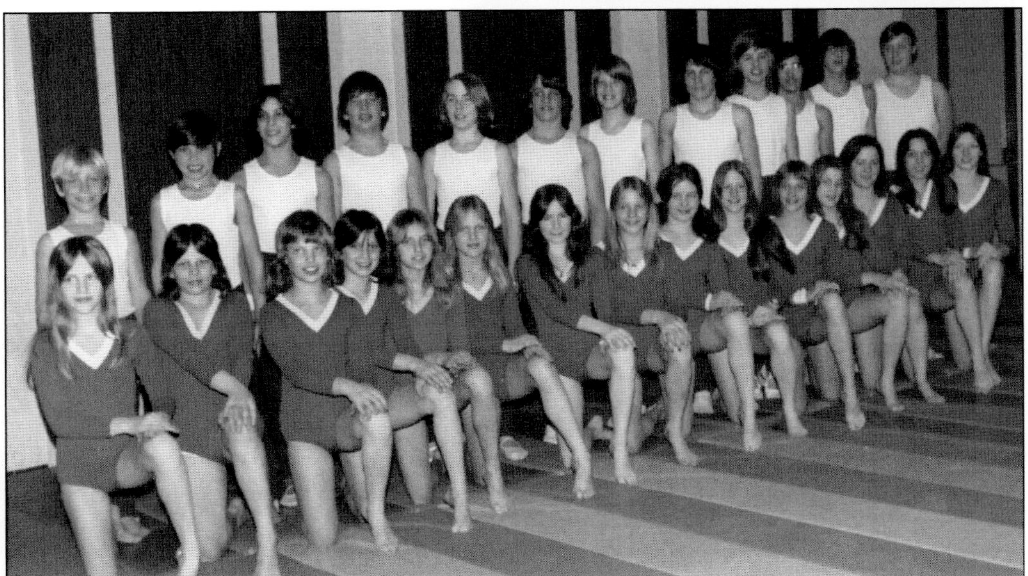

The Lamphere School District Old Tyme Hiller Circus was one of the few performing youth circuses in the country. It originated in the spring of 1971, when a circus theme was added to a gymnastics presentation given for the parents at Hiller Elementary School. Each year, it moved to larger quarters and played to increasing crowds. The original 25 Hiller performers, aged eight to 13, grew to a troupe of 80 representing the entire Madison Heights school system. A cast photograph from the early days of the circus is pictured here. (Courtesy of Robert and Sue Eller.)

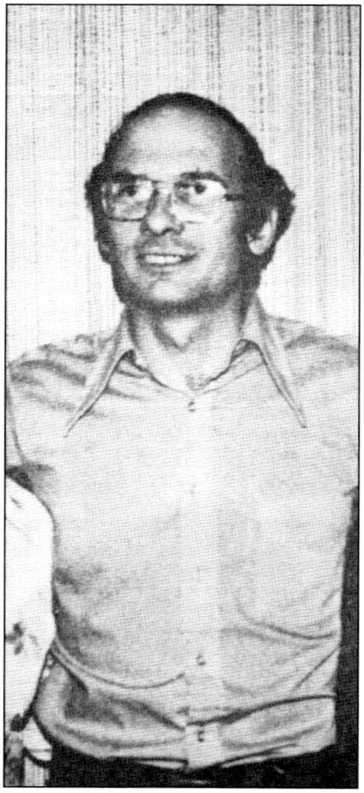

The success of the Old Tyme Hiller Circus was largely due to the enthusiasm and ability of its originator and director, Robert Eller, known throughout the schools as "Mr. Eller," a former circus performer himself. The circus was self-supporting, and proceeds went back into the program for additional equipment, costumes, and expenses. He went on to teach gymnastics for Madison Heights recreation programs, then branched out as a professional coach for gymnastics schools. He and his family retired to New Mexico, where he loves life on his ranch and trains performing horses. His son Curtis is a well-known songwriter, banjo player, yodeler, and band leader. (Courtesy of Lamphere Schools.)

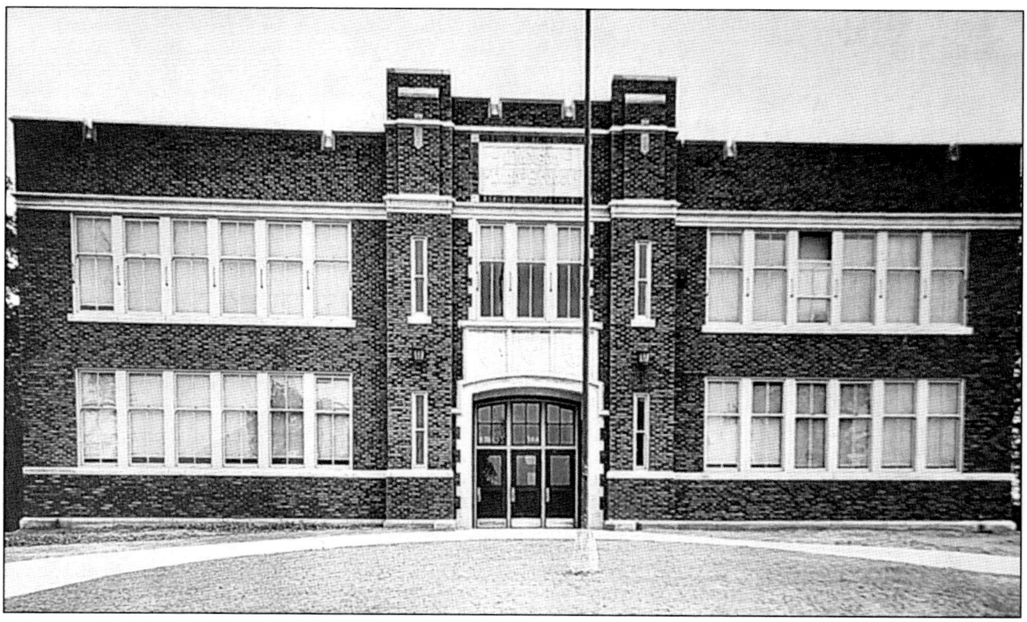

With the change from a primary to a graded school district, Madison High School was created, and in 1929, the first graduates received diplomas. The original Madison High School is pictured in this image. Later, the new Madison High School at 915 East 11 Mile Road was built and equipped through $600,000 remaining from a 1955 bond issue and a 1958 bond issue for $1 million. (Courtesy of Madison Schools.)

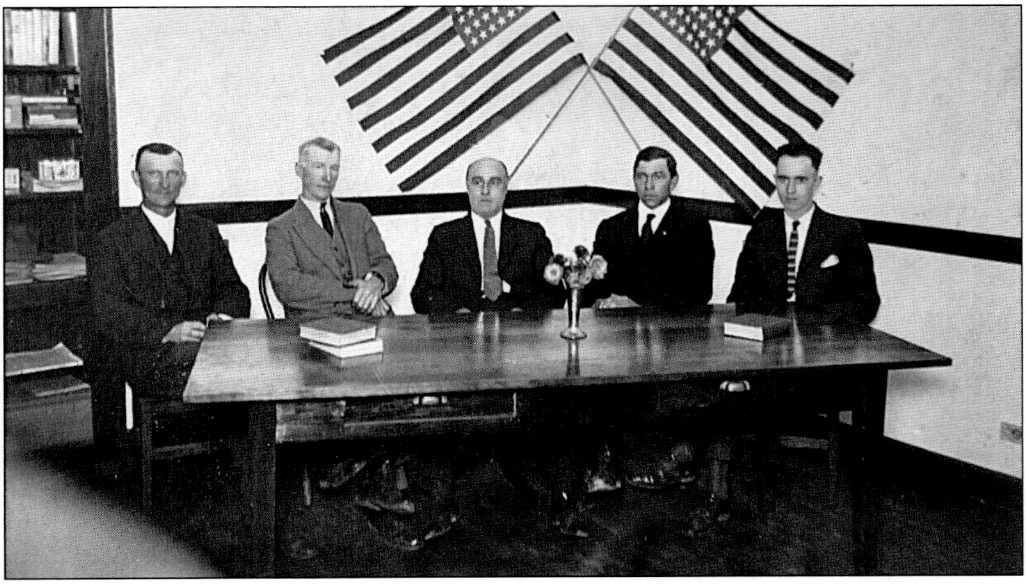

The first Madison District School Board was formed in July 1923, and this image of the five-man board appeared in the first Madison yearbook in 1929. William Kendall (left) was from the Kendall family, who gave their land to the school district for Kendall School on Wolverine Street and East Lincoln Avenue. Also in the photograph are, in unknown order, E.E. Milby, president; Daniel J. Gunter, secretary; Herbert Jackson, treasurer; and Lawrence Bartley, who along with William Kendall was a trustee. (Courtesy of Julie Halpin McMillan.)

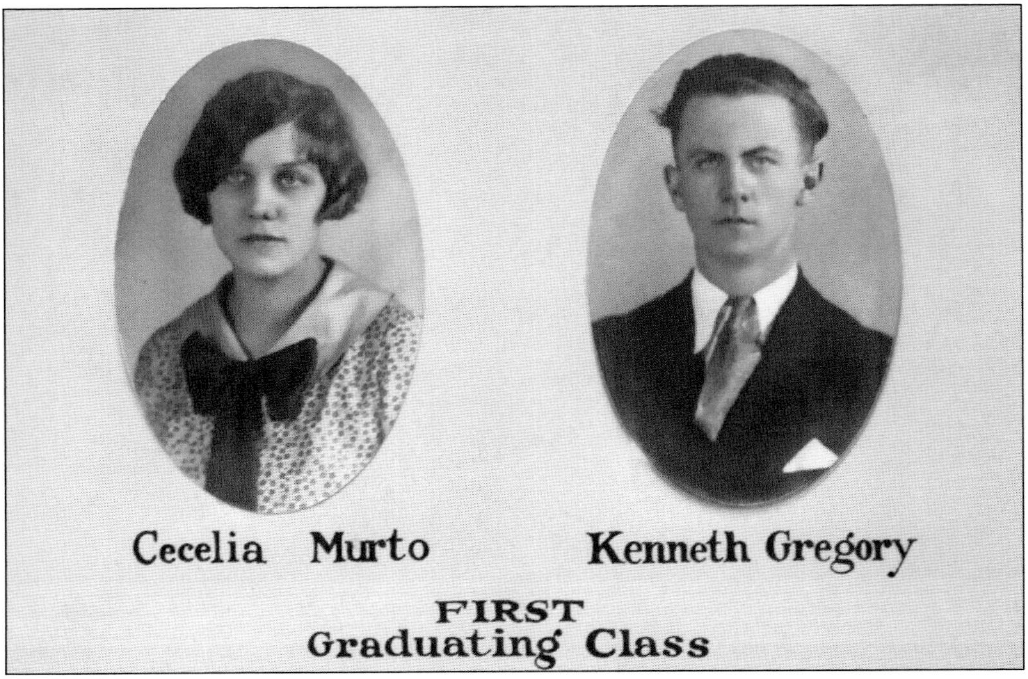

Cecelia Murto was a member of the first graduating class from Madison High School in 1929 and became a teacher for Oakland Grade School. Cecelia, who also went by her middle name of Helen, married Percy Croze. Kenneth Gregory was the other member of the class and served as a mentor to students after him. (Courtesy of Madison Schools.)

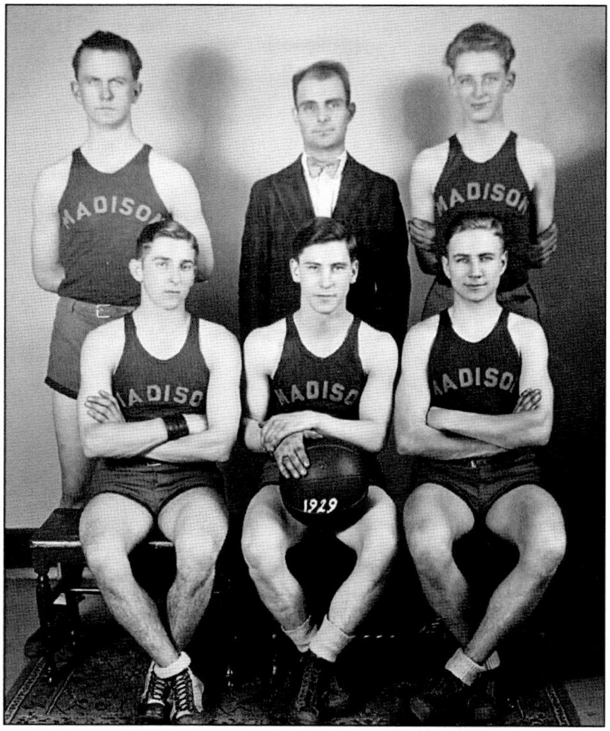

The 1929 basketball team included, from left to right, (first row) Stanford Bricker, captain Robert Stevens, and Kenneth Stahl; (second row) Kenneth Gregory, teacher and coach Mr. Tarrant, and Robert Manning. (Courtesy of Madison Schools.)

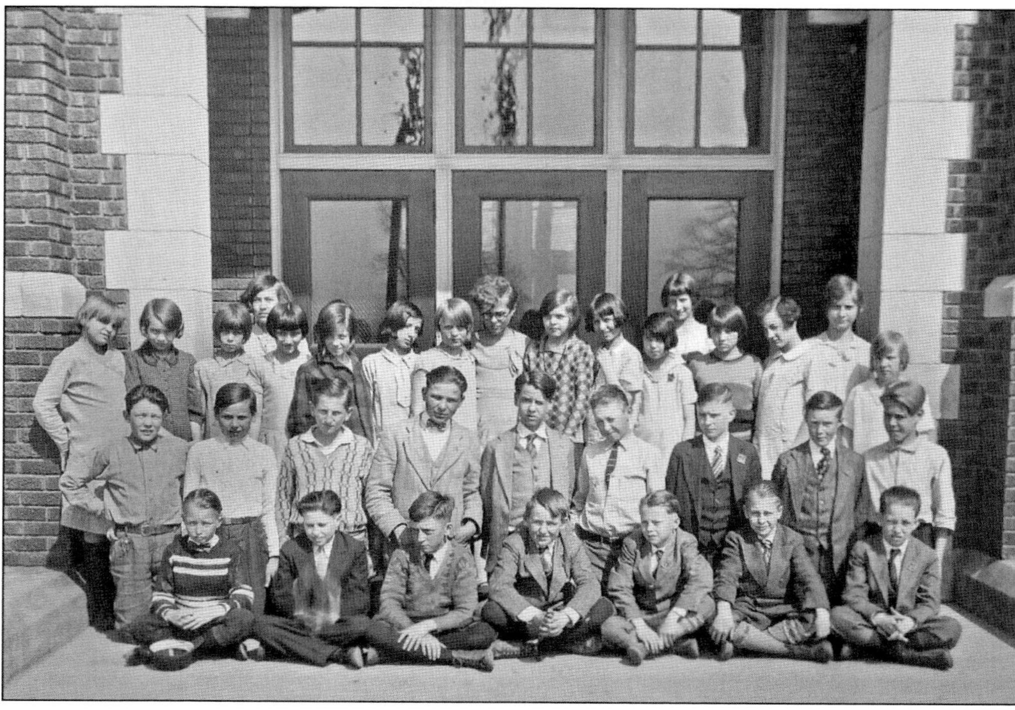

A seventh-grade class poses for a photograph in front of Madison High School in approximately 1926. Included are Bernie Travnikar (second row, third from right) and Bernice Travnikar (third row, second from right). The Travnikar family was well known in Madison Heights. (Courtesy of Madison Schools.)

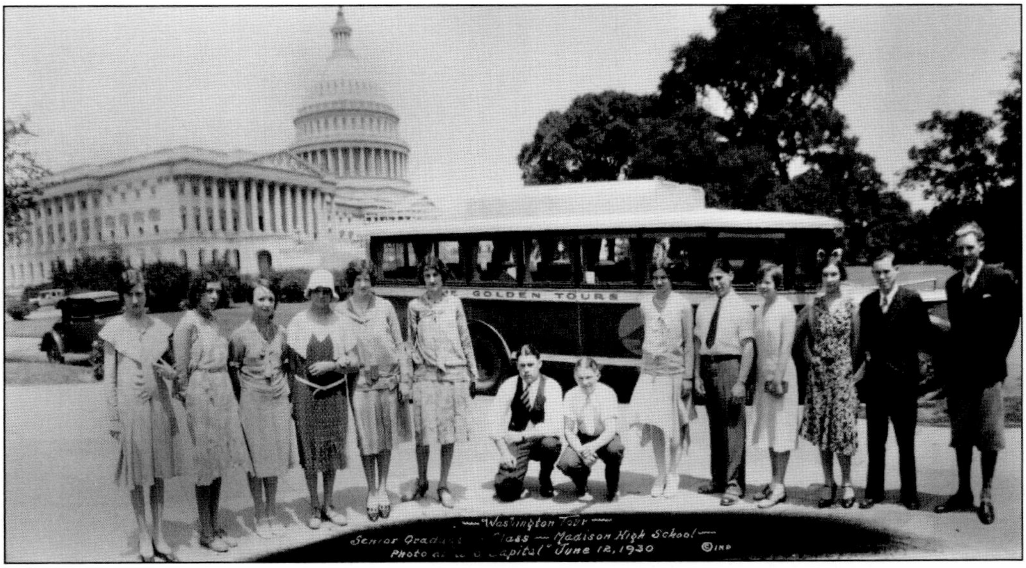

The 1930 Madison High School graduating class poses at the US Capitol during their class trip to Washington, DC. The 1930 class was the second Madison graduating class and raised money for the trip as a class project. The photograph was taken on June 12, 1930, and included class president Helena VanMeter (second from left), chaperone Miss Sonnenberg (fourth from left), secretary and treasurer Robert Stevens (fifth from right), and vice president Helen Dzienis (fourth from right). Helen Dzienis would become the future esteemed teacher Helen Hennessey. (Courtesy of Madison Schools.)

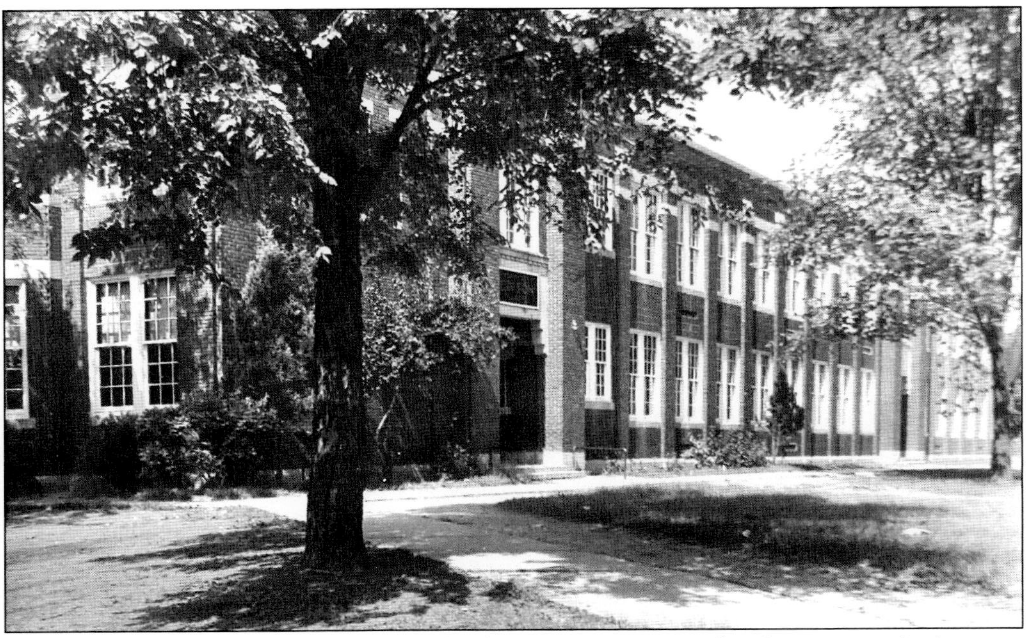

In September 1924, the Blanche Villa school site at 27321 Hampden Street, now the location of Edison School, was purchased for $18,000. An increase in school enrollment during the 1926–1927 school year resulted in the need for more classrooms, and the six-room Edison School was constructed by the fall of 1929. In 1951, a bond issue made possible additional classrooms, and bond issues in 1955 and 1962 built second and third additions. (Courtesy of Madison Schools.)

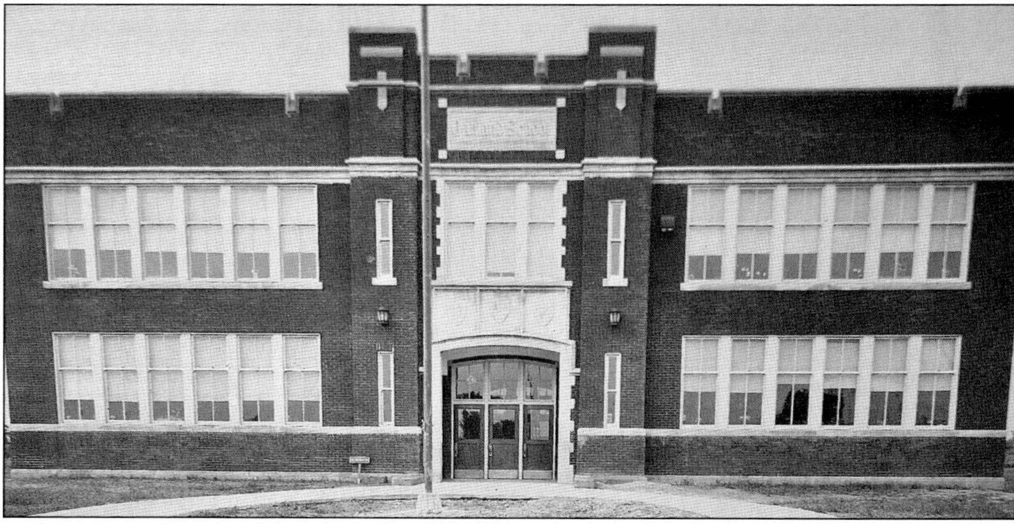

Oakland Grade School was completed in March 1924, initially located near the southwest corner of Royal Oak Township, which is now Madison Heights. It eventually became part of the Royal Oak School District. As growth necessitated the expansion of Madison Schools, a five-acre site was purchased from the John Brinkey farm and occupied by Oakland. It was located just west of Monroe on Barrett and Dallas Avenues in Royal Oak, and included kindergarten through the sixth grade. Oakland students graduated from Madison High School. (Courtesy of Madison Schools.)

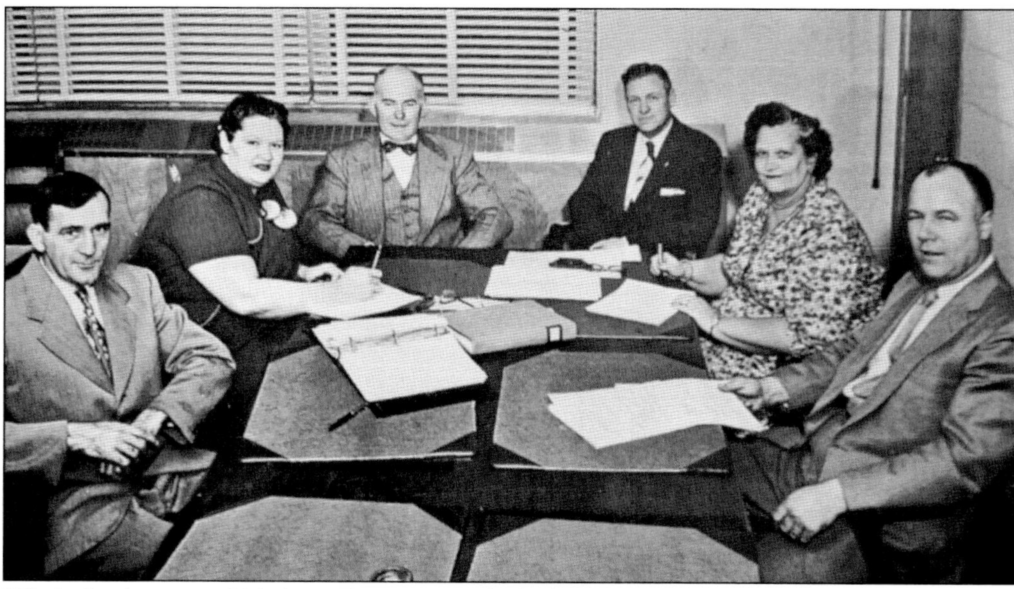

While the first actual Madison District Board of Education was established as a primary school district in 1913 and consisted of three members, Madison became a graded district in 1924, and the number of board members increased to six. In 1956, those members were, from left to right, William McCartney, trustee; Lois Myers, secretary; A.V. Frazier, president; F. Foster Wilkinson, superintendent; Elizabeth Carey, treasurer; and Leroy Comstock, trustee. (Courtesy of Madison Schools.)

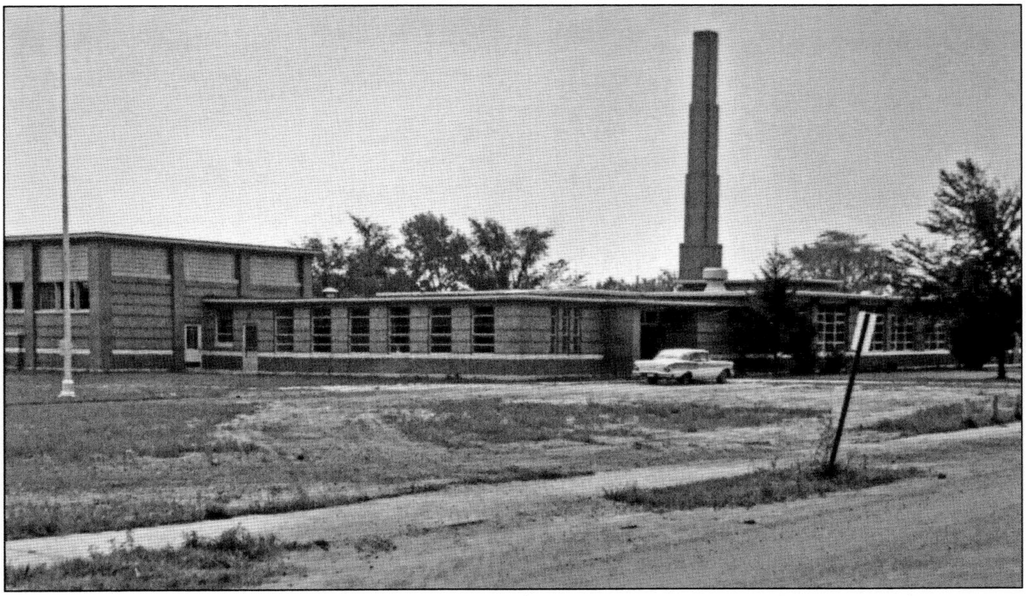

In July 1925, the Kendall site was purchased for $11,000 from the Kendall farm. In the summer of 1926, the second schoolhouse built to replace the burned Greenwood School was moved to this location. It was sometimes referred to as the "White School" or Kendall School. Following World War II, a 100-percent federal grant saw the first 10 rooms of Roosevelt School built. It was located at 26060 Wolverine Street and opened in the fall of 1946. A 1953 bond issue made possible additions to the building. (Courtesy of Madison Schools.)

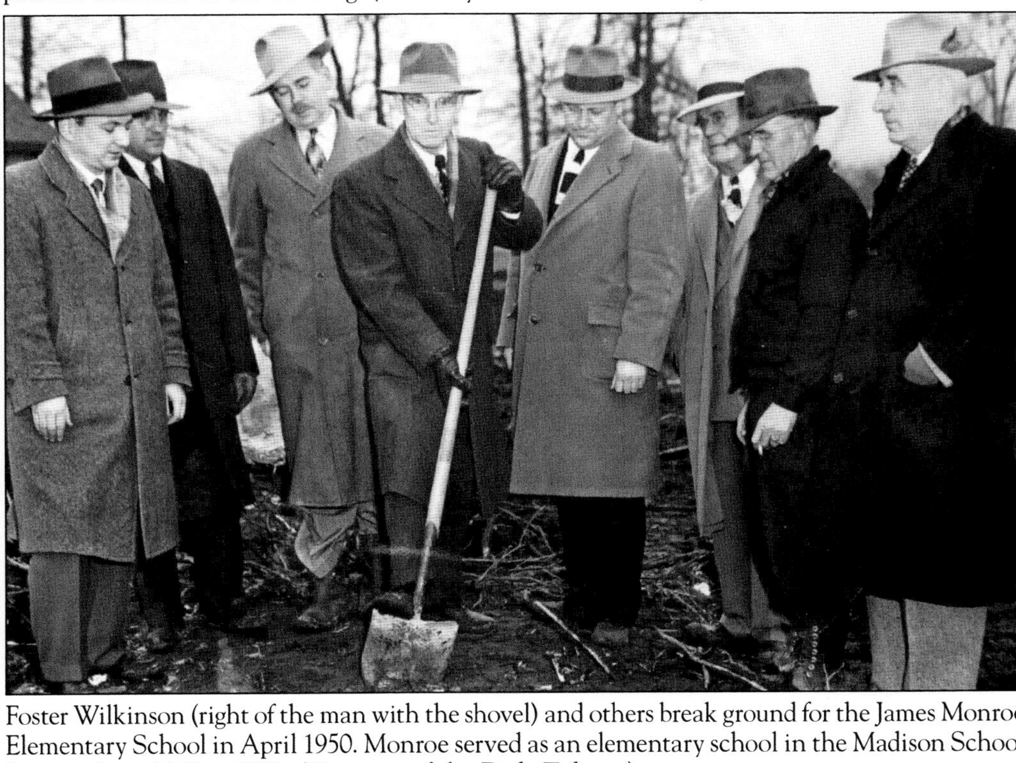

Foster Wilkinson (right of the man with the shovel) and others break ground for the James Monroe Elementary School in April 1950. Monroe served as an elementary school in the Madison School District from 1950 to 1981. (Courtesy of the *Daily Tribune*.)

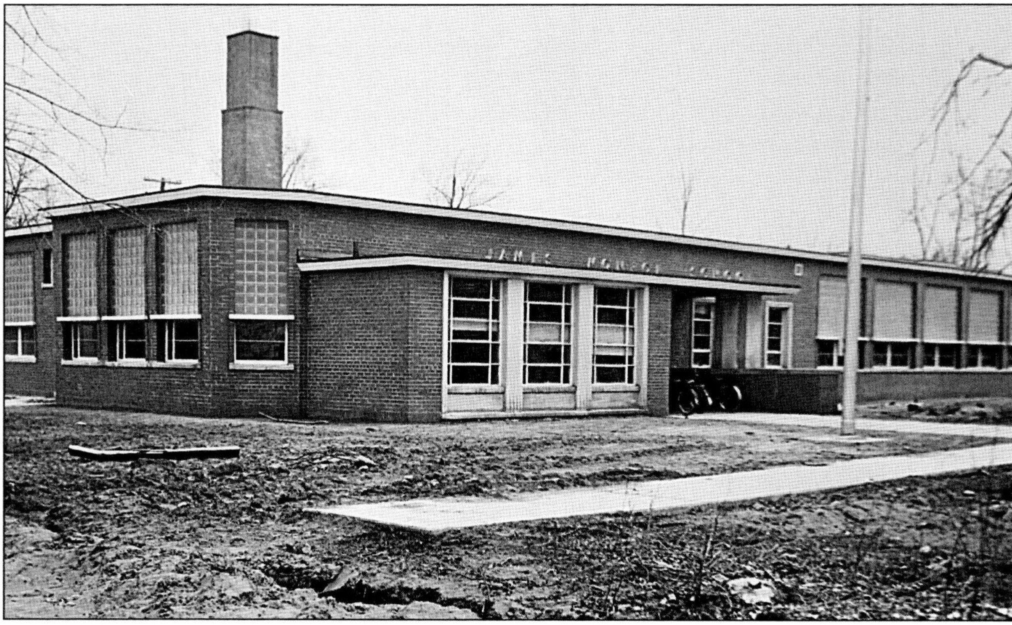

James Monroe Elementary School was used from 1950 to 1981, when declining enrollment saw Monroe and Roosevelt close and students divided between the three remaining buildings, with the sixth grade moved into the junior high school. Monroe served other uses, including home to the school board, and was eventually torn down. A park now exists on the west end of the property. (Courtesy of the *Daily Tribune*.)

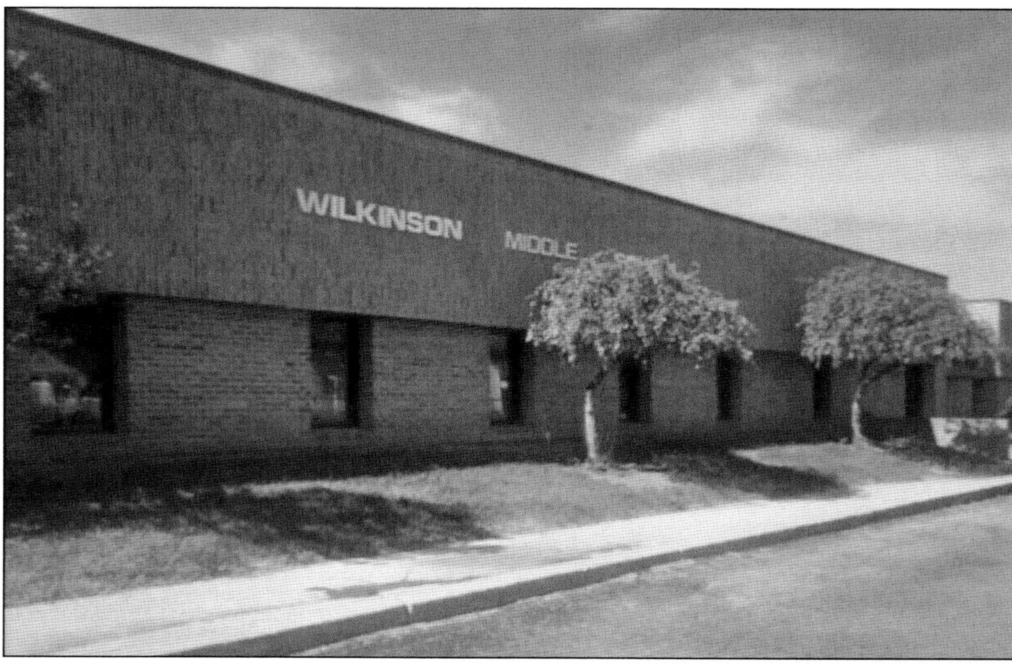

On the June 10, 1974, ballot, voters approved a proposal to replace the old junior high school. In 1975, the building was torn down, and the new Wilkinson Middle School was built; it was dedicated on April 24, 1977. The new $3 million modern education facility was built to house approximately 700 students. (Courtesy of Margene Scott.)

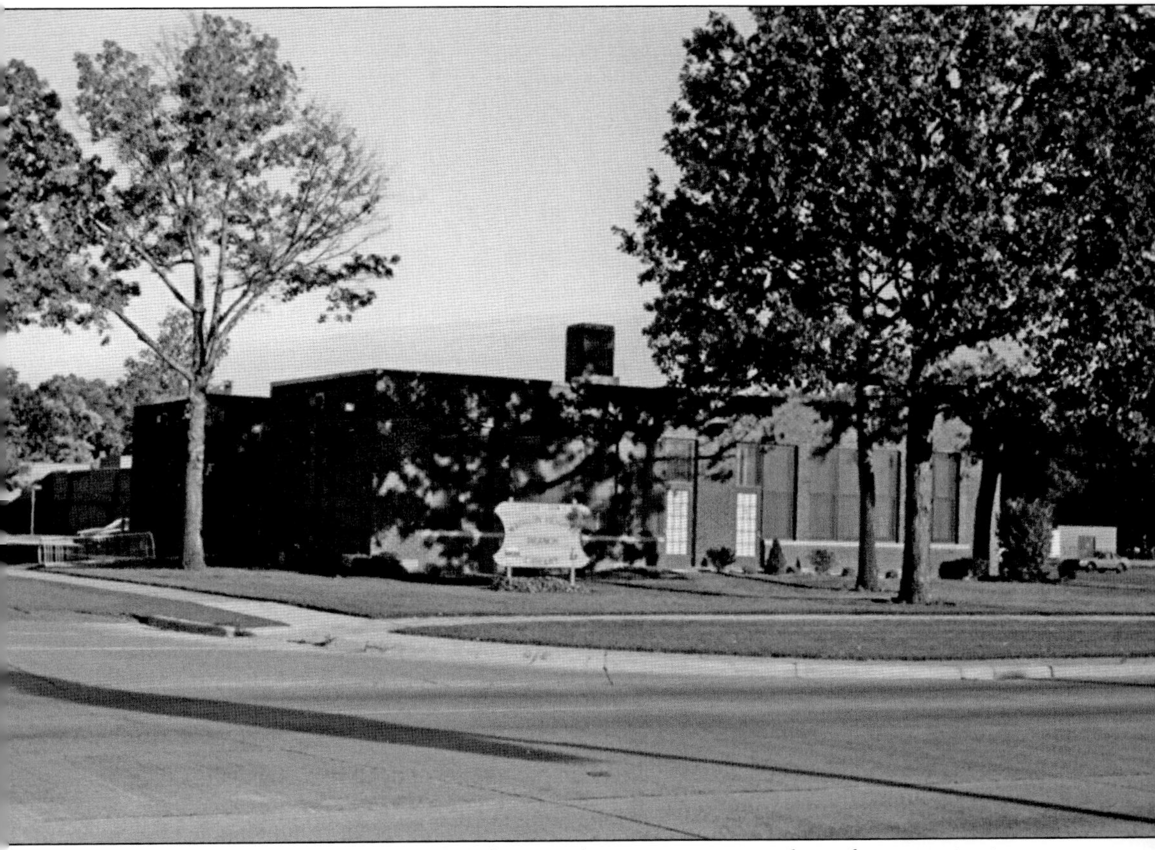

Royal Oak annexed a portion of Royal Oak Township, preventing students from continuing to attend Oakland Elementary School. The upper elementary grades were moved to the Annex, while lower elementary grades were absorbed into other schools. The Annex later became known as the Music Annex, as students from Wilkinson Junior High School would walk to the nearby building for band and choir practice. The west side, closest to John R Road, was used as the band room, and the vocal music room was located on the east side. The band director's office was sandwiched in the middle. These uses were among many the building served for Madison District Schools. (Courtesy of City of Madison Heights.)

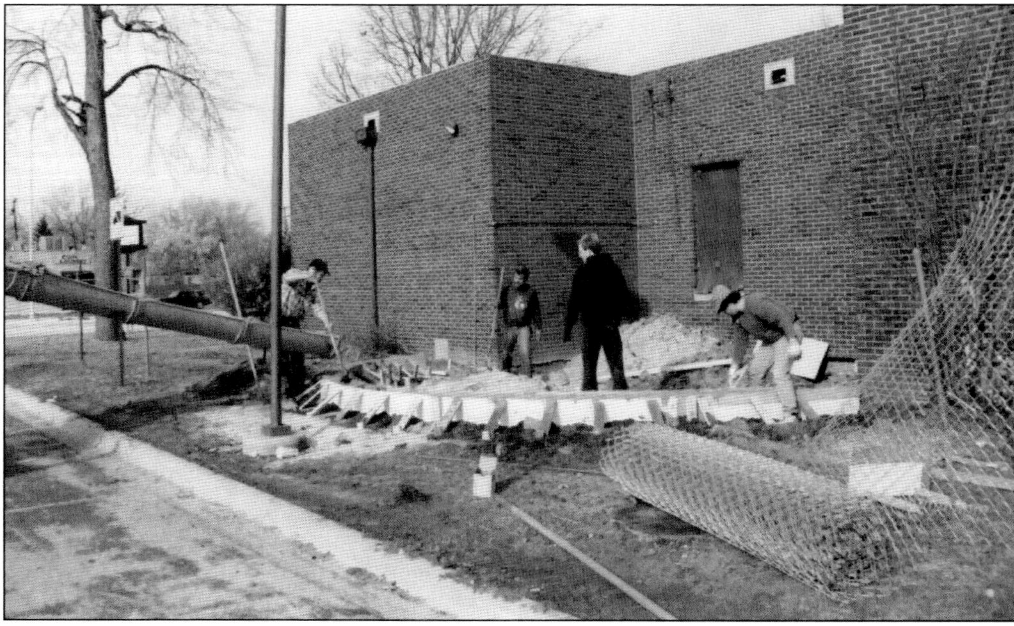

The 3,993-square-foot, four-room building was closed and used for storage with the relocation of Madison High School and the construction of Wilkinson Middle School on its site. It was purchased by the city and transformed into a branch library to reestablish library service in the south end. The branch was opened to the public in August 1992, but unfortunately, a difficult economy saw it close in 2004. (Courtesy of City of Madison Heights.)

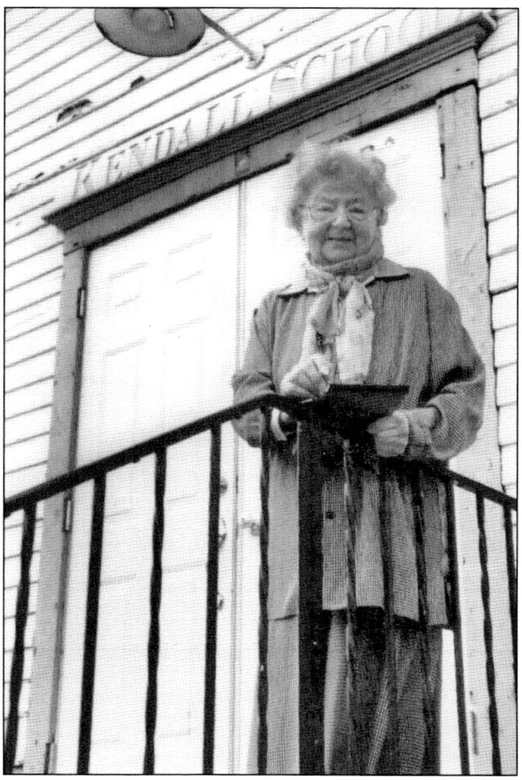

Helen Dzienis was born in 1911. Her legacy pervaded the educational field. After earning her teaching degree, she returned to the Madison Schools and was one of the primary grade instructors at Kendall School. She married and became Mrs. Hennessey, supported her family of four with her lifelong career, and even taught local history to her contemporaries as a senior. In 2000, she is shown at the old Kendall School having the classroom renamed in her honor. The Heritage Rooms museum still proudly displays her diploma, lesson books, and teaching memorabilia. (Photograph by Margene Scott.)

The Kendall Schoolhouse was used as a primary-level classroom, remaining there until 1944. This view is from the home of the Acciacca family, who lived at 950 East Lincoln Avenue. When it became the Kendall school property in 1926, there was no running water, and children used either the girl or boy outhouses behind the school. Because of their close proximity to the schoolhouse, students or the teacher would often fetch water in a bucket at the Acciacca home and carefully carry it back to Kendall. (Courtesy of Norma Acciacca Turkette.)

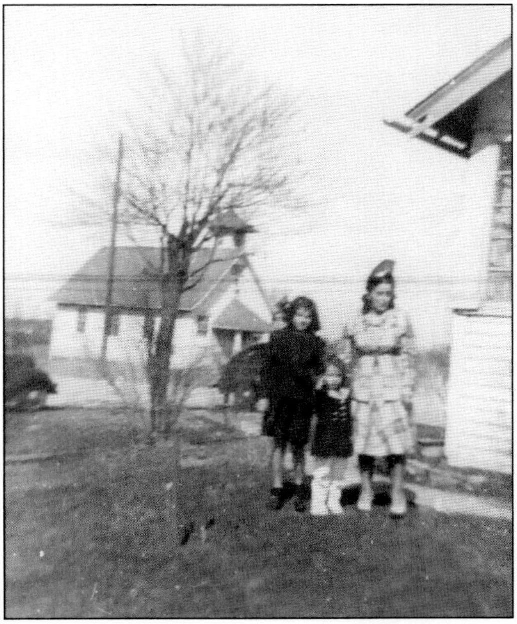

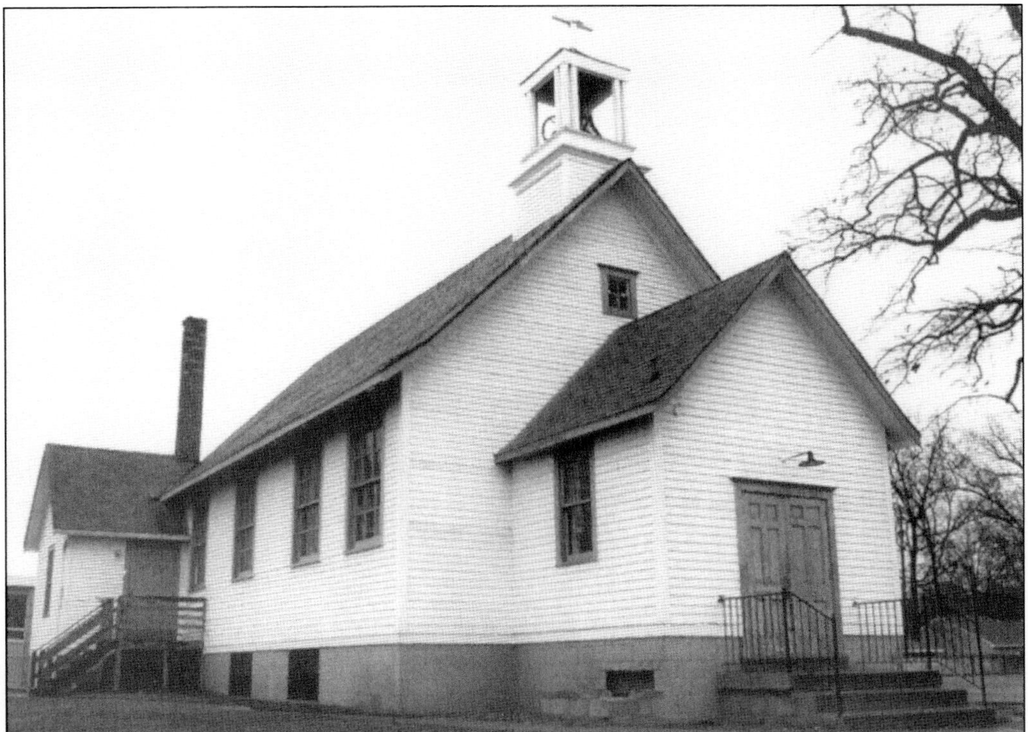

In 1913, the Madison School District was established separate from the Royal Oak District and named for Pres. James Madison. In 1944, the United Methodist Church bought the old Kendall School for a church and moved it to 11 Mile Road and Groveland Street. Many years later, an attempt was made to have Kendall School serve as a historical museum. The Kendall School Foundation was established in March 2000 for that purpose. Unfortunately, that effort was ultimately not successful, and the building was demolished. (Photograph by Margene Scott.)

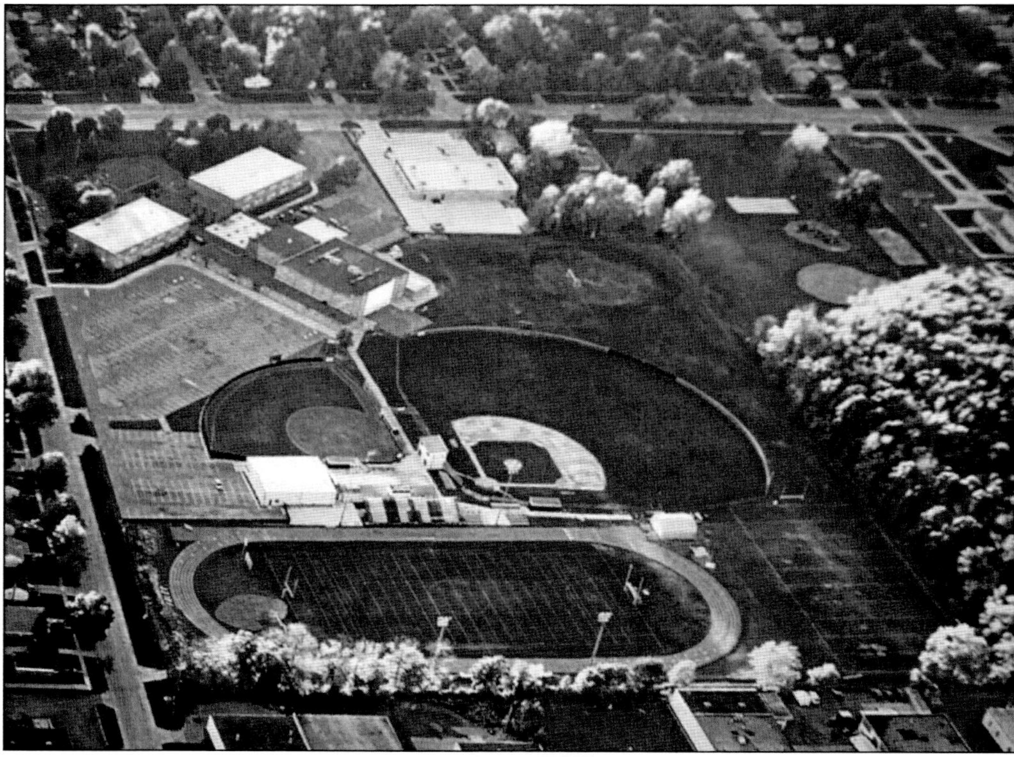

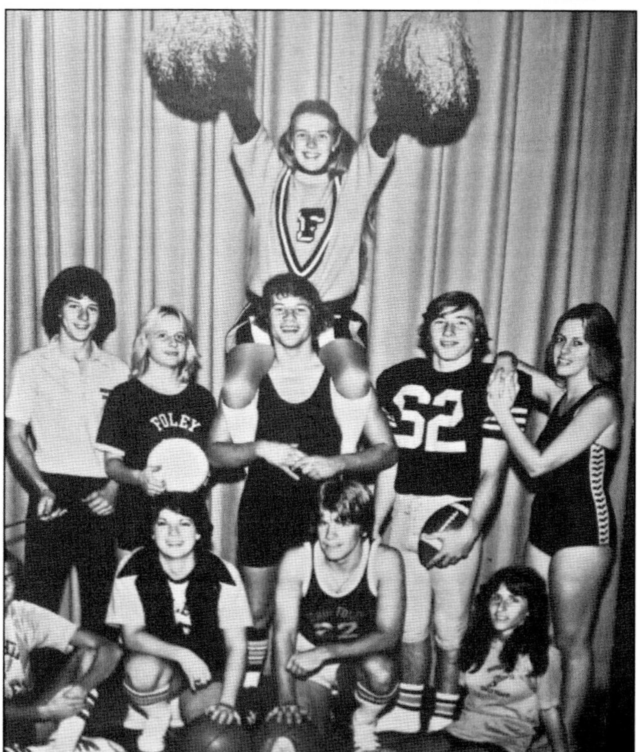

Bishop Foley is a parochial school attended by students from area parishes. The aerial view above shows the campus layout at the northeast corner of Whitcomb Avenue and Campbell Road between 13 and 14 Mile Roads. The main building is built in the shape of a cross, facing diagonally to the southwest. While it is a parochial school, there is still attention devoted to athletics, as evidenced by the athletic fields and the athletes pictured at left. (Both, courtesy of Bishop Foley School.)

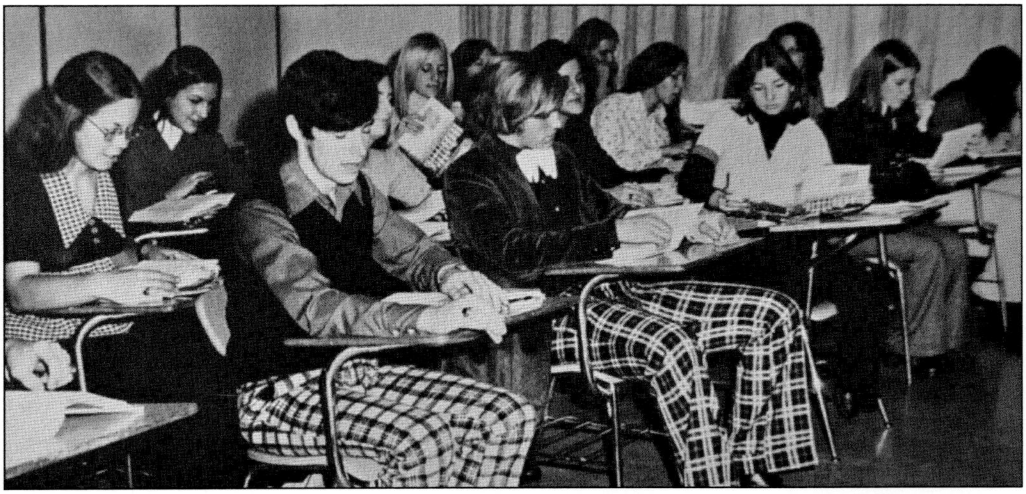

Bishop Foley High is a Catholic secondary school whose mission is to build a community of faith through a religious, academic, and social educative process. Located at 32000 Campbell Road, the building has not changed since its inception in September 1965. Bishop Foley no longer receives subsidy directly from its founding parishes but is entirely self-sustaining, with income based on tuition and fees. This 1974 classroom image features the plaid pants and bellbottoms that were fashionable at the time. (Courtesy of Bishop Foley School.)

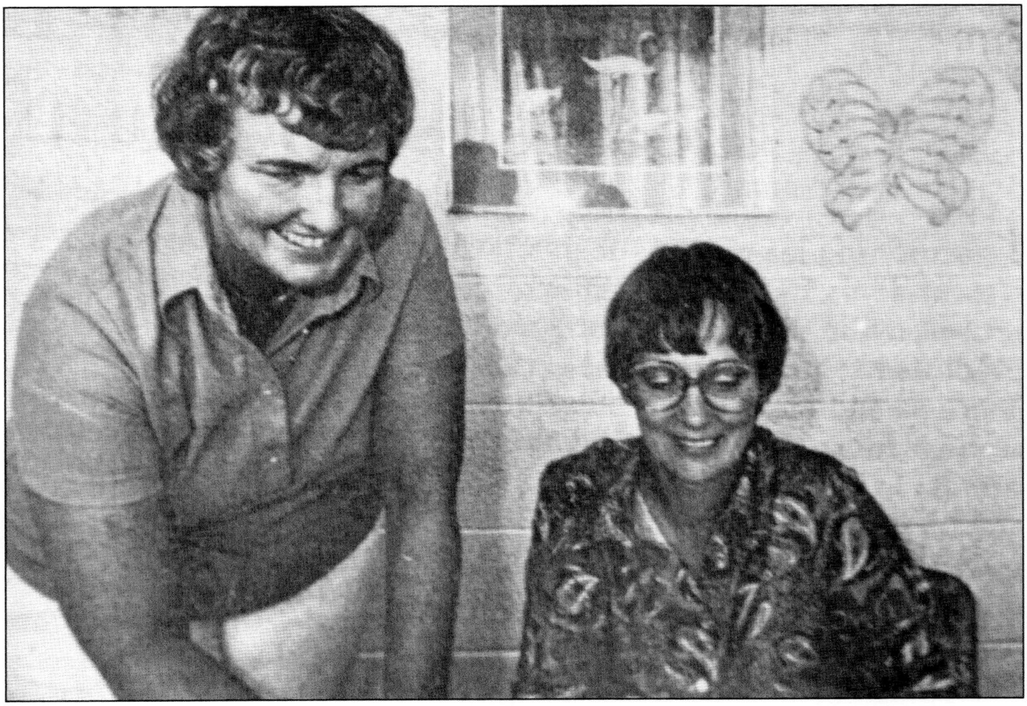

Office manager Marcia Smith (left) and Community Education Director Norma Ross are pleased at the number of registrations for an upcoming term. Madison Heights Community Education offered classes for careers and fun during its tenure in the city. The concept of community education was created to fill the needs of the business community and provide needed training for applicants. Community education also addressed the need for education of women, who were never expected to forge careers, and the need for two-paycheck families. (Photograph by Margene Scott.)

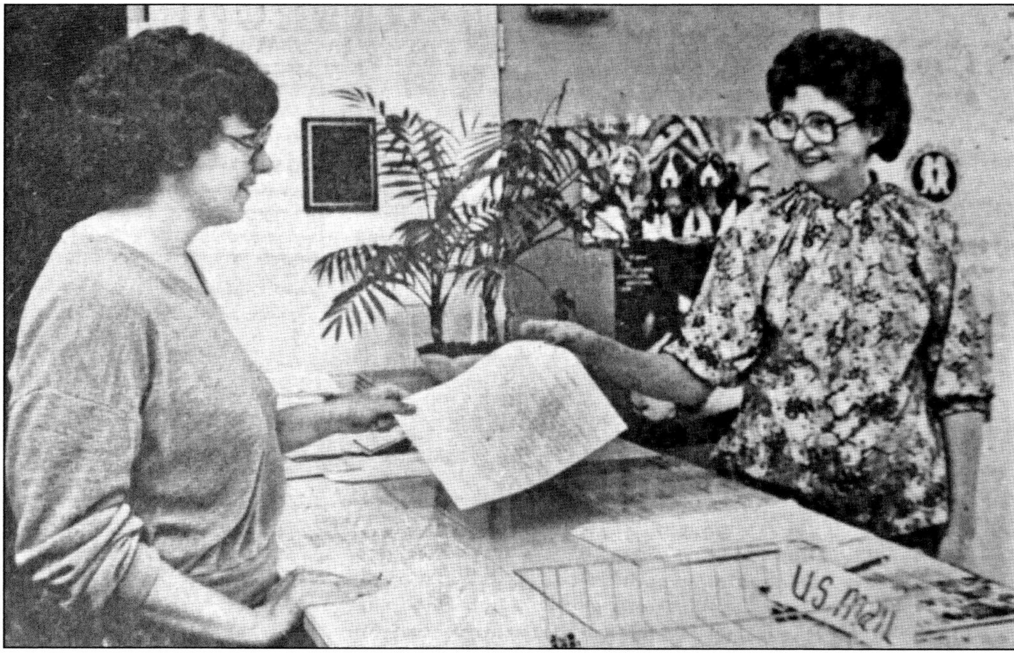

Pat Colombo (age 20, left) is one of 38 graduates from the 1979 Madison Heights Community Education program. The late Vera Morrison, community education office manager, helps her with a scholarship application. Vera Morrison's son is the current Madison School Board president Al Morrison. (Photograph by Margene Scott.)

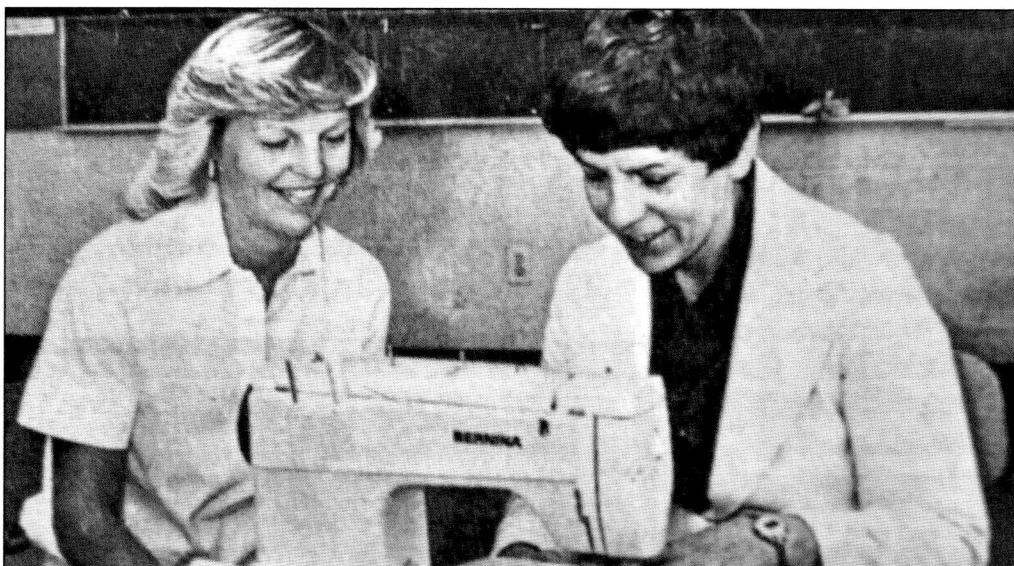

Jane Thomas (right), sewing teacher, demonstrates how to make a blazer for student Judy Grove's fall wardrobe. The community education program served residents of both Madison and Lamphere Districts. Initially, each district sponsored individual programs, but in a move designed to cut costs and consolidate educational opportunities in the city, Sixma Elementary School was used for a combined adult education program beginning with the 1977–1978 school year. (Photograph by Margene Scott.)

Seven

Community Life

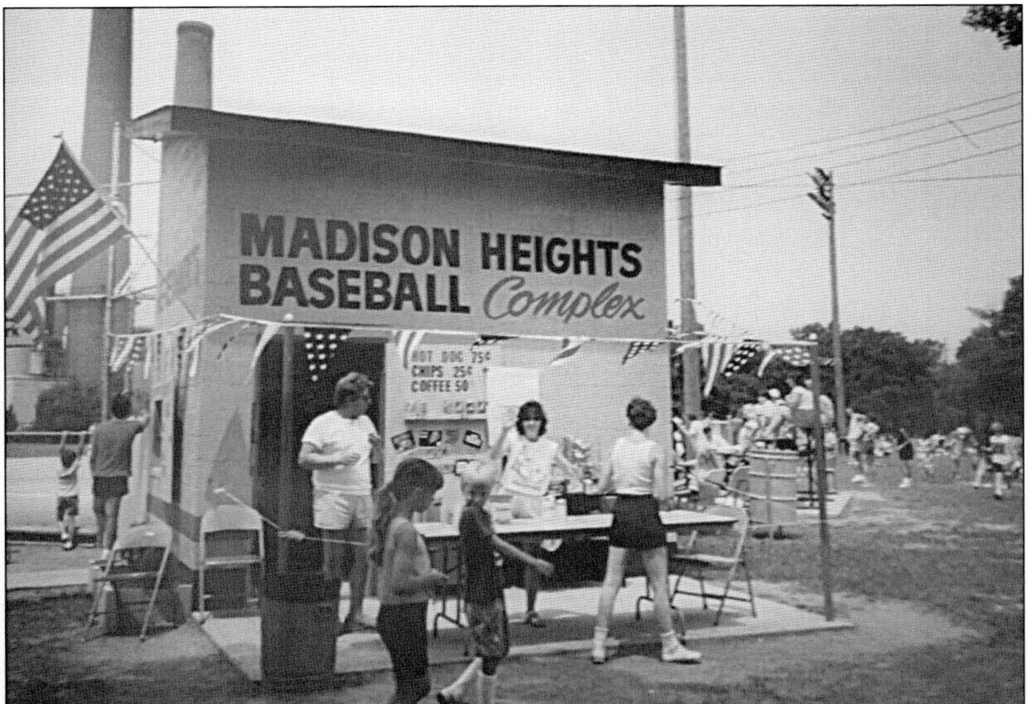

Madison Heights Little Baseball Inc. has existed since 1961 and celebrated its 50th anniversary in the city in 2011. Originally, its popular concession stand/office was a tiny cinder-block building. Twenty-two board members and four committee heads now serve the self-funding organization on a volunteer basis. The organization maintains five fields at the John Page Middle School Complex and two at the Rosie's Park complex, and operates the concession stands at both parks. Serving customers at the first food booth are (behind the table at left) league president Earl Stone and his wife, Polly. (Courtesy of Madison Heights Little Baseball.)

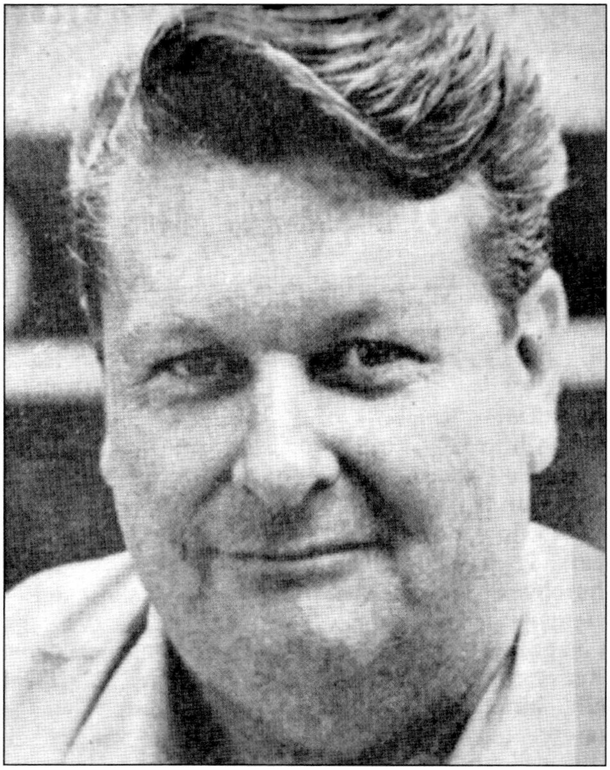

Bob Belling's dedication to Madison Heights Little Baseball and to the boys of the city is an outstanding example of parent involvement. He served both as president and as a board member for the organization, starting his volunteer work in 1969 as a coach before becoming president of the league for a year in 1973. In 1974, he met the need for programs for older boys, and in 1979, he responded to a request for an 18-and-over league. (Courtesy of Madison Heights Little Baseball.)

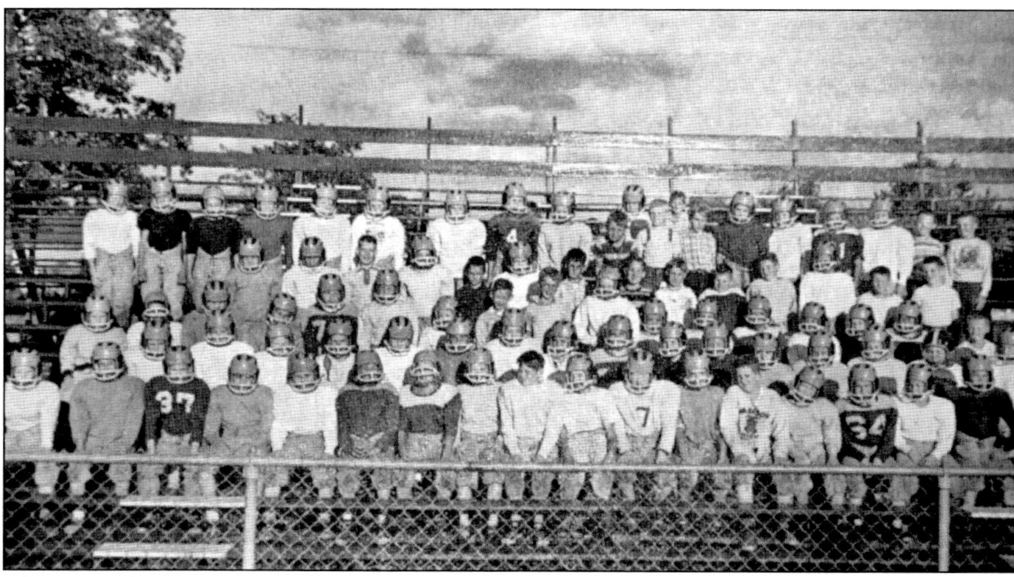

The original purpose of Madison Heights Little Football was to give community boys nine through 12 years old an opportunity to enjoy playing football with proper instruction and supervision on good fields with proper equipment. From its 1957 beginnings, the program grew to include three age divisions for three different teams. An earlier division of flag was added for the younger children and grew enormously when girls' cheerleader programs were added in the same age divisions. (Courtesy of Madison Heights Little Football.)

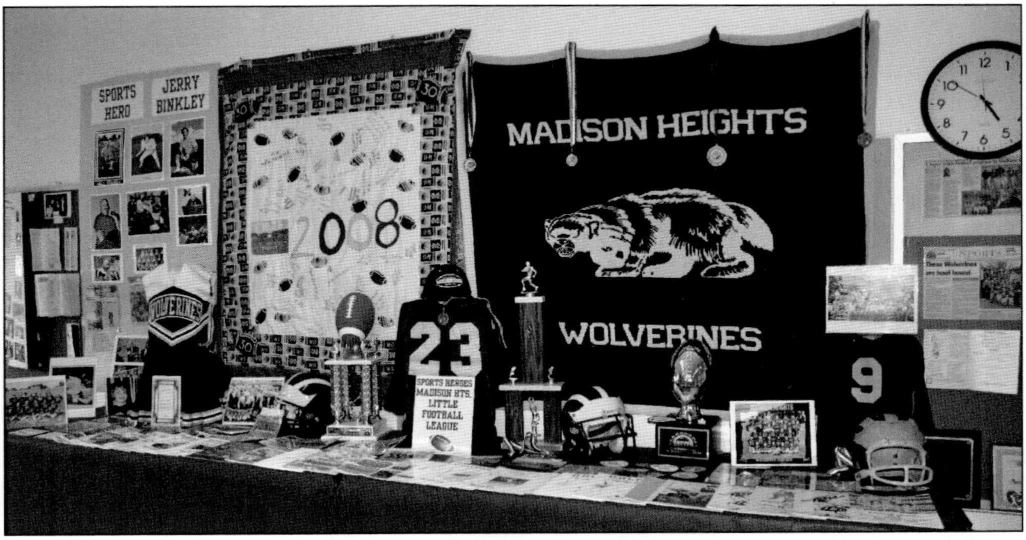

Over 50 years of Wolverine memorabilia and awards are displayed at the Sports Heroes exhibit in the Heritage Rooms museum. Teams compete with many surrounding cities, and their hard work has earned them many awards, including several Super Bowl trophies and division championships. The importance of family is stressed, and activities include an annual awards banquet and several outings. (Photograph by Margene Scott.)

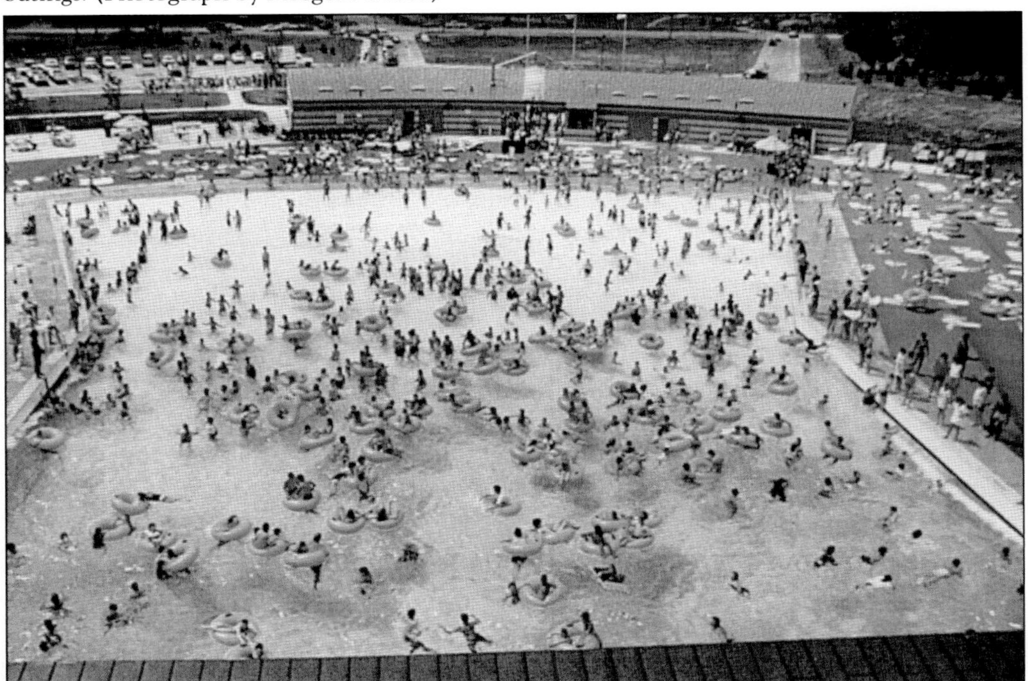

The Oakland County Red Oaks Water Park is seen from above in June 1987, near the time of the June 12, 1987, grand opening. The county originally used all yellow inner tubes, which always looked like Cheerios floating in the pool. For safety reasons, the park eventually changed to all clear tubes to enable lifeguards to see everyone in the pool all the way to the bottom. The new features, dubbed "Splashtown," opened on June 12, 2002. Red Oaks Water Park has won many accolades over the years. (Photograph by Margene Scott.)

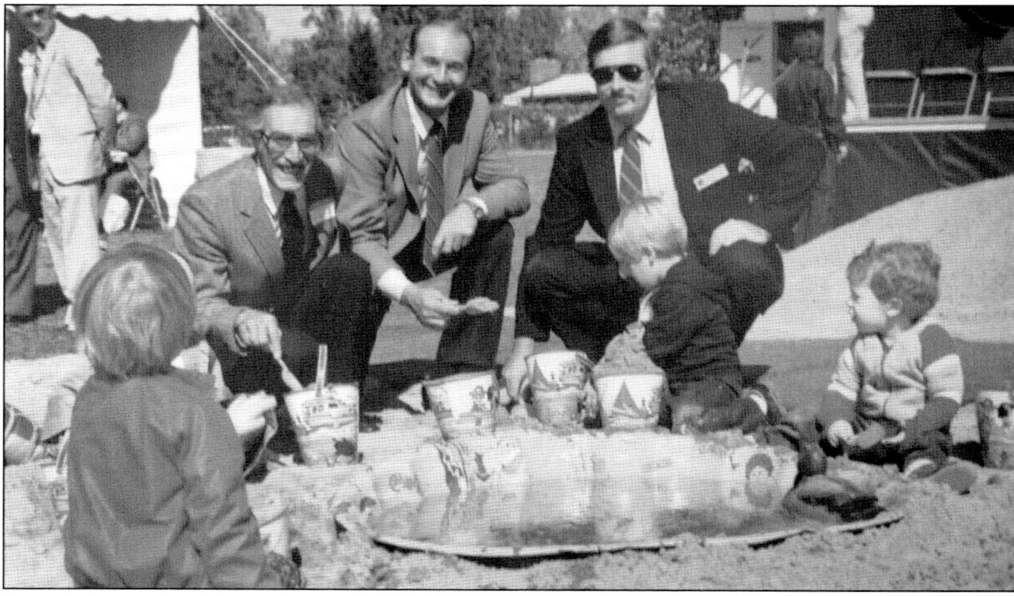

From left to right, Mayor George Suarez, Councilman Richard Van Sice, and Councilman Gary McGillivray break ground for the Oakland County Red Oaks Water Park on October 2, 1985. A smaller version of the actual ground-breaking, this picture is a photo opportunity with children present to commemorate the beginning of construction. (Photograph by Margene Scott.)

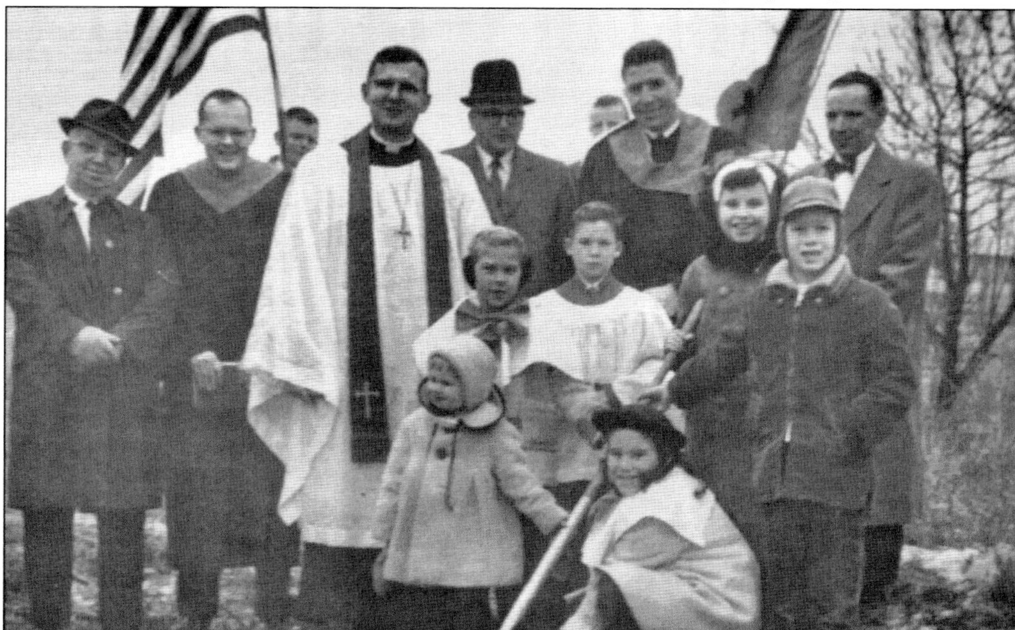

Ground was broken in January 1964 for the construction of a new Prince of Glory Lutheran Church on 14 Mile Road between Campbell and Stephenson. Participating in the service were, from left to right, (first row) Stephen Campbell, Jeff Bennethum, Diane Paquette, Larry Vergeldt, Nadine Thor, and Toni Giacobelli; (second row) John Bagley, Dexter Thor Jr., the Rev. Alan J. Kiefer (pastor), the Rev. Robert L. Robinson (assistant to the president of the Michigan Synod–Lutheran Church of America), Ed Vergeldt, and Joe Campbell. (Courtesy of the *Daily Tribune*.)

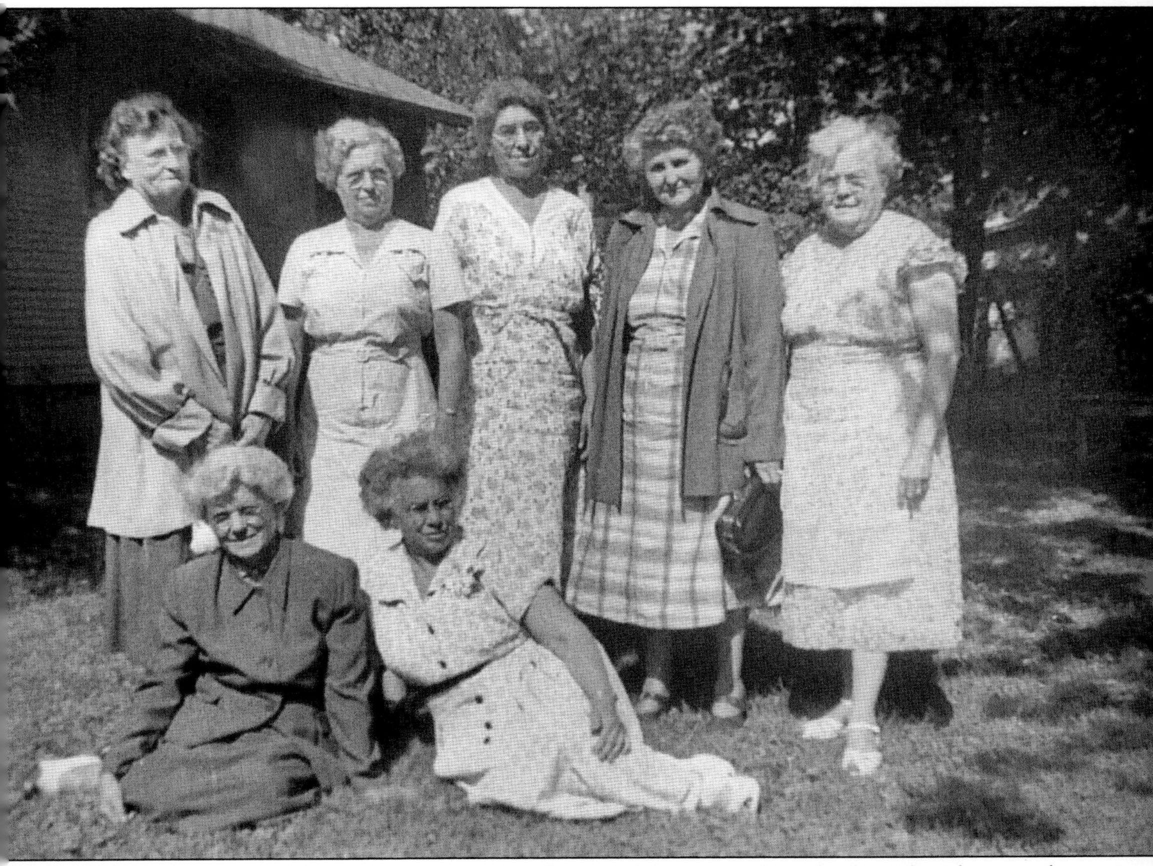

This image features the First Women of the Madison Heights United Methodist Church around the mid-1940s. In 1944, the United Methodist Church bought the old Kendall School for a church and, in April of that year, moved it to 11 Mile Road and Groveland Street. These original women of the church included, in unknown order, Jessie Thomson, Martha Rinet, Norma Fulkerson, Mrs. Patch, Mrs. Walker, Mrs. Dingwell, and Mrs. Albiston. (Courtesy of Madison Heights United Methodist Church.)

... Churches of this area welcome you. This directory will help you find a church of your religious background. If you should not find your particular faith, you and your family would be welcome at any of these churches.

On behalf of our common Lord, Jesus Christ, the Madison Heights area churches invite and welcome you into their fellowship. The pastors would welcome the opportunity to minister to the spiritual needs of your family.

BAPTIST

COMMUNITY BAPTIST
1042 E. 12 Mile
Sunday School 10 a.m.
Worship: 11 a.m. & 7 p.m.
Phone: LI 7-5890
Lewis H. Votaw Jr. -Pastor

FAITH MISSIONARY BAPTIST
27314 Barrington
Sunday School 10 a.m.
Worship: 11 a.m. & 7:30 p.m.
Phone: 548-3656
Roy Humble - Pastor

FELLOWSHIP GENERAL BAPTIST
652 E. Kenneth
Church School 9:45 a.m.
Worship: 11 a.m. & 7 p.m.
Phone: PR 1-2446
Wiley Adams - Pastor

FREE-WILL BAPTIST
302 E. 13 Mile
Church School 10 a.m.
Worship: 11 a.m. & 7:30 p.m.
Charles Dickinson -Pastor

FIRST BAPTIST
26689 Northeastern
Sunday School 10 a.m.
Worship: 11 a.m. & 7 p.m.
Phone: LI 1-3980
Martin R. Craft - Pastor

FIRST GENERAL BAPTIST
950 W. Gardenia
Church School 9:45 a.m.
Worship: 11 a.m & 7:30 p.m.
Phone: LI 2-6830
Letcher S. Bush - Pastor

MADISON HEIGHTS BAPTIST
Affiliated with S.B.C.
215 W. Eleven Mile Rd.
Sunday School 9:45 a.m.
Worship: 11 a.m. & 7:30 p.m.
Phone: LI 3-8171 or 541-0622
Douglas H. Sowards - Pastor

NORTH BIBLE BAPTIST
31329 John R.
Church School 9:45 a.m.
Worship: 11 a.m. & 7:30 p.m.
Phone: 588-6240 or 544-7222
James Passman - Pastor

TEN MILE FREE-WILL BAPTIST
74 W. Ten Mile
Sunday School 9:45 a.m.
Worship: 11 a.m. & 7:30 p.m.
Phone: LI 1-2200 or LI 7-2543
James T. Holman - Pastor

CHURCH OF CHRIST

26375 John R.
Bible Study 10 a.m.
Worship: 11 a.m. & 6 p.m.
Phone: LI 5-3190

Meeting in Lessenger Sch.
Girard and Campbell Rd.
Services 10 & 11 a.m. & 6 p.m.
Phone: LI 3-5173
Lanzo Pribble - Pastor

EPISCOPAL

ST. MARGARET'S
24120 Stephenson Hwy. H.P.
Sunday School 9:15 a.m.
Worship: 8; 9:15; & 11 a.m.
Phone: LI 3-6705 or LI 8-0097
Russel McKinsley - Vicar

ST. PATRICK'S
Meeting in Lamphere Hi. Cafe.
29615 Tawas
S.S. 10 a.m. Worship: 10 a.m.
Phone: LI 7-9589
Joe Yokota - Lay-Reader

LUTHERAN

HOLY CROSS (Missouri)
12-1/2 Mile & Rayan, Warren
Sunday School 9:30 a.m.
Worship: 10:45 a.m.
Phone: SL 7-5138
Marvin Bergman - Pastor

HOLY REDEEMER (American)
29860 Dequindre, Warren
Sunday School 9:15 a.m.
Worship: 10:30 a.m.
Phone: 754-9550 or LI 7-2755
Norbert T. Schroeder - Pastor

OUR SAVIOR'S (Missouri)
505 S. Stephenson Hwy.
Church School & Worship
9 a.m. & 10:30 a.m.
Phone: LI 5-3230 or LI 9-4141
George W. Rehkopf - Pastor

PRINCE OF GLORY (Michigan)
Meeting in Mark Twain School
Campbell near 14 Mile Road R.O.
S.S. 9:30 a.m. Worship: 11 a.m.
Parish House & Office-1325 W. 14M
Phone: 588-4652 or 588-6761
Alan J. Kieffer - Pastor

METHODIST

MADISON METHODIST
226 E. 11 Mile
Church School & Worship
9 a.m. & 11:30 a.m.
Phone: LI 4-3544 or LI 5-6882
Earl W. Downing Pastor

PRESBYTERIAN

CHRIST MEMORIAL
1318 S. Stephenson Hwy. R.O.
Jr. S.S. & Worship: 9 & 11:15 a.m.
Jr. Hi. & Sr. Hi. S.S. 10 a.m.
Phone: LI 1-1596 or LI 5-1216
Dr. Wayne L. McCoy - Pastor

REFORMED CHURCH IN AMERICA

REDEEMER REFORMED
3119 N. Campbell S. of 13 Mile R.O.
Sunday School 11:30 a.m.
Worship: 10 a.m. & 7 p.m.
Phone: 588-5488 or LI 4-5170
Roger P. Hendricks - Pastor

CHURCH OF THE BRETHREN

BETHANY
1529 E. 12 Mile
S.S. 11 a.m. Worship: 10 a.m.
Phone: LI 1-8128 or LI 8 9390
William Kidwell -Pastor

ASSEMBLY OF GOD

WAYSIDE
30728 John R.
Sunday School 9:45 a.m.
Worship: 11 a.m. & 7:30 p.m.
Phone: SL 4-2327
Edward H. Tarno -Pastor

CHRISTIAN AND MISSIONARY ALLIANCE CHURCH

315 S. Stephenson Hwy.

The multicultural diversity of Madison Heights is also reflected in the variety of denominations that have called the city home over its history. More recently, the Church at Madison Heights has been established, a coalition of churches committed to working together to share the joy, hope, and grace of Jesus Christ. The coalition is made up of a diverse collection of different denominations with unique personalities, beliefs, and goals, united for the purpose of serving the local community and sharing faith. (Courtesy of Madison Heights Public Library.)

The Easter Bunny, played by Darlene Berent, makes her annual visit to the Madison Heights Senior Center around 1980. The bunny was sponsored by the Madison Heights Junior Women's Club, predecessor of the General Federation of Women's Clubs Madison Heights Intermediate Women's Club. (Photograph by Margene Scott.)

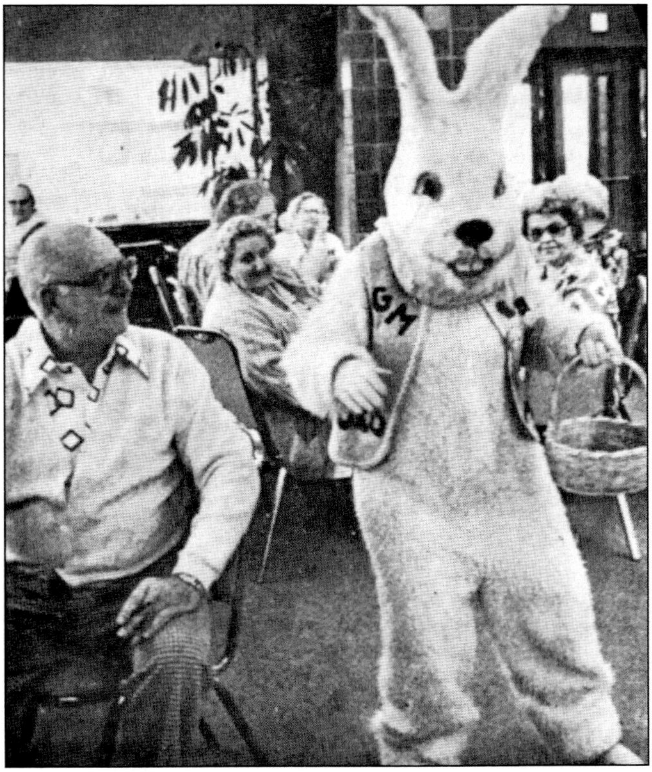

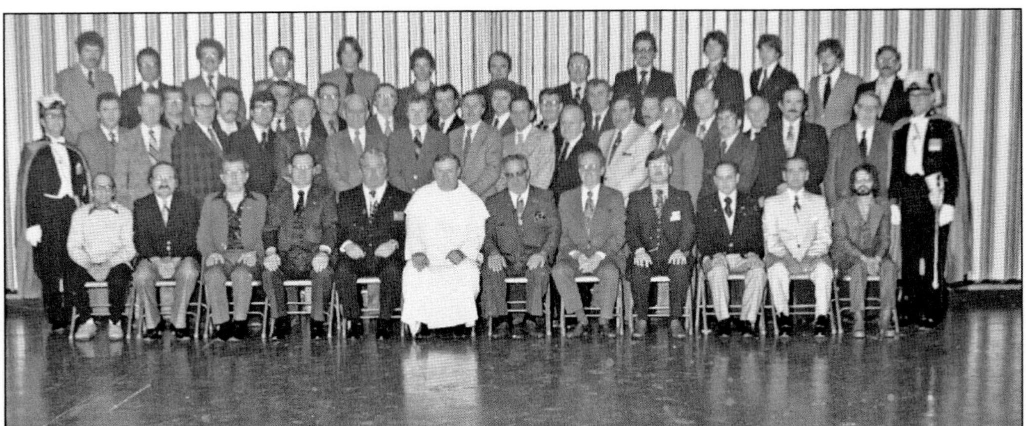

Founded in 1882, the Knights of Columbus has grown to over 1.8 million members nationally. The Father Heary Council No. 7239 was chartered in 1979 with 52 members. Primary council efforts are for the developmentally disabled, youth, and those in need in the community. (Courtesy of Knights of Columbus and Tony Bliss.)

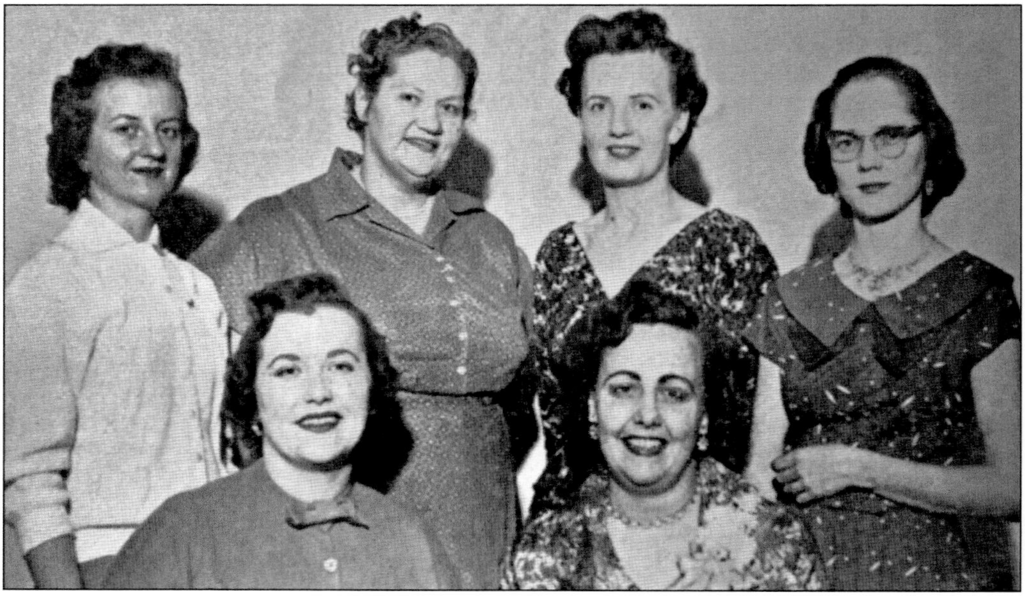

This 1959 image of the Metropolitan Club Ladies Auxiliary features, from left to right, (seated) Jean Linville and Jerry Johnston; (standing) Joyce Osantowski, Lois Meyers, Mary Cunningham, and Mary Merkel. Merkel is a member of the Madison Heights Historical Commission and a font of information about the city. Jean Linville has given almost a lifetime of service to Madison Heights, from serving as the Gold Star Mother in the City's Memorial Day Parade to playing Mrs. Claus as part of the city tree lighting. (Courtesy of Madison Heights Metropolitan Club No. 69.)

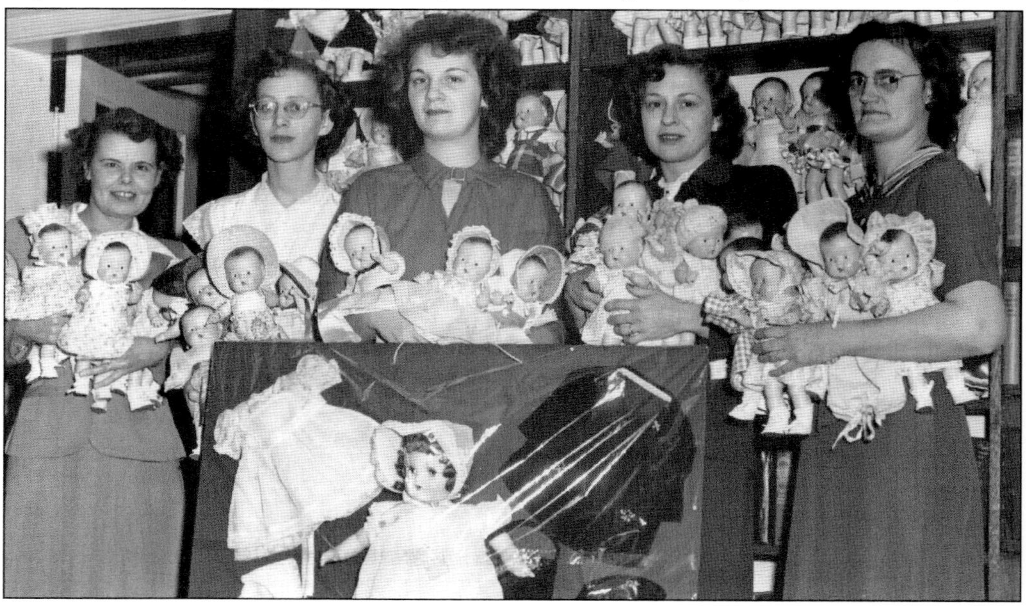

The Metropolitan Club Ladies Auxiliary always bought and dressed dolls for the Goodfellows, among the many ways they assisted. This Christmas 1950 image shows some of the ladies with dolls; from left to right are Ellen Bradford, grand lady and township clerk for many years; Arlene Sloan, the fire chief's wife; Delores Podobnikar, the fire lieutenant's wife; Marge Travnikar, Bernie Travnikar's wife; and Dorothy Griffith. (Courtesy of Cheryl Charpentier Hankins and John Charpentier.)

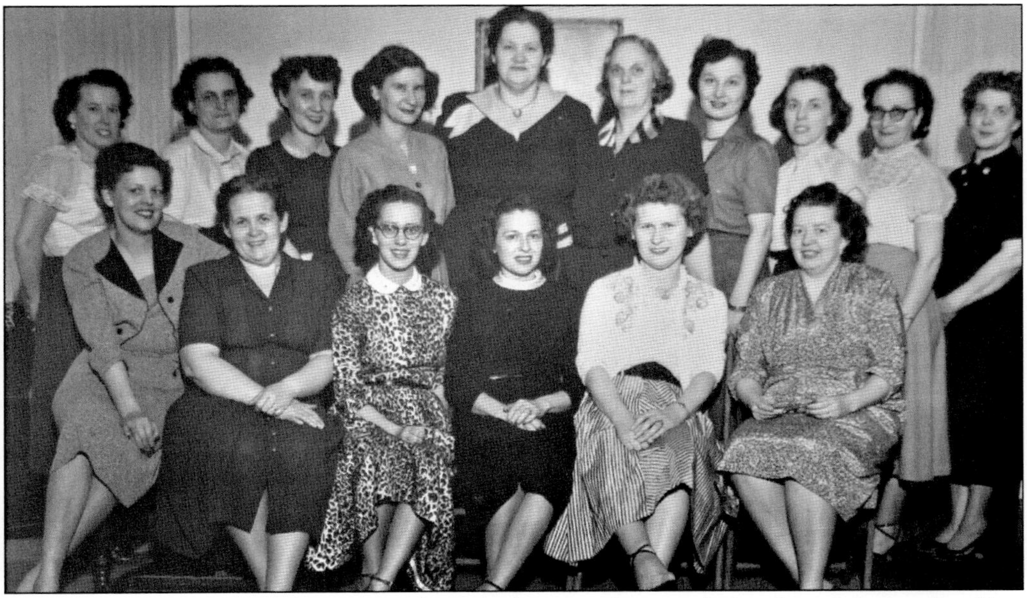

This 1950s group shot of the Metropolitan Ladies Auxiliary includes, from left to right, (first row) unidentified, Virginia Solberg, Arlene Sloan, Margaret Travnikar, Bernice Travnikar, and Peg Richardson; (second row) unidentified, Dorothy Griffith, unidentified, Emma Hartwell, Lois Myers, Mrs. Christianson, Angelina Bucciarelli Joyce, Helen Osantowski, Reva Kendall, and Mildred Neville. Lela Campbell and Lucille Brand are also in the photograph but are not identified. (Courtesy of Cheryl Charpentier Hankins and John Charpentier.)

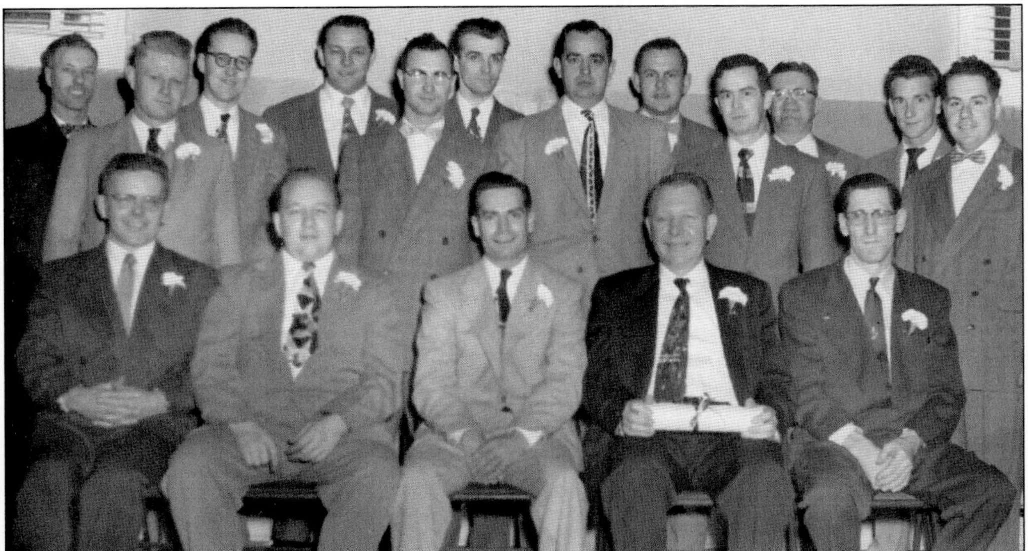

The Madison Heights Metropolitan Club annually gave financial aid to many worthwhile community projects. This 1950s group picture of the Metropolitan Club men includes, from left to right, (first row) two unidentified, fire chief Joseph Sloan, William Myers, and Wilbur Griffin; (second row) Don Osantowski, Albert Hartwell, Lt. Fred Johnson, unidentified, Neil Osantowski, Ralph Merkel, police chief Ralph Richardson, two unidentified, Chester Campbell, unidentified, and John Charpentier. Edward Miller, John Eddy, and Ray Todd are also in the photograph but are not identified. (Courtesy of Cheryl Charpentier Hankins and John Charpentier.)

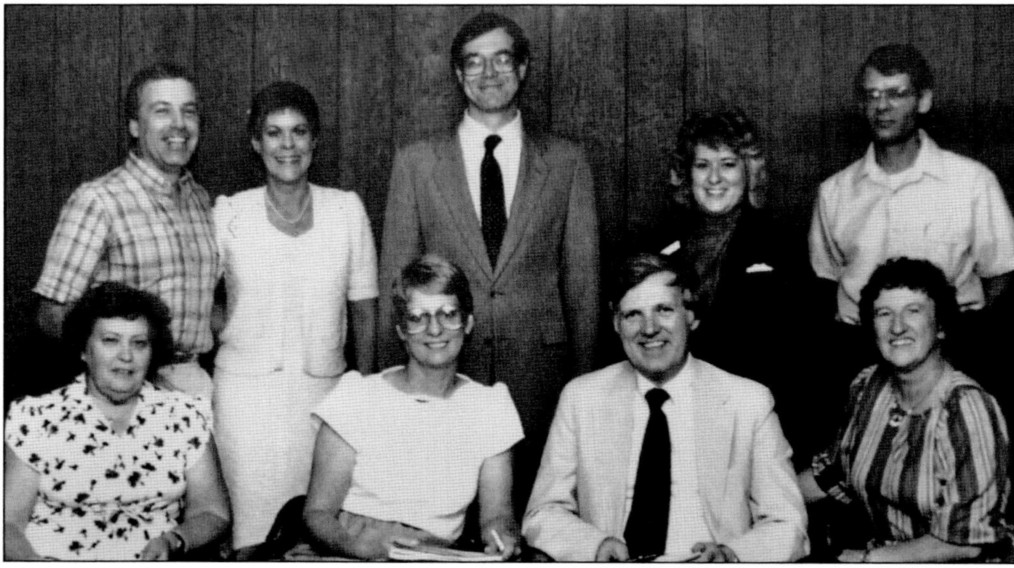

The Madison Heights Community Round Table was formed in 1984 and incorporated in 1986. John Schaible Jr. was the first chairman from 1984 to 1985, followed by Norma Ross from 1985 to 1986. Board members and others pictured include, from left to right (first row) Nell Pendergrass, Noma Ross, A. Michael Deller, and Darlene Berent; (second row) county commissioner James Doyon, Kay Brady, John Schaible Jr., Margene Johnston, and Dan Jones. This board and the one that followed began the annual awards banquet as a community event. Prior to that time, the selection of an annual award was made just within this group. (Courtesy of Madison Heights Community Round Table.)

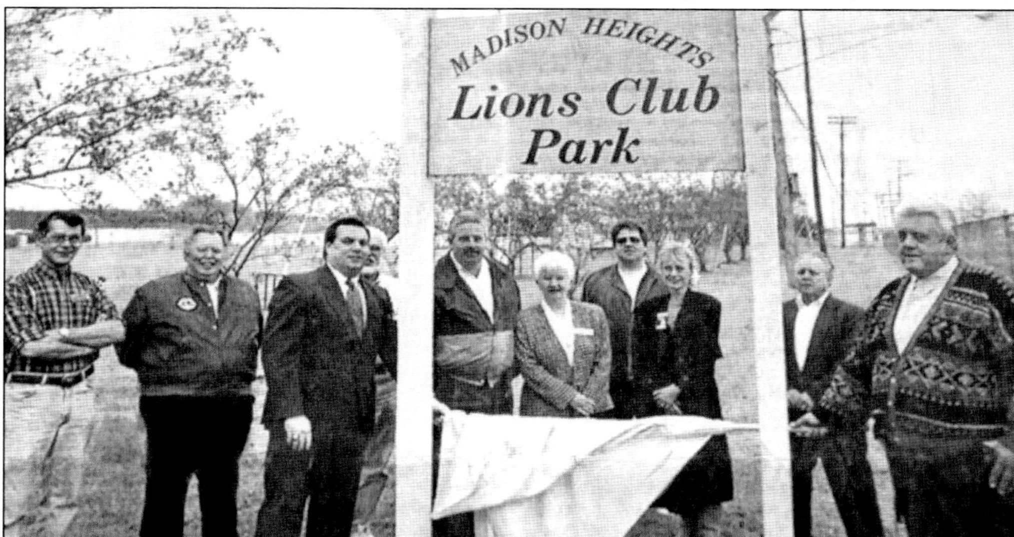

Twelve Sherry Park was officially renamed Lions Club Park with the 1998 unveiling of a carved wooden sign. Service clubs were approached about adopting city parks to upgrade and maintain them in times of tight budgets. The Lions Club aids sight-impaired individuals by means of glasses or assistance in the Leader Dog program. Pictured just after the unveiling are, from left to right, Dan Jones, Maynard Heck, Dennis Swanson, Councilman Gary McGillivray, Councilwoman Elva Mills, Ed Jacobs, Councilwoman Mary Stema, Ray Meischeid, and Don Nagel. (Courtesy of the *Daily Tribune*.)

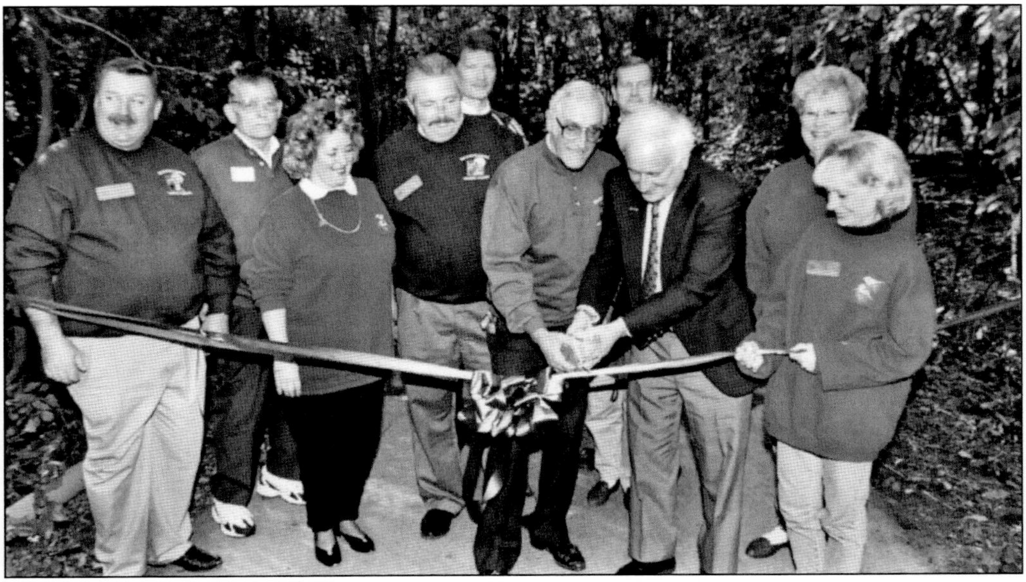

The Madison Heights Nature Center at George W. Suarez Woods opened with a ribbon-cutting on October 5, 1996. The nature center was designated as part of the city's five-year parks and recreation plan. Mayor George W. Suarez cuts the ribbon with US Rep. Sander Levin, while from left to right, Councilman Doug MacLean, Councilman Russell Pearce, Councilwoman Margene Scott, Councilman Gary McGillivray, city manager Jon R. Austin, deputy city manager Pete Connors, Mayor pro tem Marilyn Russell, and Councilwoman Mary Stema look on. (Courtesy of City of Madison Heights.)

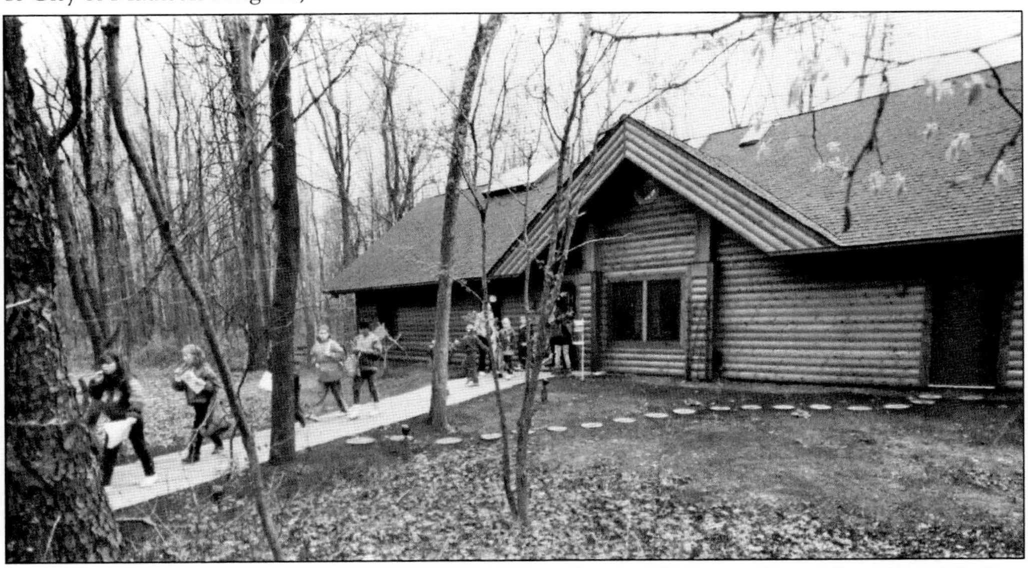

Visitors leave the Madison Heights Nature Center at George W. Suarez Friendship Woods before the addition of a pond and waterfall in the spring of 2002. The water features were built next to the east entrance. Unfortunately, the nature center was not immune to the challenges faced by the city in light of Michigan's recession. However, access to this treasure has been maintained, with the county now running the renamed Red Oaks Nature Center as part of the Red Oaks County Park, which also includes a water park, golf course, dog park, and soccer complex. (Photograph by Margene Scott.)

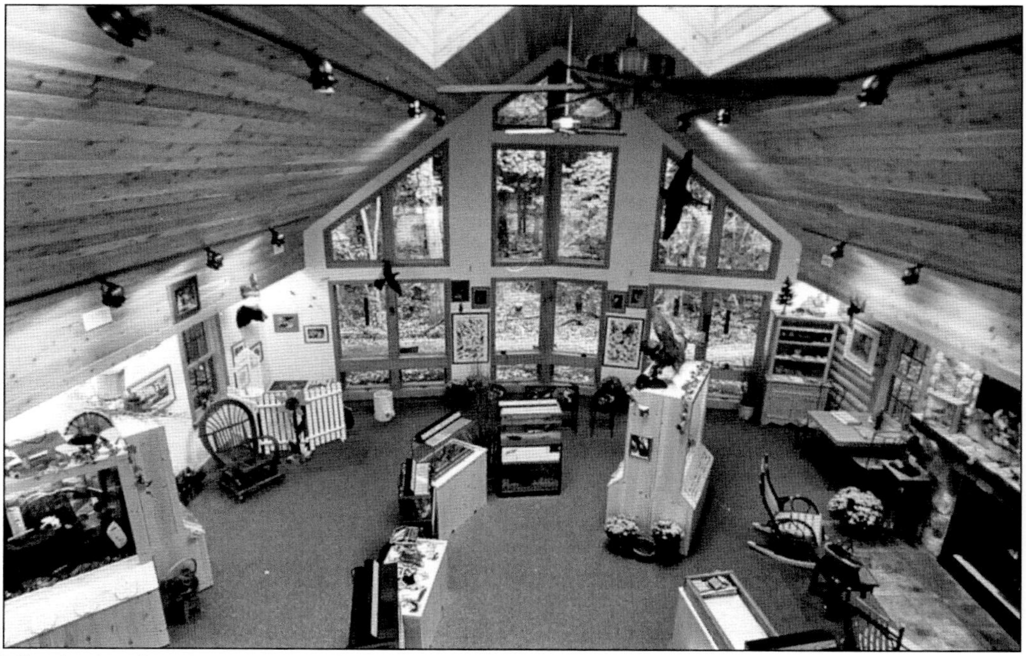

The facility has 2,400 square feet of public space, including the gift shop, exhibit room, and auditorium. Displays within the center change seasonally. Live reptiles and amphibians are featured year-round, with numerous tree species, spring woodland flowers, and nesting and migrating birds. The property is accessed by over 1.5 miles of paved trails. (Photograph by Margene Scott.)

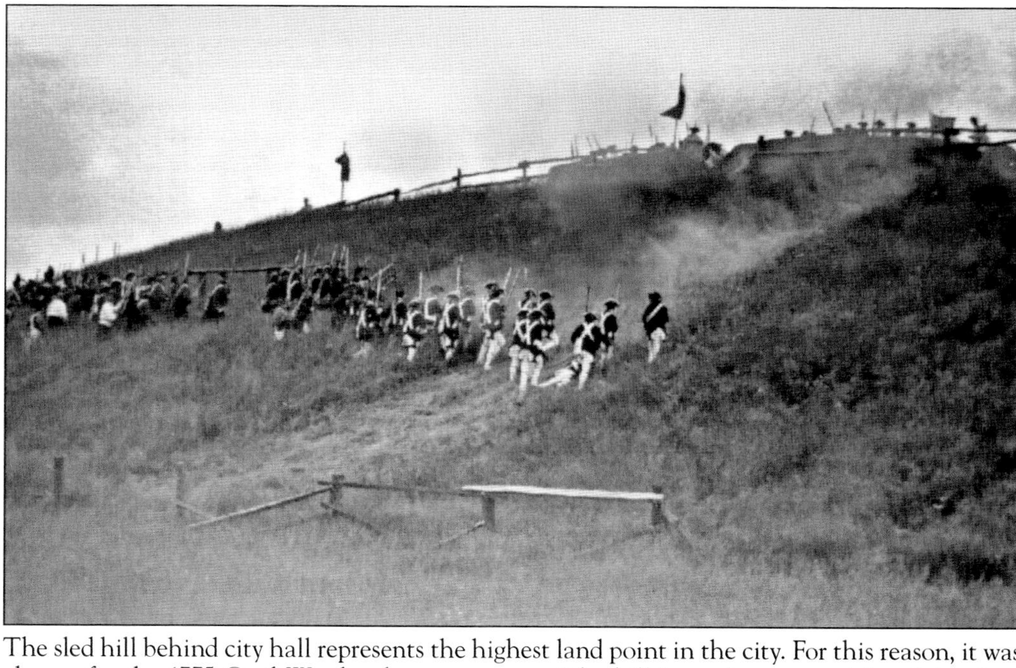

The sled hill behind city hall represents the highest land point in the city. For this reason, it was chosen for the 1775 Civil War battle reenactment. The hill is used year-round for all kinds of sports and exercise. The name originates from the fact that it's an extremely popular destination for this activity following a significant snowfall. The hill is also used routinely by walkers and joggers on the path through Civic Center Park. (Photograph by Doug MacLean.)

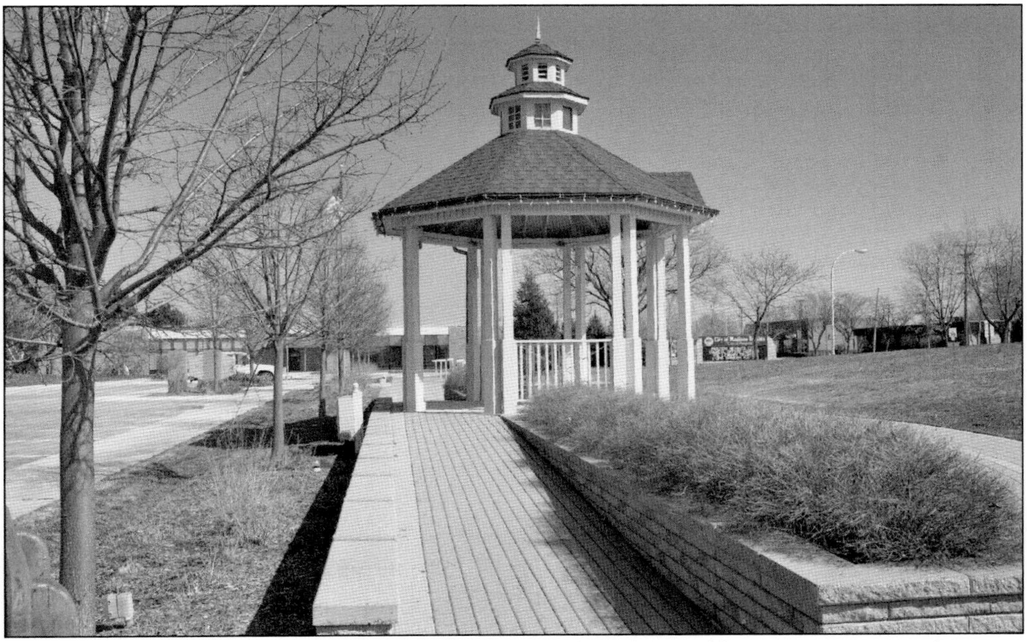

The gazebo in front of city hall was built in 1992 and made possible as a joint project between the Madison Heights Jaycees and the City of Madison Heights. The public library is visible in the background. The gazebo is a beautiful addition to the civic center complex landscape and serves many purposes. During the city's annual tree lighting event, Santa receives the key to the city and to the hearts of good little boys and girls. In late May, the gazebo serves a more somber role as the site of the memorial service that follows the Memorial Day Parade. The gazebo also served as a picturesque setting for weddings conducted by the mayor. (Both photographs by Margene Scott.)

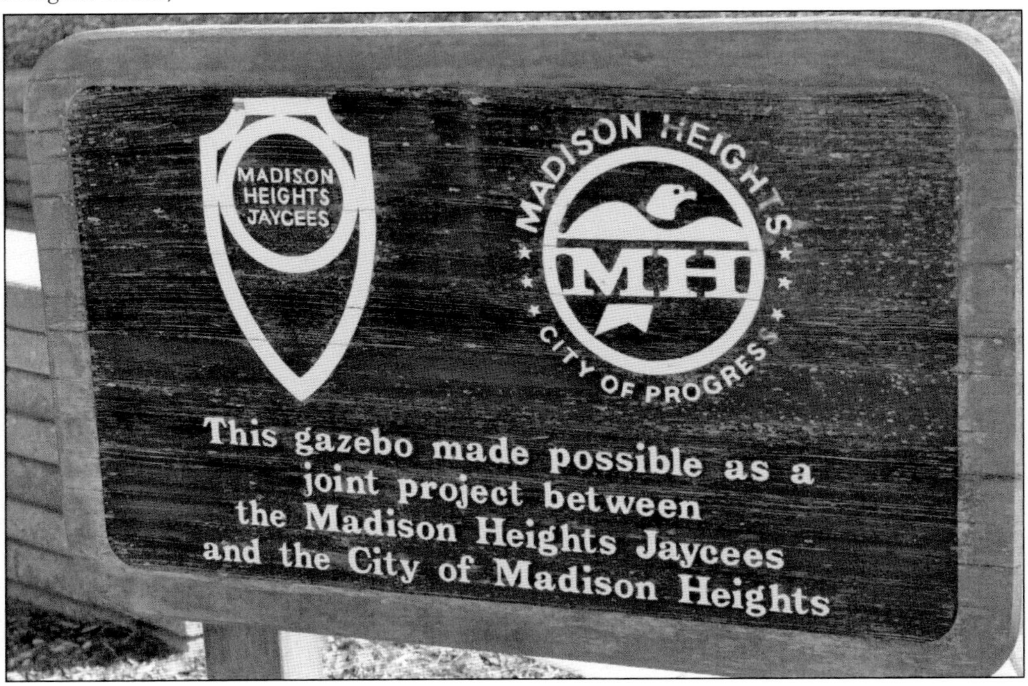

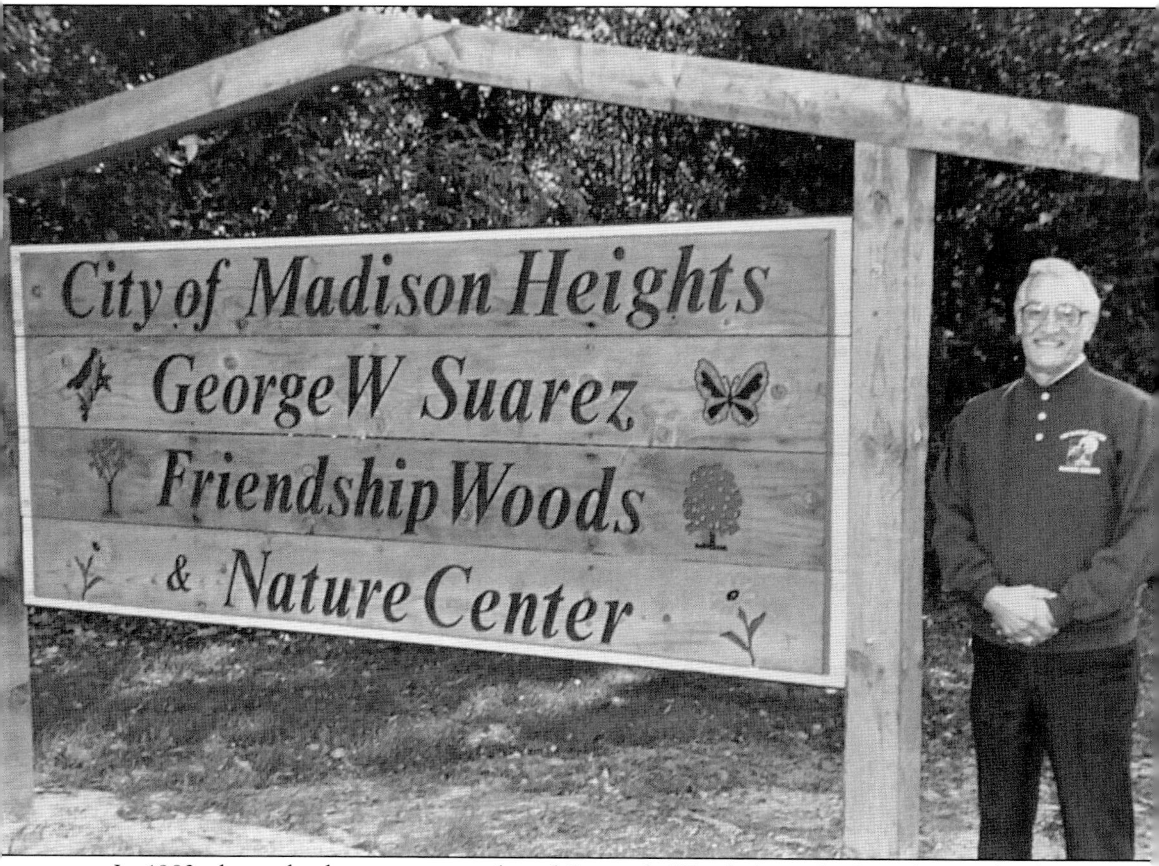

In 1983, the parks department purchased Simonds Woods from the Lamphere School District through a $403,000 state grant. In 1987, to honor the longest serving mayor of Madison Heights, Simonds Woods became George W. Suarez Friendship Woods. George Suarez poses with the sign that bears his name. (Photograph by Margene Scott.)

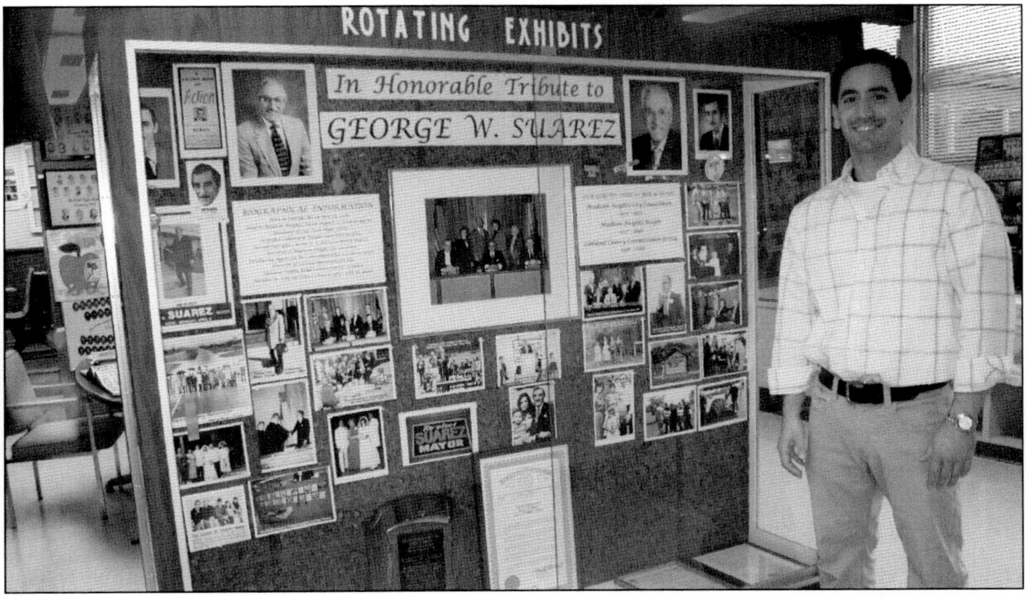

Two generations of the Suarez family are represented, as Justin Suarez, a member of the Madison Heights Historical Commission, stands next to a display honoring his father, the late George W. Suarez, longtime mayor and Oakland County commissioner, in October 2008, following his father's passing earlier that year. The display case is located in the Madison Heights Heritage Rooms, the city's first museum, and the case serves as a rotating exhibit featuring noteworthy individuals. (Photograph by Margene Scott.)

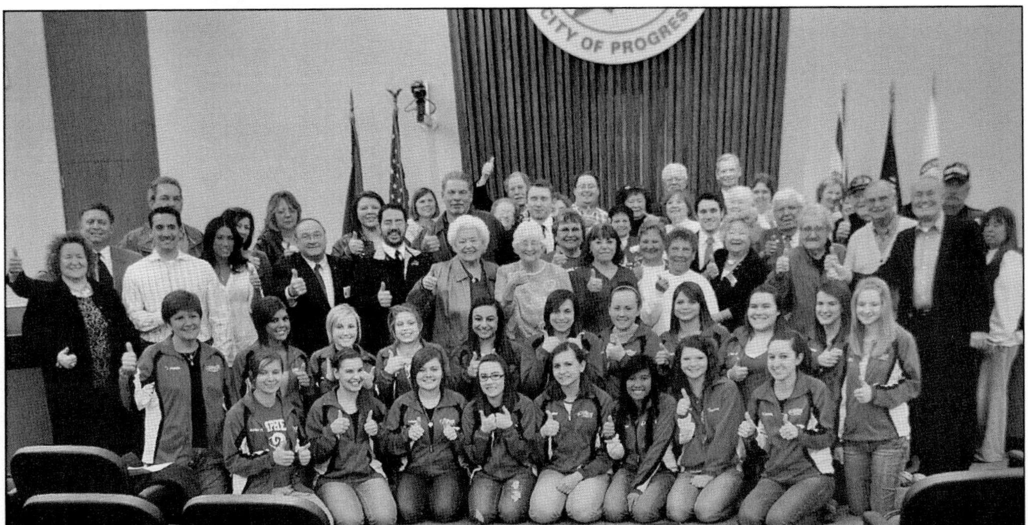

The Madison Heights Memorial Day Parade is a long-standing community event that represents a cooperative effort between local businesses, service clubs, and government representatives to pay homage to veterans. A memorial service afterward further affords residents the opportunity to pay their respects. When the challenges of the Michigan economy meant that the city could no longer fund this event, a group of dedicated residents formed the Save the Parade Committee. Martha Kehoe, Dolly Ferries, Andy McGillivray, and Monte Geralds were a big part of this effort. This image at a city council meeting captured the moment when the committee reached the funding needed to continue the parade. (Photograph by Jack Scott.)

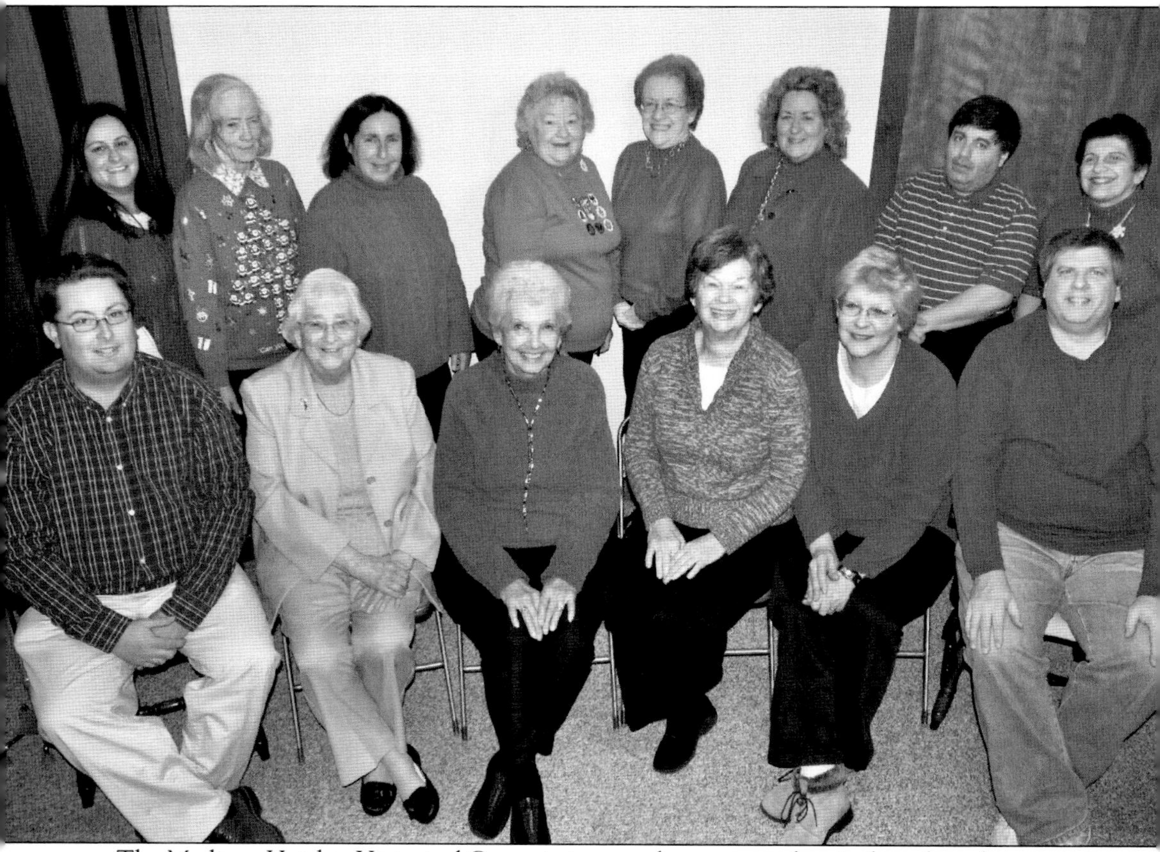

The Madison Heights Historical Commission numbers among the city boards and commissions, with a goal to preserve the history of Madison Heights. Established in 1984, the first appointed members included Frank James Cagle Sr. and Darrel K. Davis, both founders of the city. The commission has authored three local *Heritage Books* covering the city's history through 2005. The commission also maintains the Heritage Rooms. Pictured in this 2010 photograph are, from left to right, (first row) Andy McGillivray, Dolly Ferries, Lila Richards, Sue Price, Cheryl Suiter, and Tony Bliss; (second row) Stacey Karwoski, Mary Merkel, library director Roslyn Yerman, Martha Kehoe, Barbara Geralds, Councilwoman Margene Scott, Robert Scheere, and Connie Schmelzle. (Photograph by Jack Scott.)

Eight

EVENTS

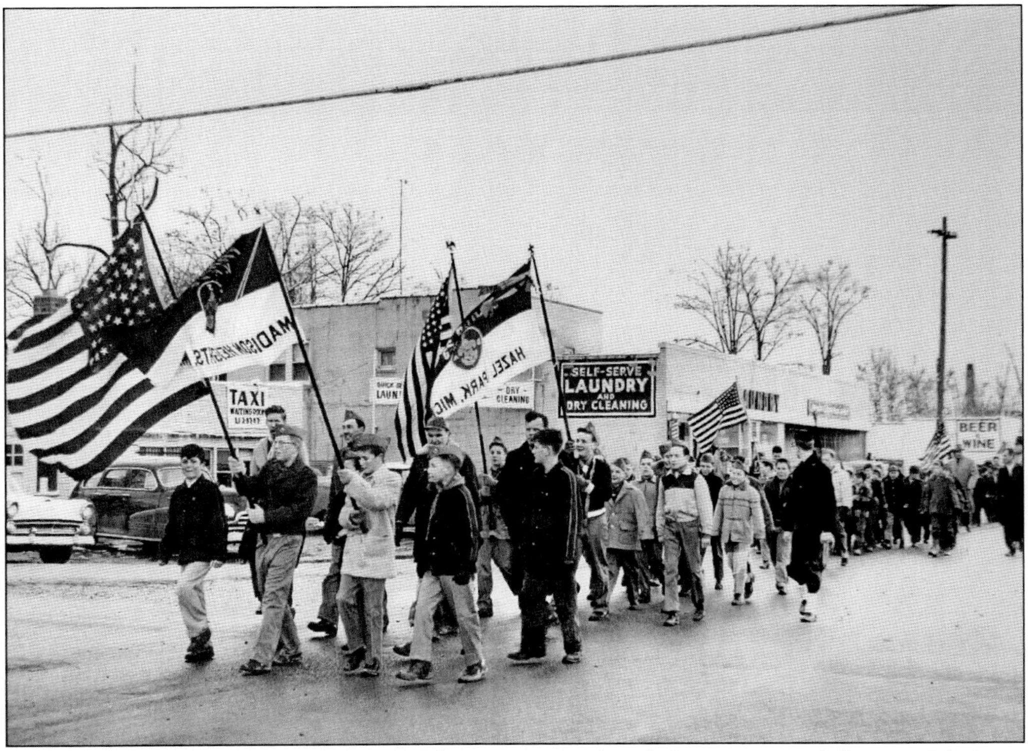

To mark the first birthday of the city charter approval and the opening of the new Madison Heights Recreation Center at John R Road and Gardenia Avenue, the city held a birthday celebration and parade on December 9, 1956, preceded by a Christmas tree lighting ceremony and carol sing at the city hall at John R and Sixth Street. The parade moved north from the city hall to the recreation center. The parade marshal was Councilman George Sargeant. He was assisted by John B. Michrina, deputy marshal, and Edwin Morgan, chief of staff. (Courtesy of City of Madison Heights.)

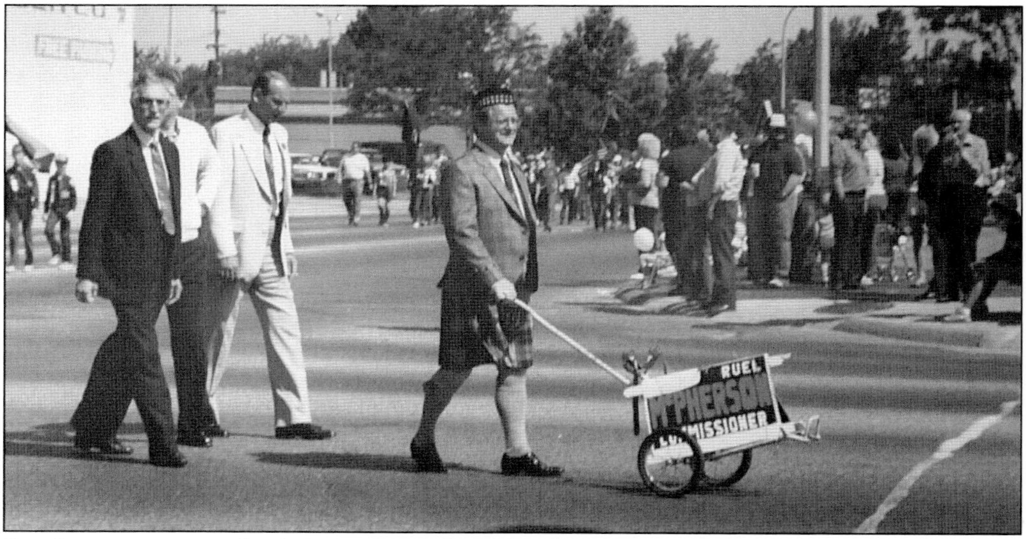

Parade participants make their way from John R Road to 11 Mile Road during an annual Memorial Day Parade in the mid-1980s. Turning the corner from left to right are Mayor George Suarez, Councilman John Claya (partially hidden), Councilman Richard Van Sice, and county commissioner Ruel McPherson (pushing wagon). The parade route took participants from around 12 Mile Road, south on John R for at least a mile, then east on 11 Mile. The memorial service was held at the Madison football field and stadium on East 11 Mile and Lorenz Street. The parade route has since changed, and elected officials now ride in or are accompanied by vehicles. (Photograph by Margene Scott.)

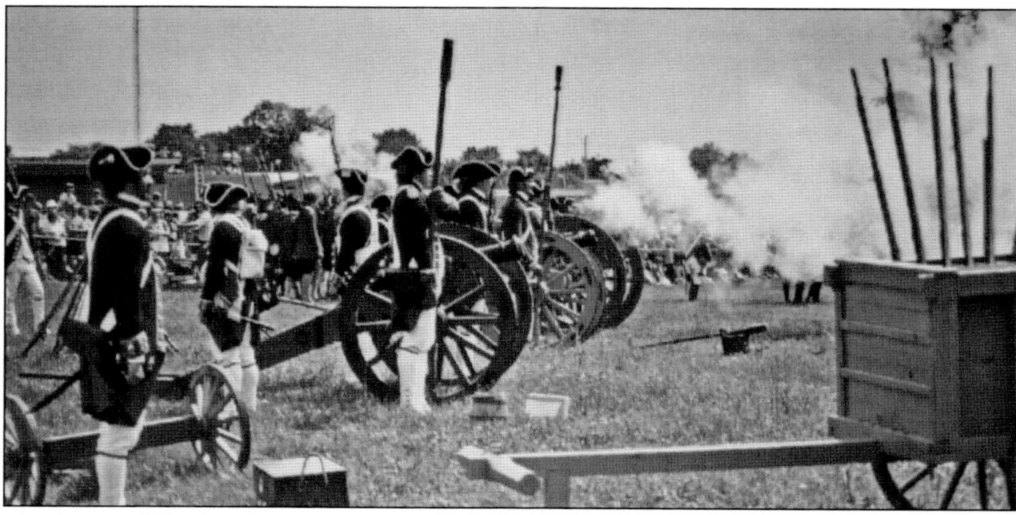

The Battle of Bunker Hill was reenacted on the Madison Heights sled hill behind city hall on June 14, 1975, three days before the June 17, 1775, battle's 200th anniversary. According to Al Koch, the city's youth assistance worker, the battle was actually fought on Breed's Hill. Koch was the commander of the 3rd Artillery Regiment Continental Line, based in Pontiac. The group sent about 20 soldiers, and British and American units totaling more than 100 soldiers also participated. Members of a committee chaired by MaryAnne Yemec raised $3,000 for what was anticipated to be the best Revolutionary War reenactment of the year in Michigan. Social and civic groups in the city made donations and operated food booths while dressed in period clothes. (Photograph by Doug MacLean.)

Ground was broken in June 1985 for the construction of the New Horizons Cooperative Senior Apartments to be built at 31101 Edward Street. This photograph, facing south, was taken from the top floor of the existing Madison Heights Cooperative Apartments senior living facility at 500 East Irving Avenue. The city remains committed to meeting the needs of a growing senior population. (Photograph by Margene Scott.)

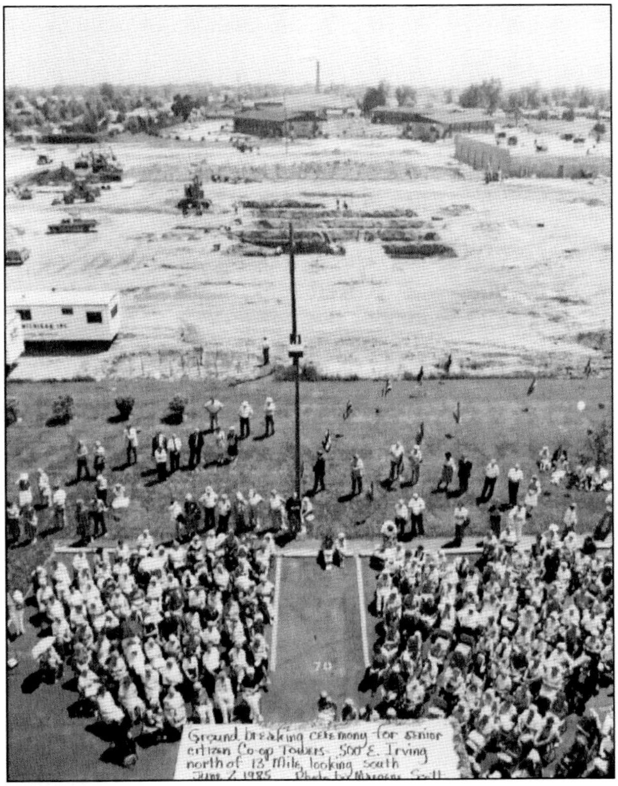

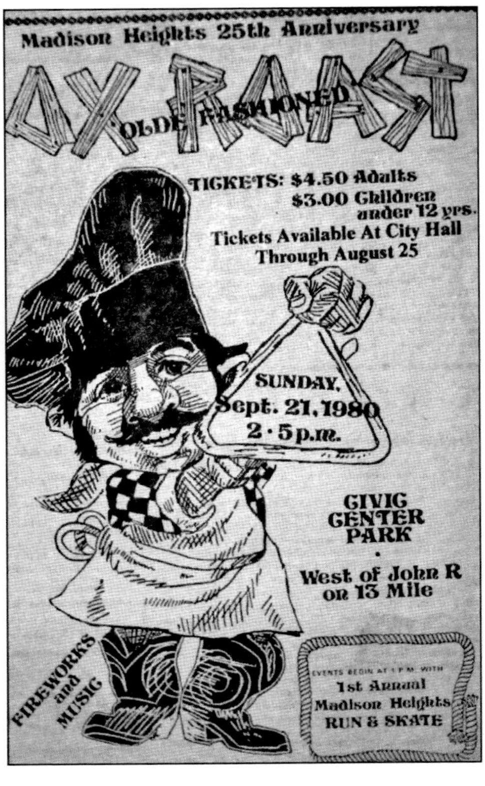

The highlight of the city's 25th anniversary celebration was an ox roast held on September 21, 1980. The event also included booths and activities sponsored and run by various community groups and civic organizations. A February 2 concert and dance in the Lamphere High School cafeteria kicked off the anniversary, featuring the Big Band sound of Warney Ruhl and his Orchestra, and was preceded by a concert by the Parks and Recreation Jazz Ensemble in the auditorium. (Courtesy of City of Madison Heights.)

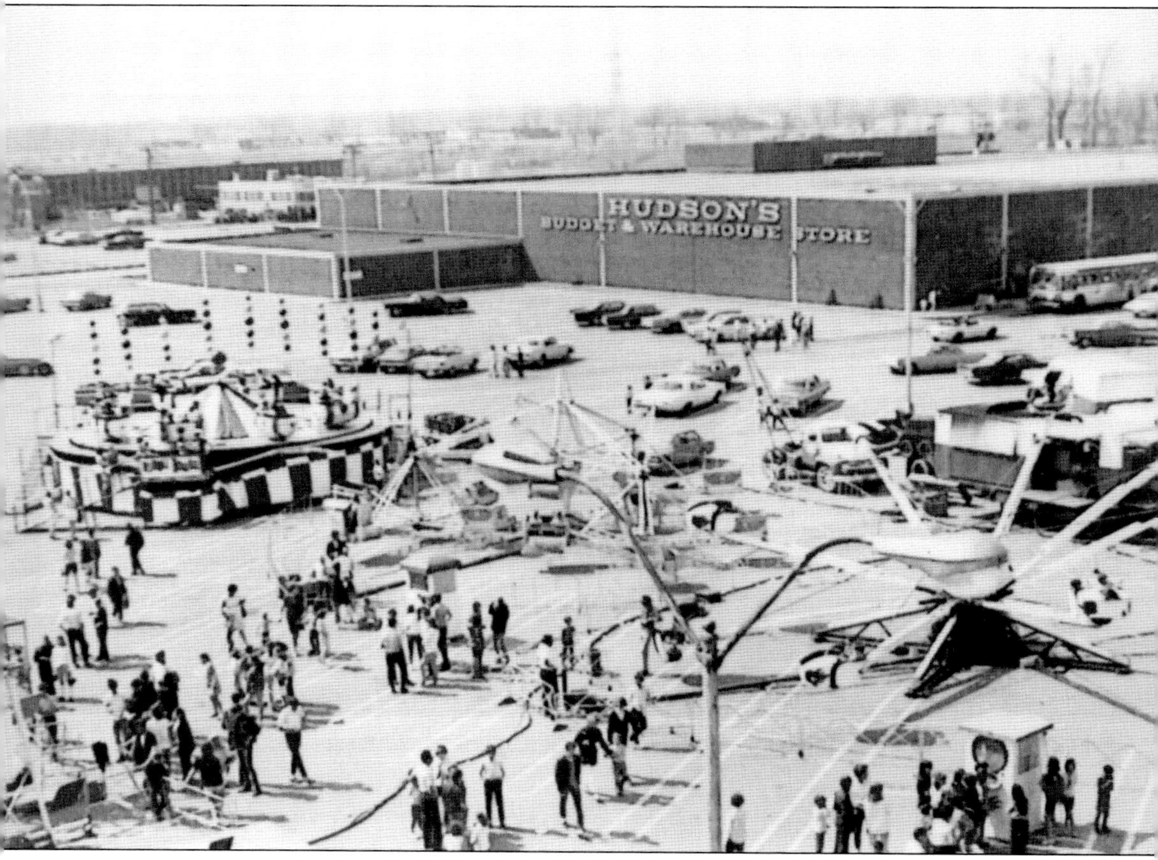

Hudson's Budget Store featured an annual fair in the store's parking lot. Wade Rides offered the attraction, which provided many memories. While it may or may not have been a forerunner of the Jaycee fair, the service organization held an annual fair of its own in the summer in Civic Center Park for many years. (Courtesy of Mary Merkel.)

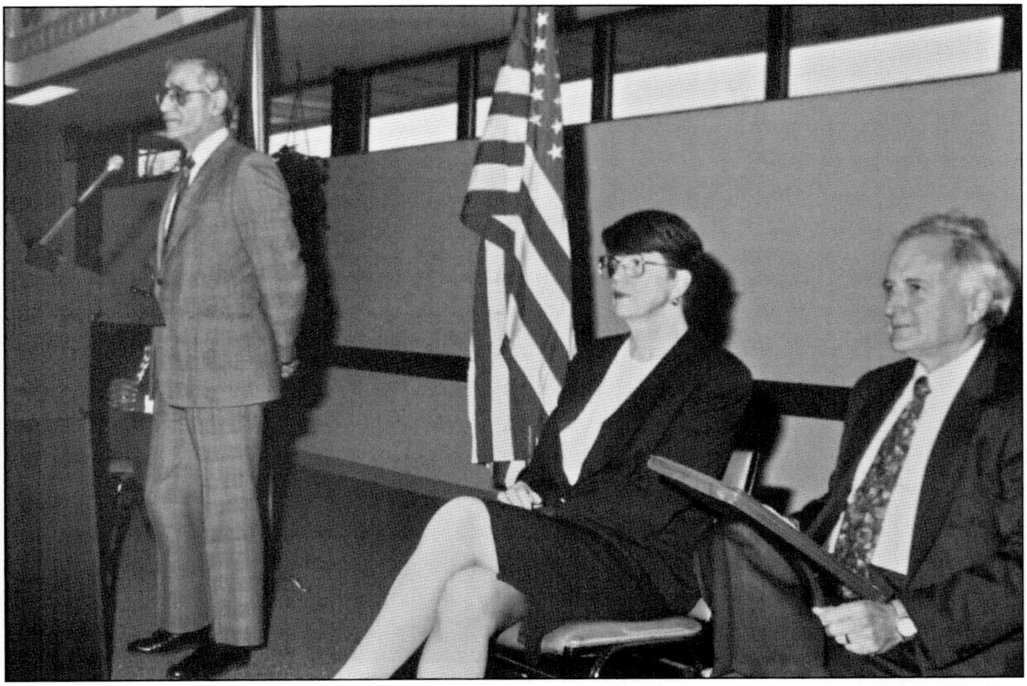

Attorney General Janet Reno spoke at the Madison Heights Senior Center on April 9, 1994, as part of a weeklong tour to rally support for President Clinton's anti-crime bill. While a focal point of the bill was to put up to 100,000 community police officers on the streets, crime remained a pressing problem. Above, the attorney general and Congressman Sander Levin listen to Mayor George W. Suarez. Below, Reno visits with city council. From left to right below are Councilwoman Mary Frances Stema, Councilwoman Elva Mills, Councilman Gary R. McGillivray, Councilwoman Margene Johnston Scott, Councilwoman Marilyn Russell, Reno, Chief of Police Ronald Pearce, and Mayor George W. Suarez. (Above, photograph by Margene Scott; below, photograph by Benjamin I. Myers.)

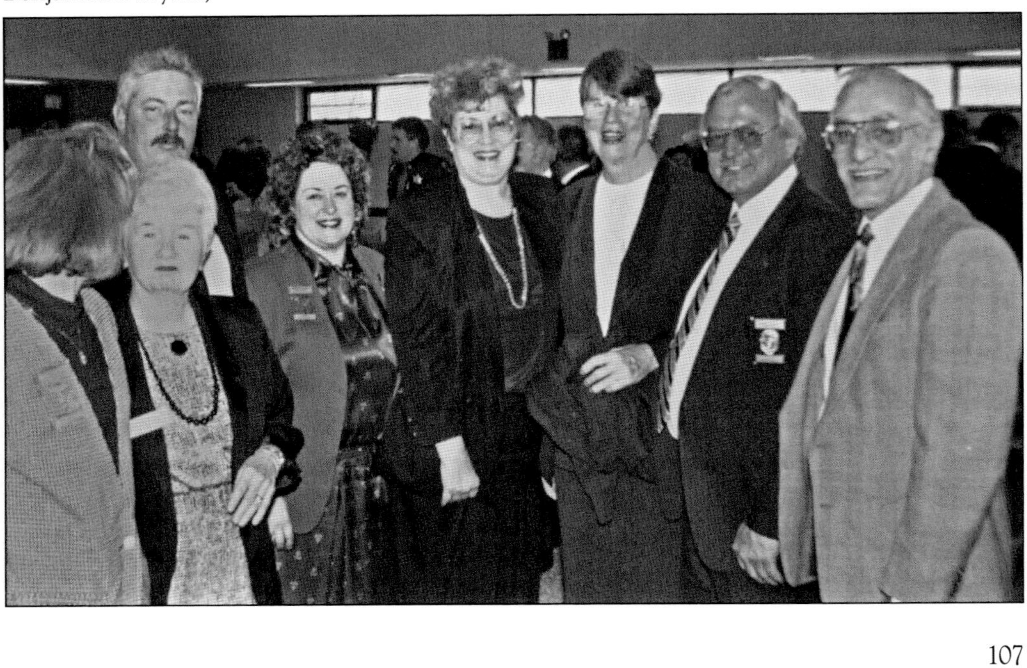

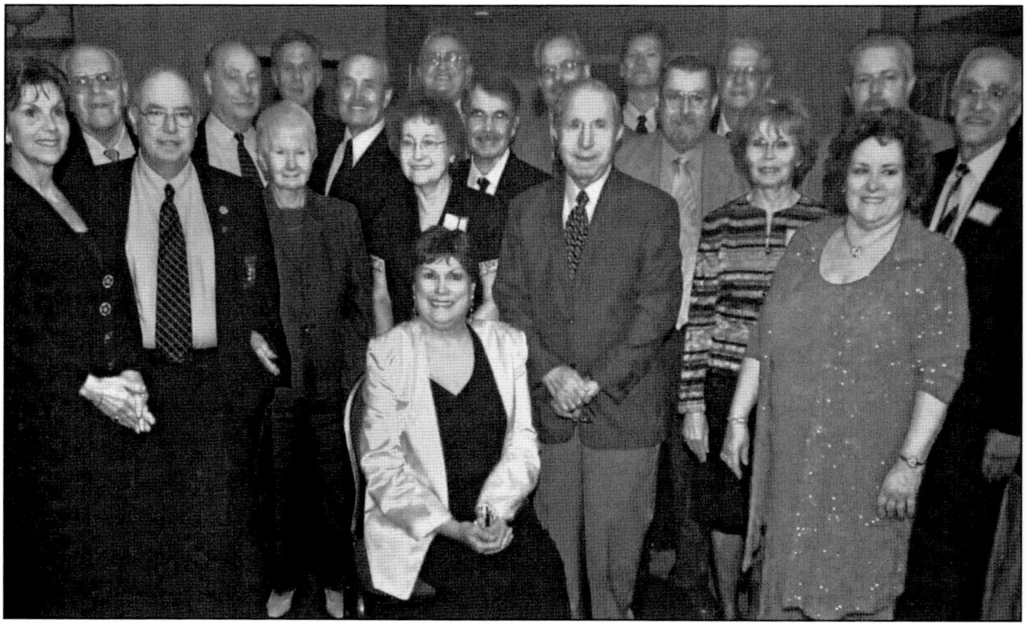

Until it was eliminated as a budget measure, the city held an annual Boards and Commissions Dinner in the spring to thank the citizens who volunteered their time to serve on the city's boards and commissions. This photograph was taken at the 50th anniversary dinner held in May 2005. City staff liaisons to a board or committee were also invited to attend, as well as city council and all former elected officials. (Photograph by Jack Scott.)

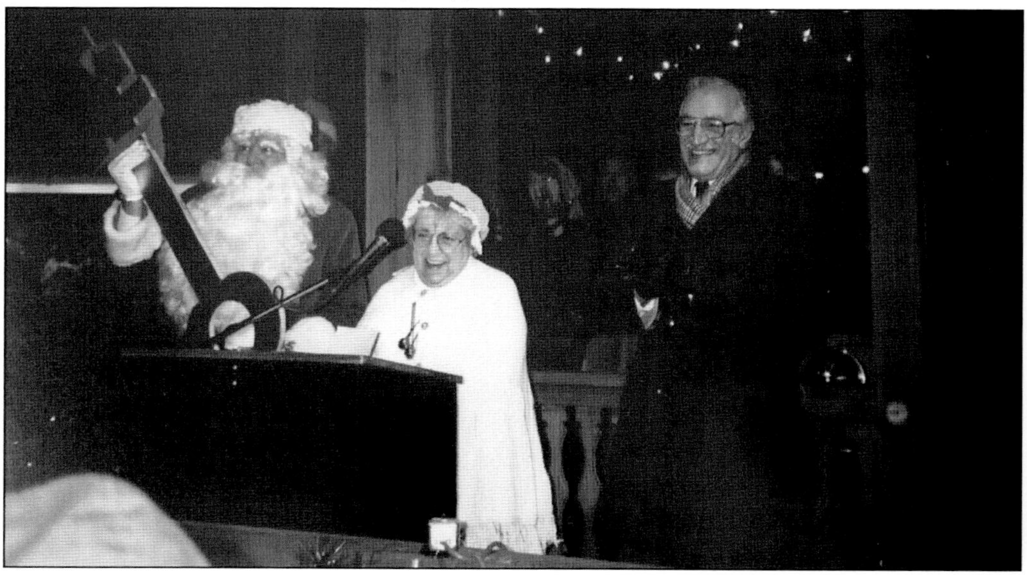

Santa and Mrs. Claus, otherwise known as Dick and Mary Sliwoski, accept the key to the city from Mayor George Suarez at the gazebo in front of city hall. The couple reprised the roles for the city tree lighting ceremony for over 10 years beginning in 1986, stopping only when health issues prevented Dick from continuing. It was a genuine blow to the man who portrayed the true essence of Santa Claus, as the man not in the red suit but in one's heart. Mary made the four suits Dick wore in 48 years in the role, and the skirt she wore herself starting in 1965 when she took on the role of Mrs. Claus. (Photograph by Margene Scott.)

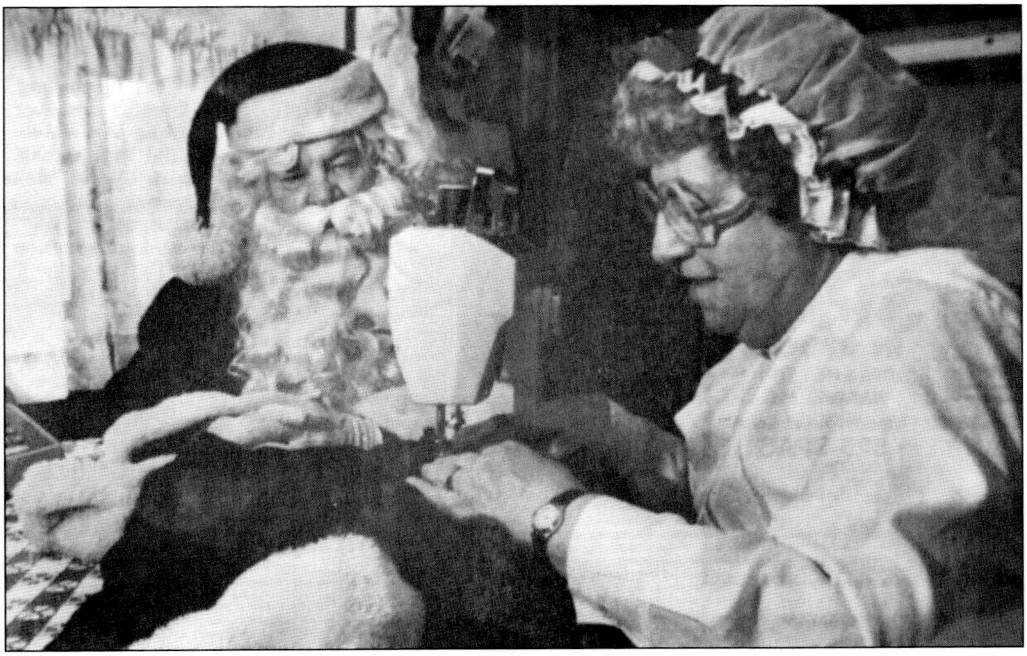

Santa, otherwise known as Dick Sliwoski, watches as Mrs. Claus, Mary Sliwoski, works on his suit in this May 18, 1980, *Daily Tribune* photograph. The two were beloved in the community for embodying the true spirit of Santa and of the season. (Photograph by Craig Gaffield, courtesy of the *Daily Tribune*.)

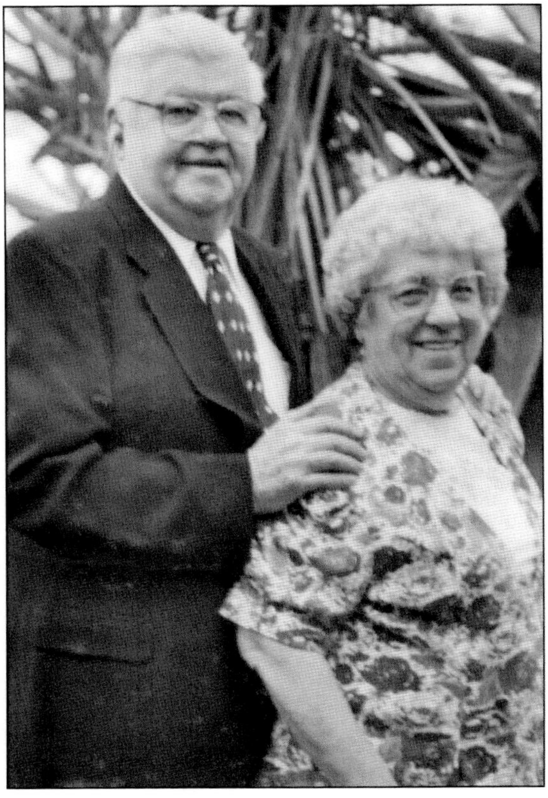

The smiling faces of Dick and Mary Sliwoski are shown, otherwise known as Santa and Mrs. Claus to both the residents of Madison Heights and others throughout the state. Dick and Mary had no children of their own but displayed equal compassion to those they encountered, never talking down to someone because of their age. Richard Ernest Sliwoski passed away on February 24, 2005, and Mary Sliwoski passed away on January 21, 2013. (Courtesy of the Sliwoski family.)

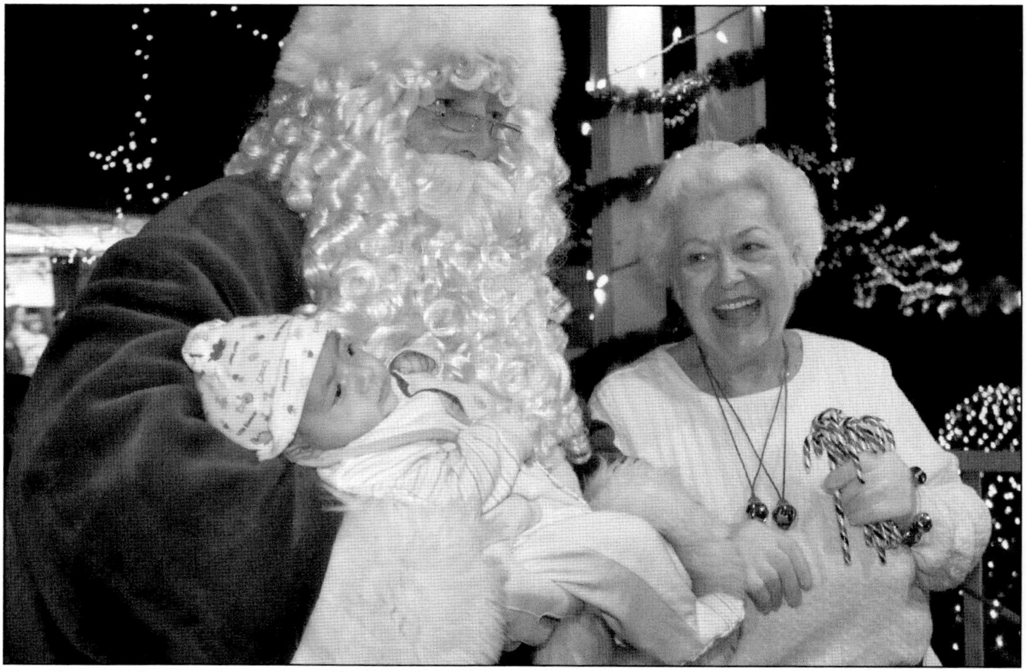

For almost 10 years, Jean Linville has donned a red and white outfit complete with bells to play the part of Mrs. Claus to the delight of the city's younger residents. She and her husband, Santa, played by Oakland County commissioner and former mayor and city councilman Gary McGillivray, accept the key to the city from the mayor at the gazebo in front of city hall as part of the city's annual tree lighting ceremony for use in visiting the homes of all the good little boys and girls. The two are pictured here on November 22, 2010, at the gazebo with one of the city's youngest residents. (Photograph by Margene Scott.)

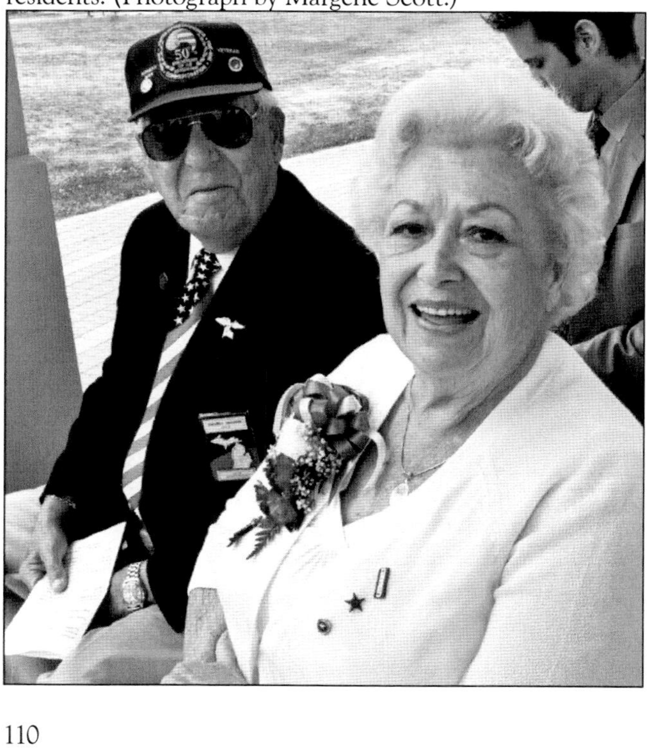

Jean Linville has served countless years as the city's honorary Gold Star Mother in the Memorial Day Parade. Gold Star Mothers have lost a child in military combat. Each year, she participates in the memorial service following the parade and lays a wreath at the city monument honoring departed soldiers. Here she is pictured with Mayor Edward Swanson on May 26, 2012. (Photograph by Margene Scott.)

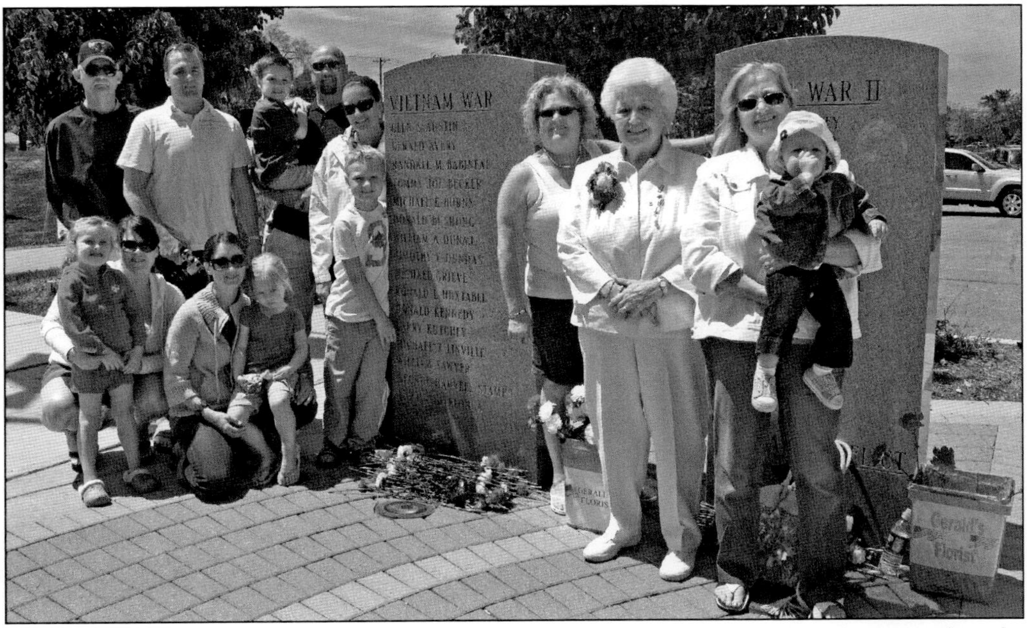

Family members point to the name of Michael Linville on the city monument, honoring him for the ultimate sacrifice in giving his life for his country in 1970 during the Vietnam War. Michael was the son of Jean, Madison Heights resident and Gold Star Mother. Absent from the family photograph is Michael's father, the late Tom Linville, who worked for the City of Madison Heights, as did his wife. (Photograph by Margene Scott.)

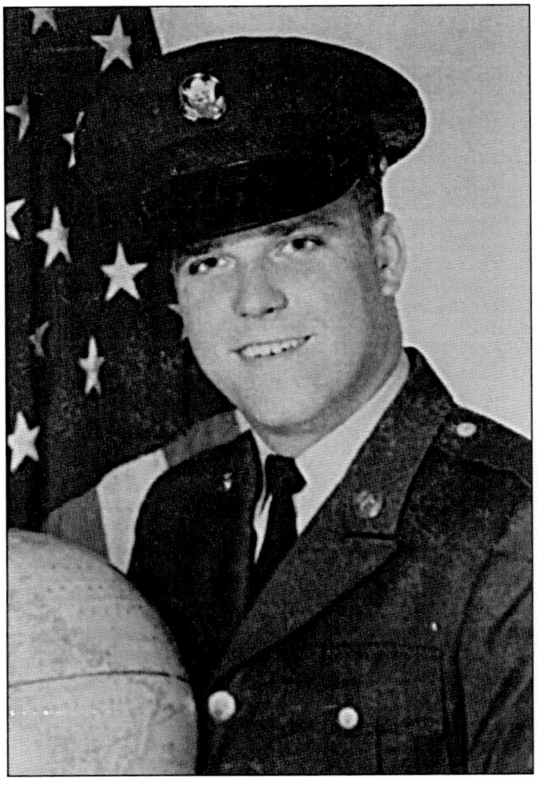

This photograph of Michael T. Linville is included with others on the city's Wall of Heroes, a montage of those who gave their lives in battle. Housed in the city's Heritage Rooms museum, the montage is displayed at the annual memorial service following the Memorial Day Parade. (Courtesy of the Linville family.)

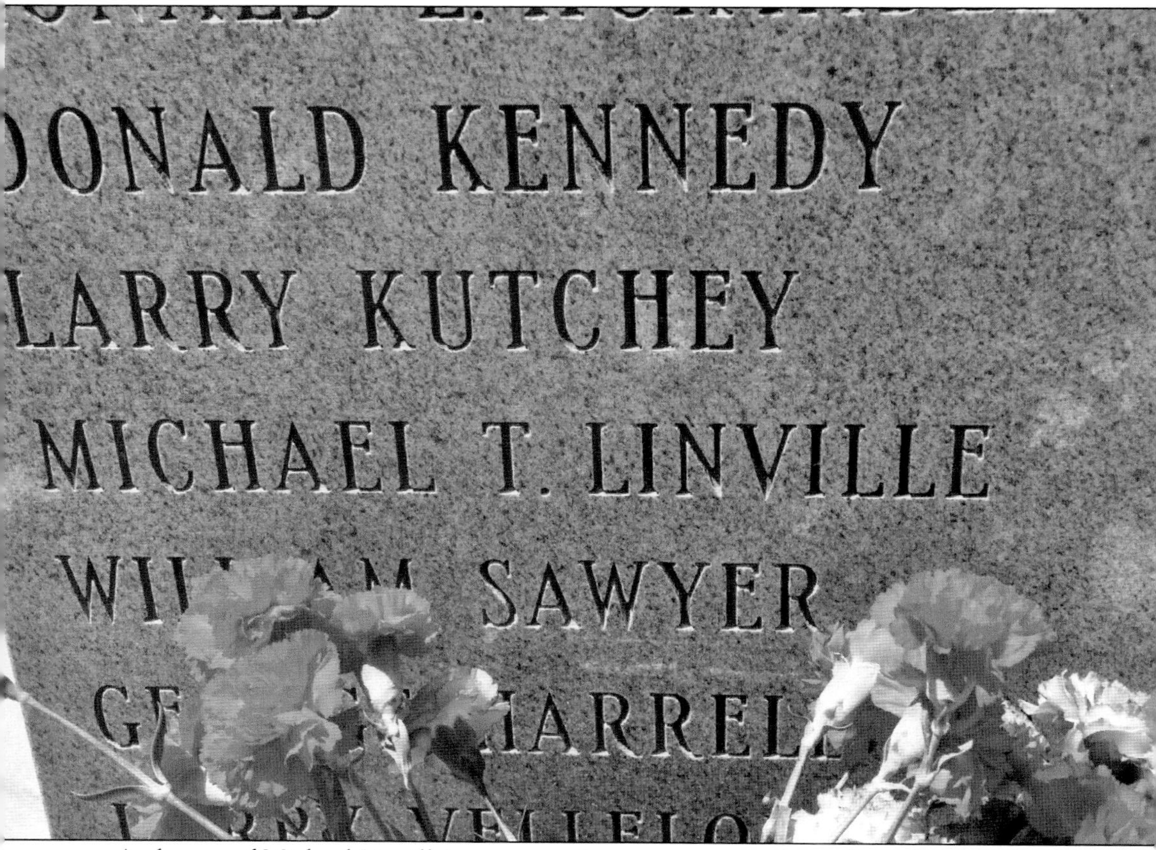

A closeup of Michael Linville's name on the monument is shown here. During the services, residents have the opportunity to place red, white, and blue flowers at the monument in honor of those who served. (Photograph by Margene Scott.)

Bernard "Bernie" Plummer was the longtime owner of Gerald's Florist at the corner of 12 Mile and Dequindre Roads. The business was named after Plummer's father, Wilford, whose middle name was Gerald. The business has been in Madison Heights for 45 years, and Bernie is known as the big, loveable guy with a heart of gold. He often gave away flowers, including for the annual Memorial Day Parade, where he would provide complimentary carnations for participants in the memorial service to place on the monument in front of city hall. Following Bernie's passing, Gerald's Florist continues to be run by Mary Zalewski, his longtime partner. (Photograph by Margene Scott.)

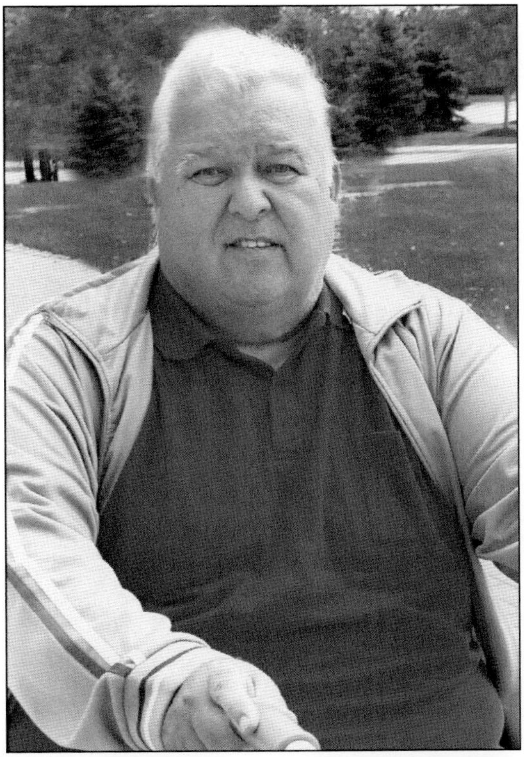

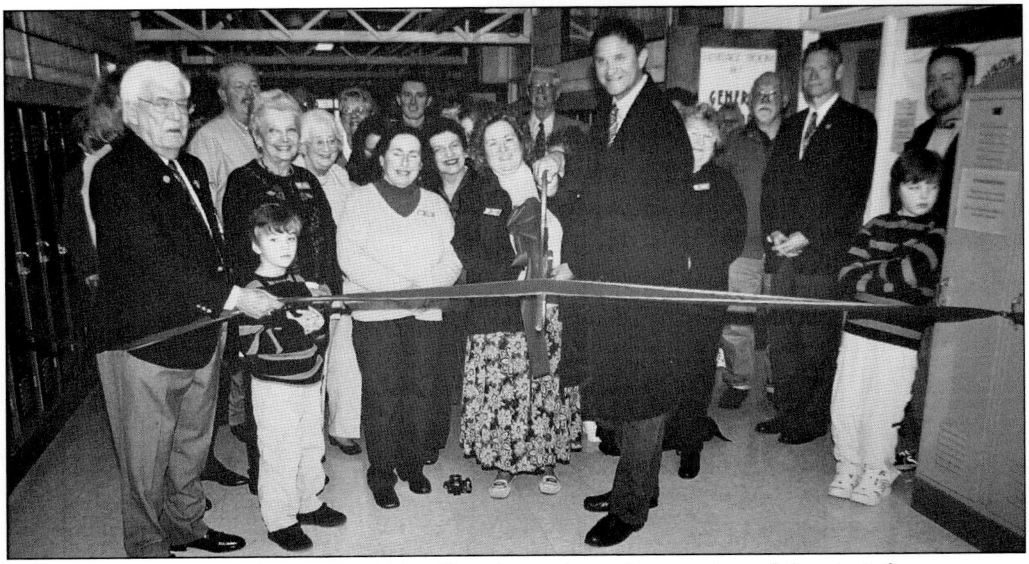

The ribbon is cut on February 5, 2008, officially marking the opening of the city's first museum, the Heritage Rooms, a partnership between the city and Madison Schools. City council members and administration, along with Madison Heights Historical Commission members, were present for the moment when David Hurnevich, principal of Schoenhals, the school housing the rooms, does the honors. Among those included in the image are Mayor Edward Swanson (left), library director and historical commission staff representative Roslyn Yerman (second to the left of Hurnevich) and Margene Scott, historical commission council representative (left of Hurnevich). (Photograph by Jack Scott.)

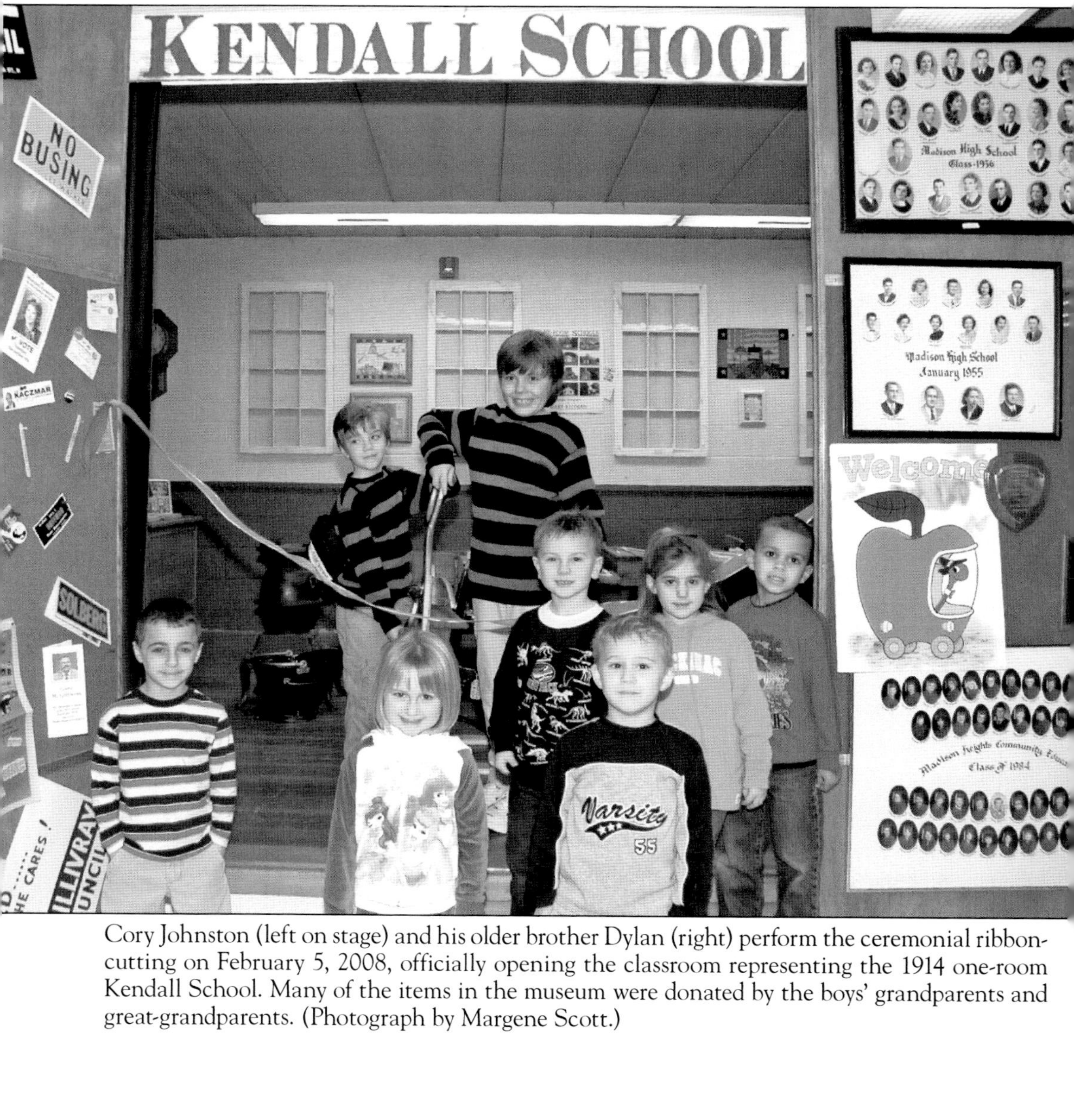

Cory Johnston (left on stage) and his older brother Dylan (right) perform the ceremonial ribbon-cutting on February 5, 2008, officially opening the classroom representing the 1914 one-room Kendall School. Many of the items in the museum were donated by the boys' grandparents and great-grandparents. (Photograph by Margene Scott.)

Nine

NOTABLES

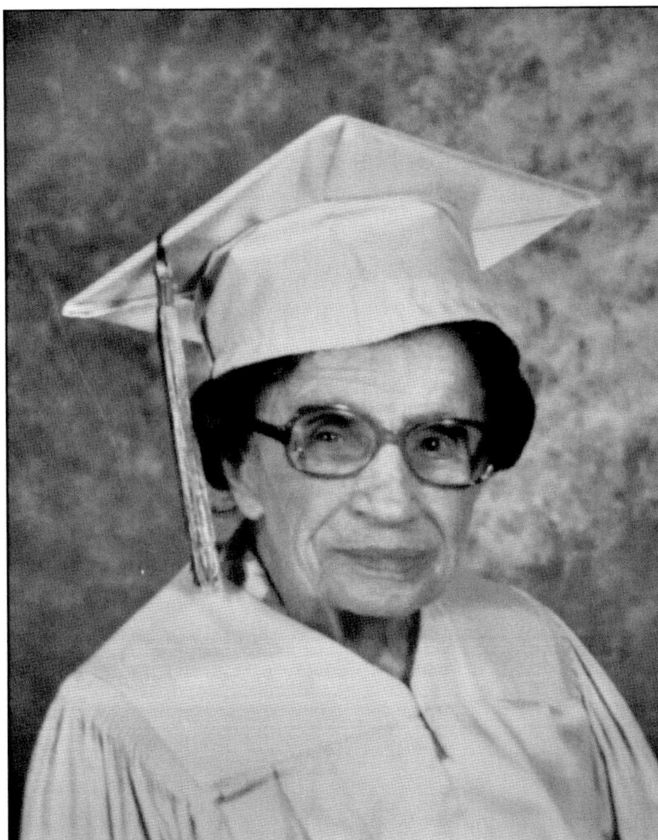

Jessie May Moore Byam was born 1891 in New York and received her high school diploma on May 21, 1982, at the age of 98, making her the oldest person in the United States to graduate from high school at the time. She took classes at the senior center through the community education diploma program after having left school after the 10th grade and going to work in her father's greenhouse business. She took classes with her younger friends in their 70s, only intending to learn more, before deciding to graduate. (Courtesy of the Jessie Byam family.)

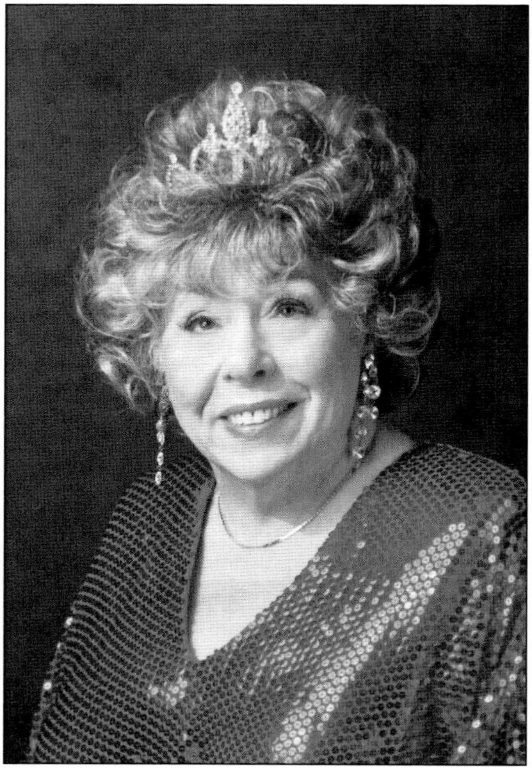

Edna Brown won the title of Miss Senior Michigan 1991. The personable Edna Brown's talent was jokes. A talent for singing transitioned into jokes, and a highlight of her career was entertaining with legendary fan dancer Sally Rand. Edna Brown was a social organizer at the Madison Heights Senior Co-Op Center where she lived and learned of the pageant through neighbors who thought she'd be a natural. April 10, 1991, was declared Edna Brown Day in Madison Heights, and she was the 1990 Madison Heights Senior of the Year. Edna Brown died on September 11, 2004. (Courtesy of Edna Brown.)

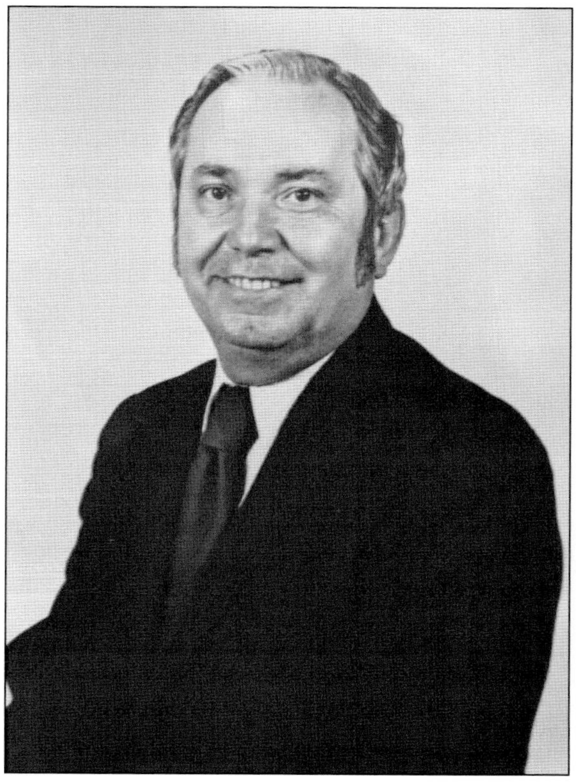

Charles "Chuck" Maloney practiced law for 52 years, serving nine years as an associate municipal judge in Madison Heights. He was involved with the early development of the city's municipal facilities through over 21 years of service on the municipal building authority. Judge Maloney issued the oath of office to his nephew Robert Corbett Jr. with his 2003 reelection to city council. Maloney died in June 2013. (Courtesy of Steve Maloney.)

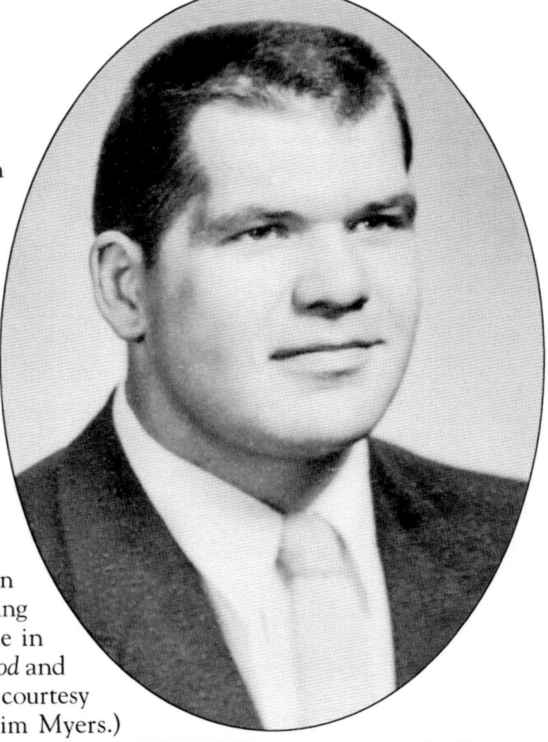

Jim Myers is a 1956 graduate of Madison High School, where he earned 16 varsity sports letters. He graduated from Michigan State University and earned a master's degree from Central Michigan. He was a Madison High School physical education teacher and coach for 25 years and started the Madison wrestling team, coaching for 16 years and winning the state title in 1969. Myers was named to the Michigan Coaches and Michigan Football Coach Hall of Fame. Yet his biggest claim to fame was as the world-famous professional wrestler George "The Animal" Steele. In 1995, he entered World Wrestling Entertainment's Hall of Fame, and in 2005, he was elected to the Professional Wrestling Hall of Fame. Jim Myers had a starring role in the Academy Award–winning movie *Ed Wood* and appeared in movies and commercials. (Right, courtesy of Madison Schools; below, courtesy of Jim Myers.)

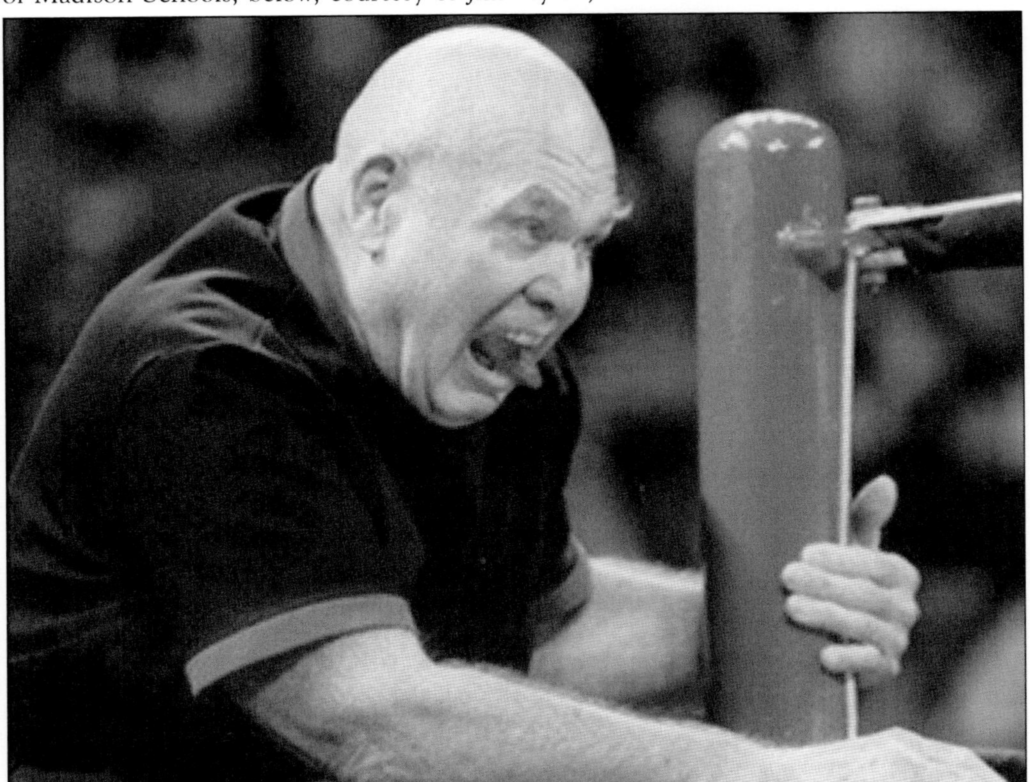

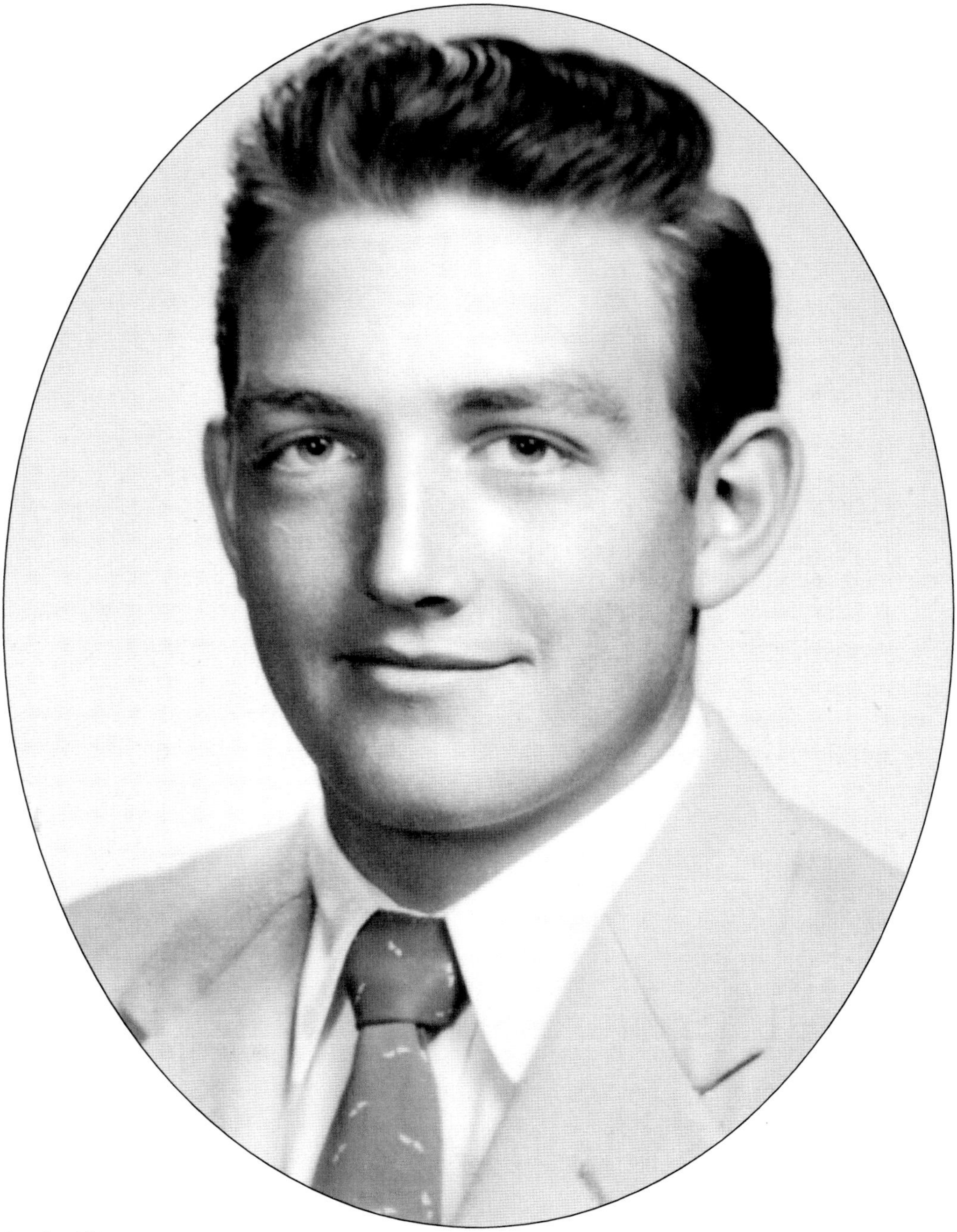

Grady Alderman is a 1956 Madison High School graduate and a noted football player. He played Madison Eagles football for three years and was named First Team All Pro as a lineman. Alderman graduated on a full scholarship from the University of Detroit–Mercy, where he played right tackle, and was named to the school's hall of fame. He was a 1960 NFL draft pick and played 16 seasons in the NFL as an offensive lineman, including with the Detroit Lions. However, he played most of his career with the Minnesota Vikings, and was noted for being the last of the original Vikings. (Courtesy of Madison Schools.)

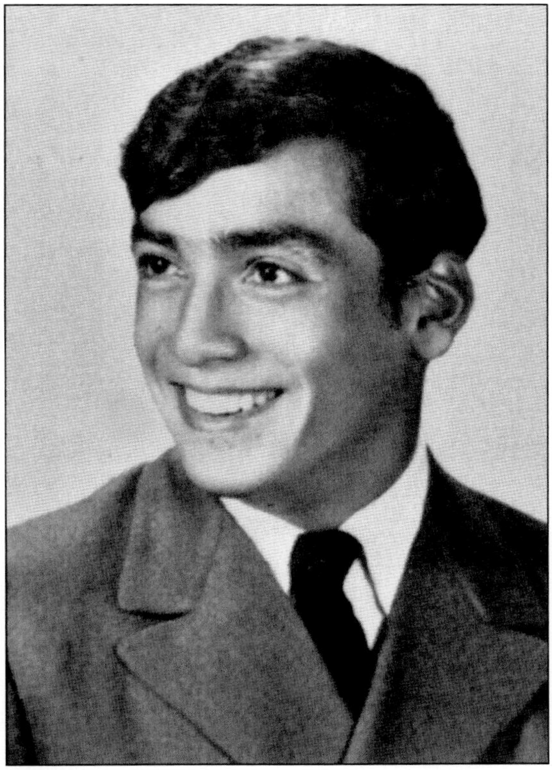

Berney Gonzales is a 1971 Madison High School graduate and renowned wrestler. He is the 1971 Junior World Olympic Greco-Roman Wrestling Champion, the first American to win a gold medal in international competition in Greco-Roman style. He was honored with a Michigan state legislature proclamation from state senator Bill Huffman, a key to the city from Mayor Monte Geralds, and a telegram from astronaut Jim Lovell, head of the President's Physical Fitness Program. A day was also proclaimed in his honor by the city, and in 2010, he was a Michigan Chapter of Wrestling Hall of Fame inductee with a Lifetime Service Award. (Right, courtesy of Madison Schools; below, photograph by Margene Scott.)

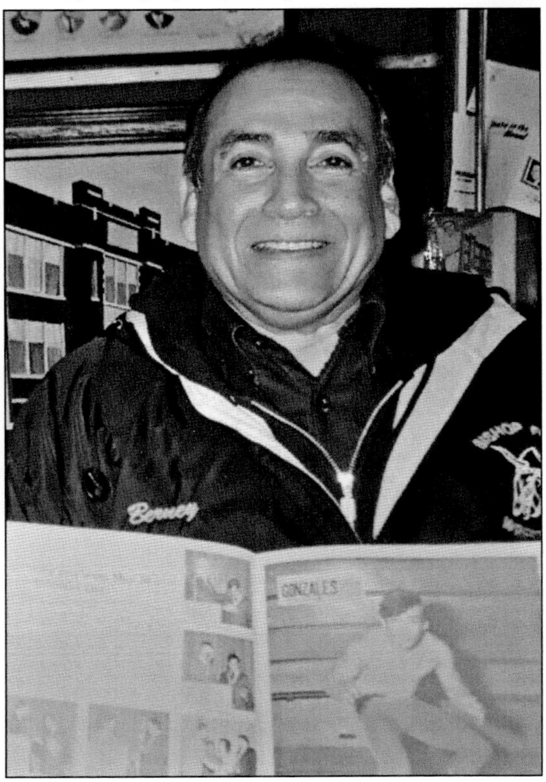

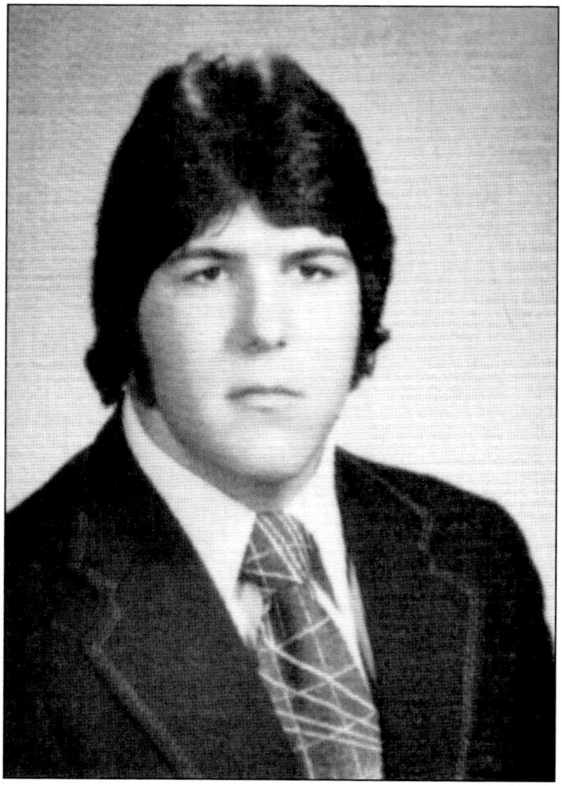

Ken Dallafior is a 1977 Madison High School graduate who played football and wrestled for the Madison Eagles and was coached by Jim Myers in both sports. He graduated from the University of Minnesota, where he played football for the Golden Gophers and was named All–Big Ten Offensive Tackle. He played for the San Diego Chargers from 1985 to 1988 and for the Detroit Lions from 1989 to 1992. Ken Dallafior has also worked as a Lions analyst and founded the Detroit Lions Courage House. (Left, courtesy of Madison Schools; below, courtesy of Ken Dallafior.)

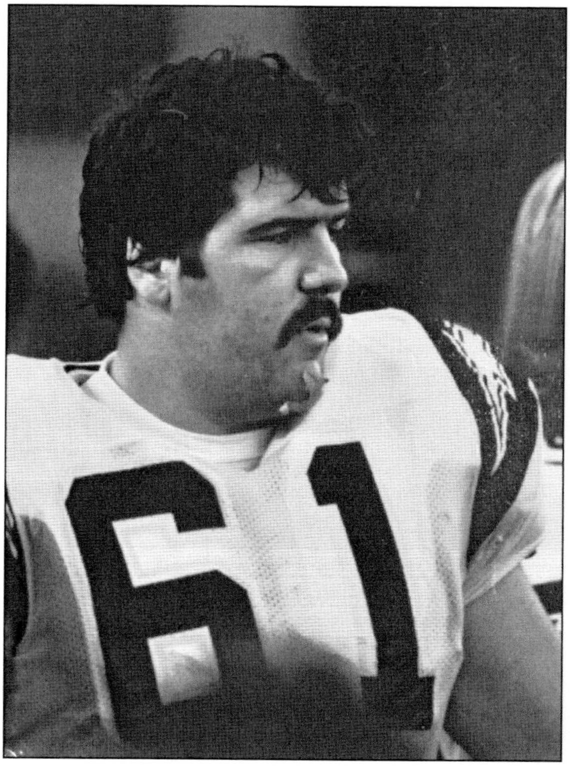

Jerry Binkley is a 1977 Madison High School graduate who played for the Madison Eagles football team and was coached by Jim Myers. Binkley coached Madison High School junior varsity football in 1984 and served as the Madison High School wrestling coach from 1985 to 1986 and in 1988, when he coached with noted wrestler Bernie Gonzalez. Binkley has been a Madison Heights Little Football coach since 1979. He has an unprecedented record of more than 200 wins, coaching his teams to 13 Super Bowls and winning nine. (Right, courtesy of Madison Schools; below, photograph by Margene Scott.)

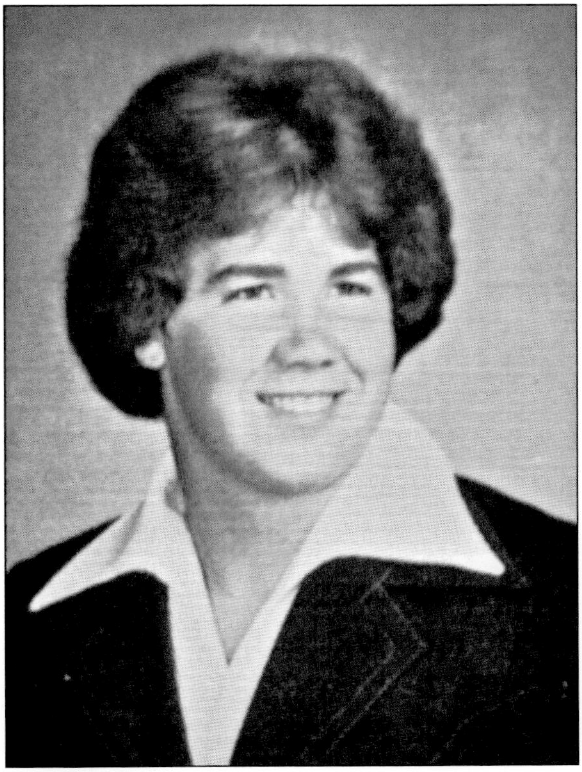

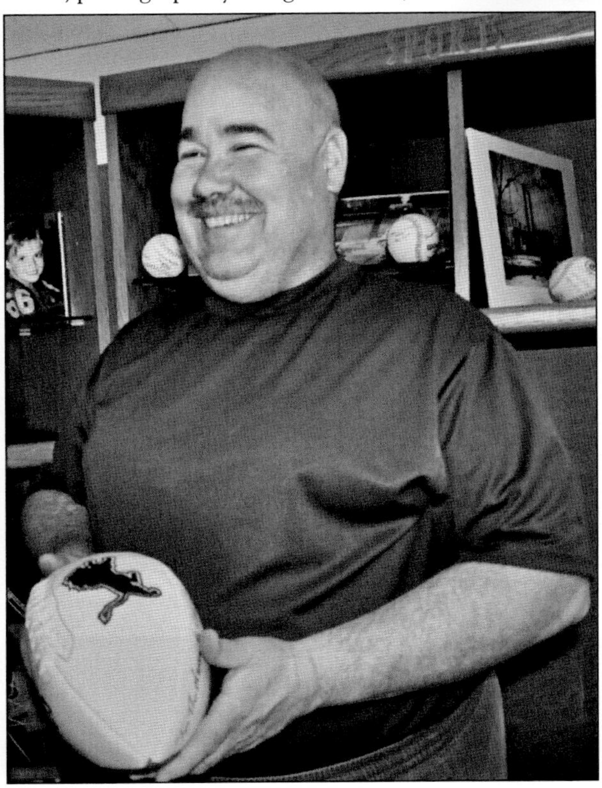

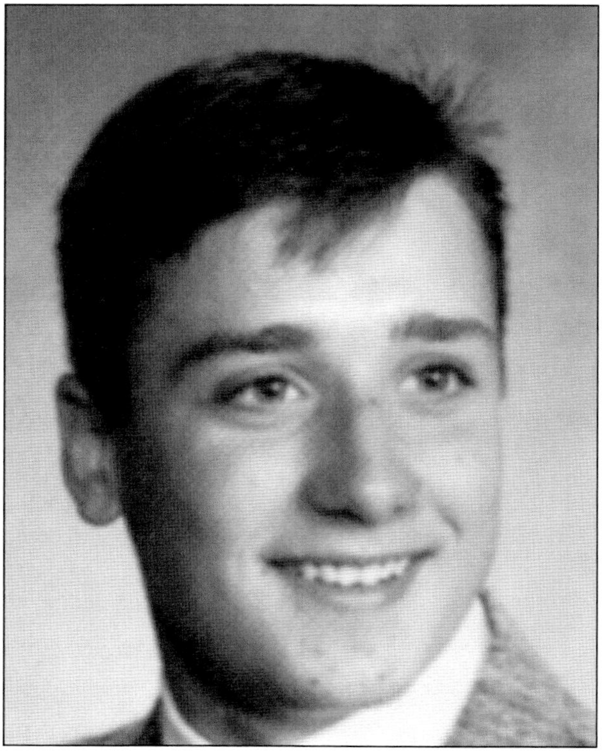

Shawn Penn is a 1989 graduate of Lamphere High School and a noted hockey player. He played both ice and roller hockey from 1991 to 1997. Penn played ice hockey for Miami University in Ohio from 1991 to 1994 and in the minor/junior leagues, where he played left wing. He played for the Toledo Storm from 1994 to 1996 and the Chicago Wolves from 1996 to 1997, then for the Long Beach Ice Dogs from 1997 to 1998, the Fort Wayne Komets from 1998 to 1999, the San Antonio Iguanas from 1999 to 2000, and the Utah Grizzlies from 1999 to 2000. Penn played roller hockey for the Detroit Motor City Mustangs in 1995 and for the Los Angeles Blade from 1996 to 1997. (Courtesy of Lamphere Schools.)

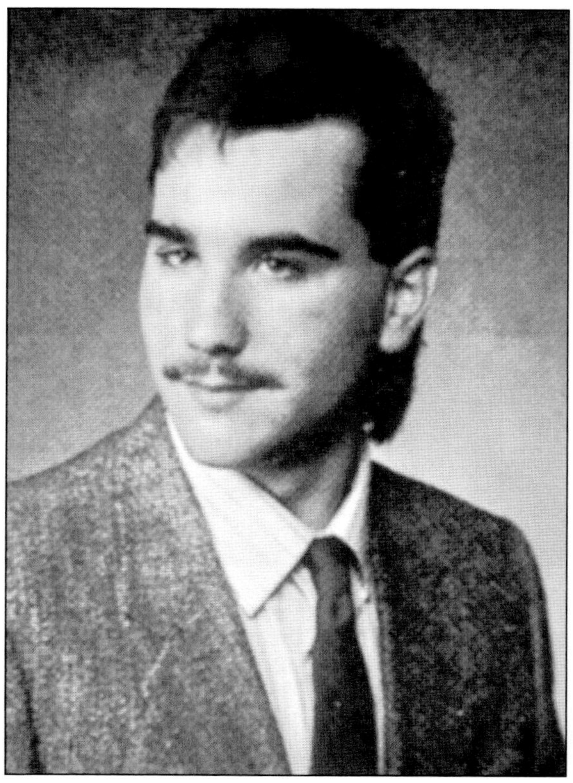

Pat Peake is a 1991 graduate of Lamphere High School and a noted ice hockey player. He played for the Detroit Junior Red Wings, where he scored 136 goals in 46 games. He played for the Detroit Compuware Ambassadors and Plymouth Whalers, leading the Whalers in scoring with 319 career points, and saw his number 14 retired. In his junior career, Peake was chosen as the first-round pick for the 1991 NHL Entry Draft, playing for the Junior Washington Capitals and then in the National Hockey League itself. He played for the Washington Capitals from 1993 to 1998. Peake now works for the Detroit Red Wing Alumni Association and as a scout for the Plymouth Whalers. (Courtesy of Lamphere Schools.)

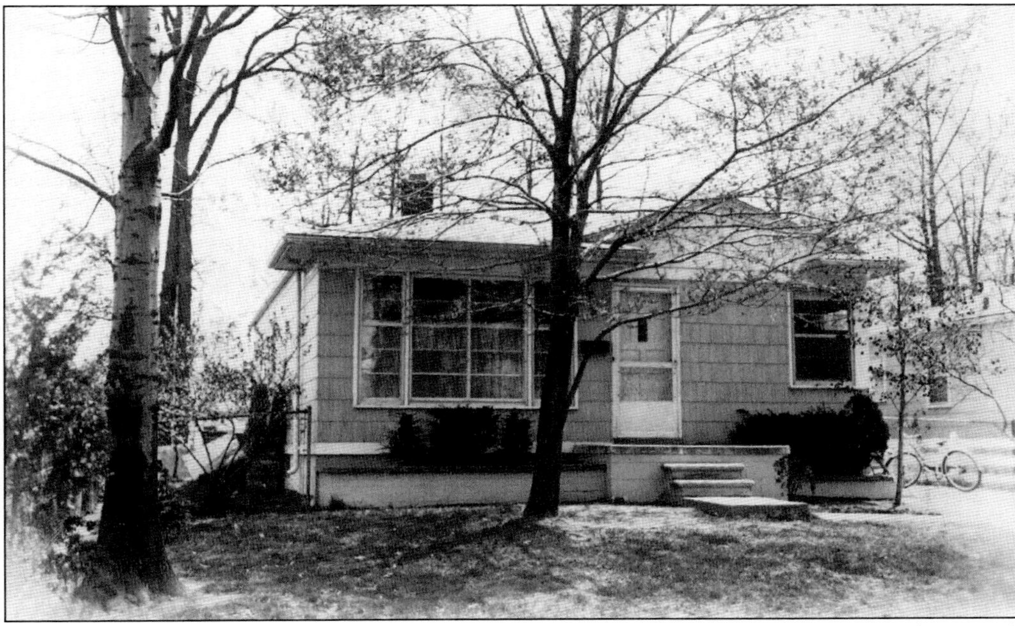

Renowned marine life artist Robert Wyland, who goes by "Wyland," is a 1975 Lamphere High School graduate who hasn't forgotten his beginnings. The artist grew up on Edwards Street, immediately south of Page Middle School, with his parents and his three brothers. Wyland was determined to use his art to work away from the poverty he observed through numerous earlier moves within Detroit. (Courtesy of the Wyland Worldwide LLC "WWW.")

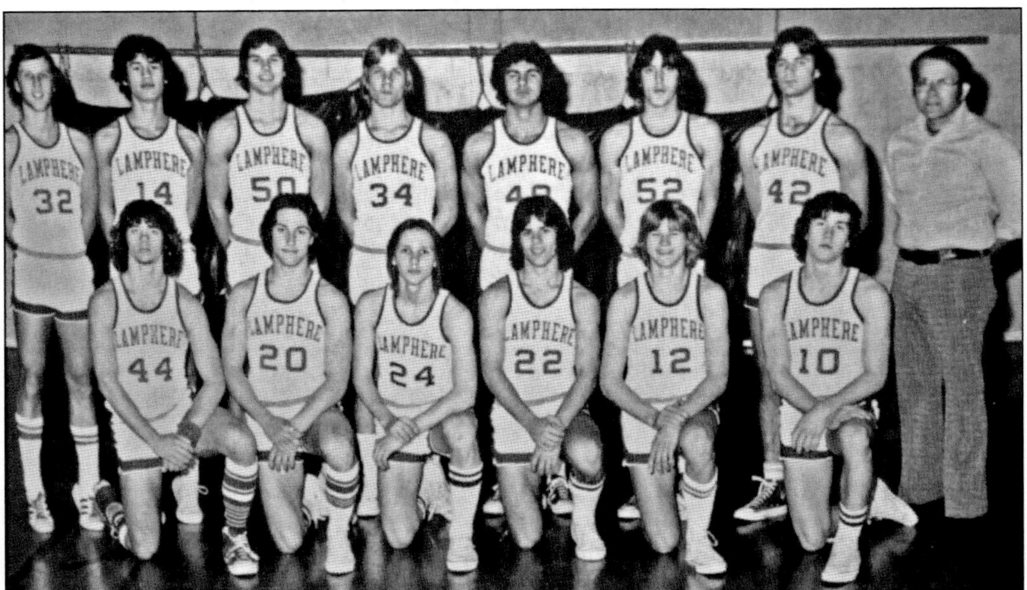

Born with a severe clubfoot, Wyland underwent numerous major surgeries at a young age. The energy that came with the inspiration to become involved in saving whales also contributed to his excelling in sports despite the handicap he had overcome. He was a starter for the Lamphere High School football team and a captain on the basketball team. Wyland is No. 44 in this image. He also served as captain of the school's track team, setting records in the high jump and the 440-yard relay. Yet his passion for art ultimately won out. (Courtesy of the Wyland Worldwide LLC "WWW.")

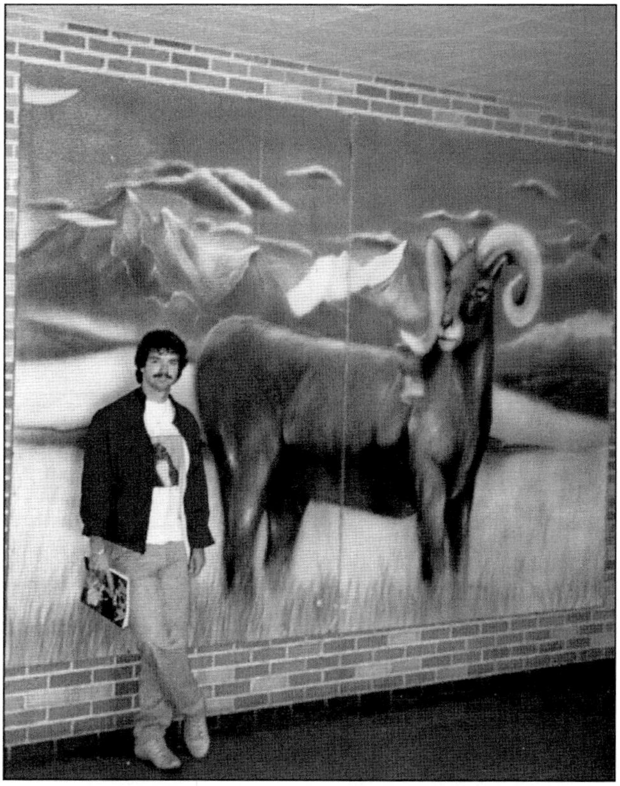

Wyland's constant passion for drawing and painting began at an early age. It was encouraged by a grade-school teacher and further encouraged by Kay Schwartzberg, a supportive junior high art teacher who later transferred to Lamphere High School and continued to work with Wyland. He credits her with being one of the greatest influences on his early development as an artist. His older brother, Steve, instilled the ethic of hard work when Steve won an early citywide poster contest that Wyland believed he would win. (Courtesy of the Wyland Worldwide LLC "WWW.")

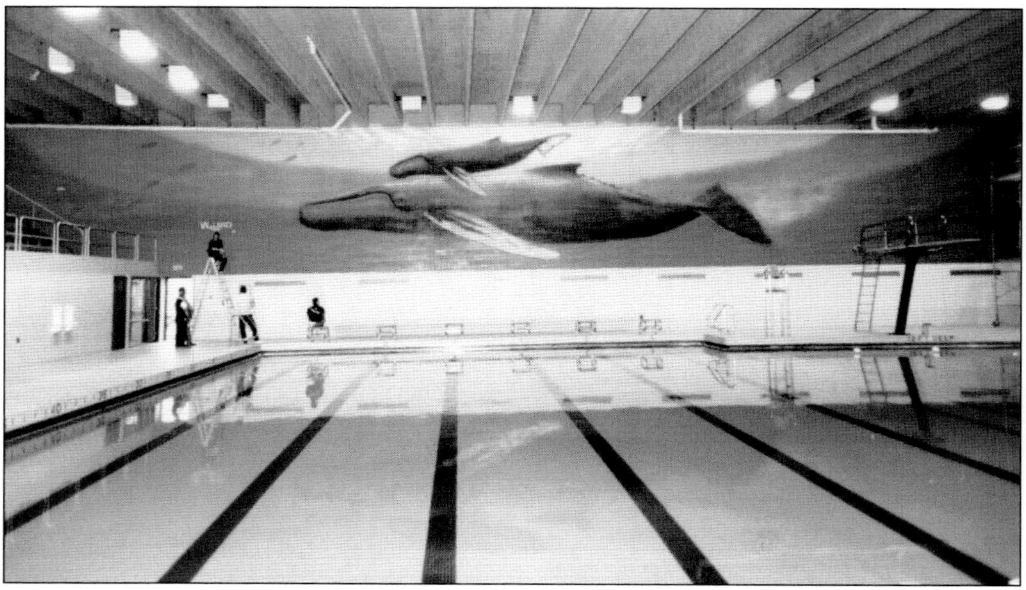

Wyland met his goal to paint 100 Whaling Walls in various places in the world by the year 2011. The wall he painted at his former high school was number 25 and was painted in 1990, when Wyland returned for his 15-year reunion. He can be seen on the top of the ladder under his name. Wyland has visited Lamphere many times to promote the arts to children. Former superintendent James McCann and former deputy superintendent George Jesko have supported and promoted Wyland extensively. (Courtesy of the Wyland Worldwide LLC "WWW.")

Whaling Wall No. 76 in downtown Detroit is pictured here. Wyland's goal was to paint 100 of these walls in various places in the world by 2011, and he succeeded. Wyland was drawn to the ocean from a young age and maintains that he should have been born instead on the West Coast, closer to marine life. A summer trip to California and the opportunity to see his first whale and the Jacques Cousteau television programs were major influences. Learning about the whales' plight and the fishing threat to dolphins moved Wyland to be involved in the save the whales movement. (Courtesy of the Wyland Worldwide LLC "WWW.")

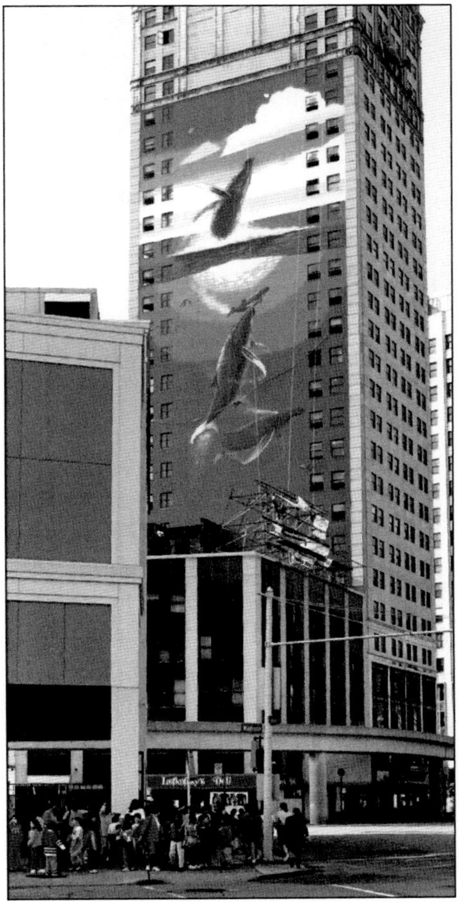

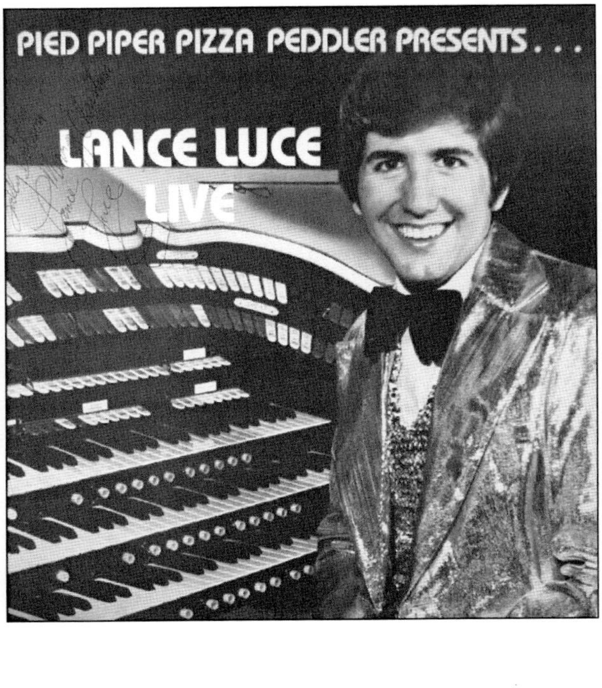

Lance Luce is an internationally acclaimed theater organist. He learned to play at the Royal Oak Theatre, and by age 13, was playing at the intermissions. In 1979, he was the chief organist at Radio City Music Hall at 19, an accomplishment recognized in *Ripley's Believe it or Not*. His many recordings include the one pictured. Lance and his wife, Nancy, were married in Toronto before moving home to Michigan in 1991. They bought a home in Madison Heights, planning for their children to attend Lamphere schools. Nancy's father, Harry Gibson, served on the Lamphere School Board for years. (Courtesy of Lance Luce.)

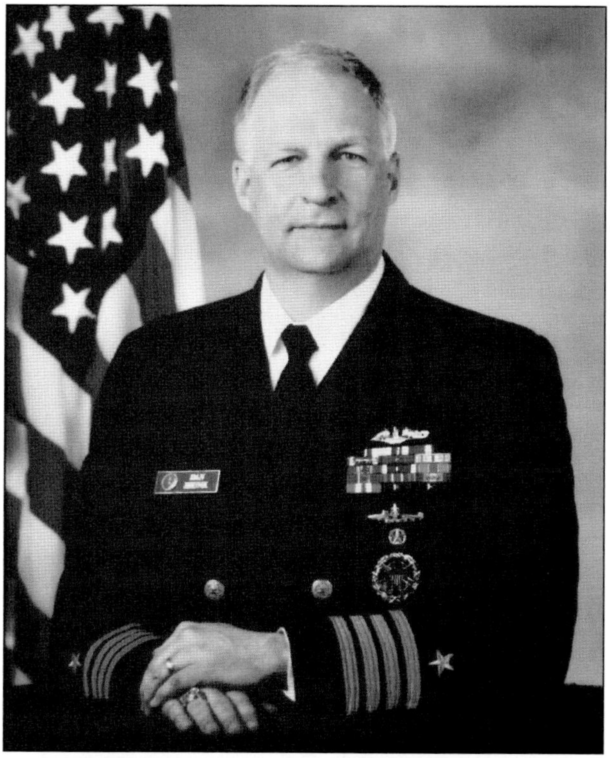

Commander Dan Brunk is a 1986 Lamphere graduate who graduated from the Naval Academy in 1990 with distinction and received a master's degree from George Washington University. He was an honored commander of a submarine while under the Arctic ice with the Pacific fleet. Brunk made captain in September 2011 and is in security with the Joint Chiefs of Staff at the Pentagon. (Courtesy of Bob and Ann Brunk.)

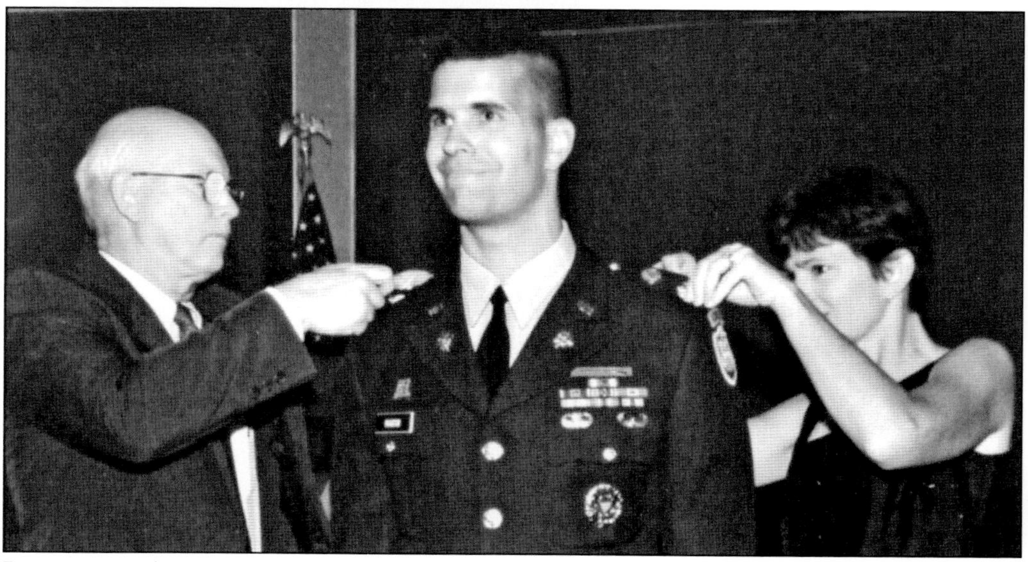

Roger Marin (center) is pictured with his father, William, and his wife, Diedre, as they pin on his colonel wings. Colonel Marin was born in West Germany when his father was serving in the Army. The Marin family moved to Madison Heights in 1968, and Roger and his three siblings attended Lamphere Schools. After graduating from Lamphere High School in 1981, he graduated with a finance degree and received a 1985 Army commission from Western Michigan University, followed by a 1994 master's degree. He was serving in the Pentagon on September 11, 2001, and retired in 2011 from a 26-year career including high-profile assignments and decorations. (Courtesy of William and Judy Marin.)

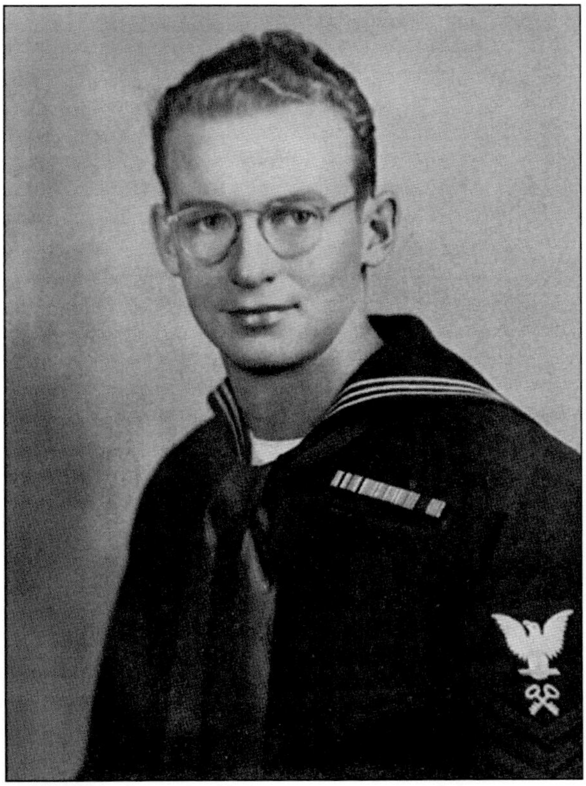

Capt. Dan Brunk followed in the footsteps of his parents in service to his country with his appointment to the US Naval Academy. Bob Brunk (right) met Ann Mager (below) in the Navy. Both parents were an influence on all three of their boys, Dan and his brothers Timothy and David. All three were Eagle Scouts, and Bob was their Scout leader all through school. Ann is a charter member of the General Federation of Women's Clubs Madison Heights Intermediate Women's Club and plays with the Banjos of Michigan. (Both, courtesy of Bob and Ann Brunk.)

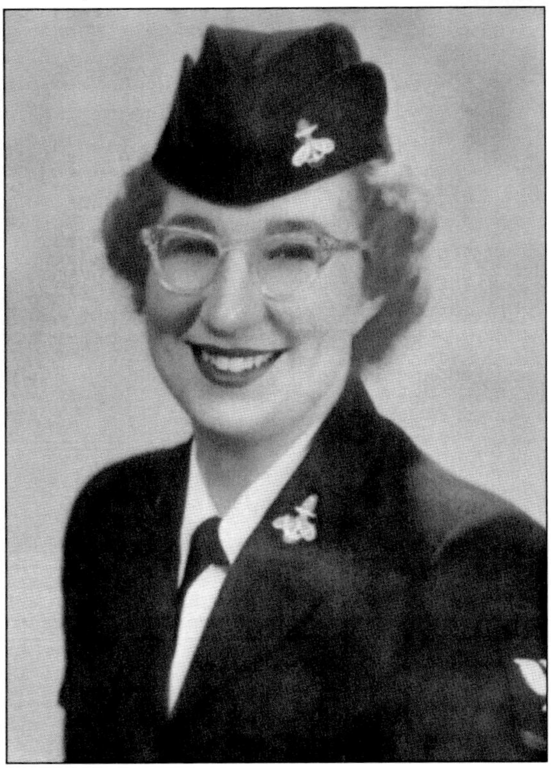

Consistent with our mission to preserve history on a local level, this book was printed in South Carolina on American-made paper and manufactured entirely in the United States. Products carrying the accredited Forest Stewardship Council (FSC) label are printed on 100 percent FSC-certified paper.

MADE IN THE USA